Oriental Memoirs

Oriental Memoirs

Selected from a Series of Familiar Letters Written During Seventeen Years Residence in India

James Forbes

A new introduction by **W.H. SIDDIQUI**

In 4 Vols.

VOL. I

GYAN PUBLISHING HOUSE
Delhi-110 007

GYAN PUBLISHING HOUSE
Publishers of Books on Human Civilization
5, Ansari Road, Daryaganj, Delhi

First Published in 1813 (London)
First reprint in India, 1988

ISBN: 9788121201117 (Set)
ISBN: 9788121201810 (Vol 1)

Published by Smt. Gayatri Garg for Gyan Publishing House, Delhi-110007, and Printed at Goyal Offset Printers, Delhi-110035

" Seeing the Almighty hath given me grace to return to my native country, after having for " eighteen years coasted and travelled in the Indies, I thought it good, as briefly as I could, to write " and set forth this voyage made by me, with the marvellous things I have seen in my travels. The mighty " princes that govern those countries, their religion and faith that they have: the rites and customs which " they use and live by: of the divers success that happened unto me; and how many of these countries " are abounding with spices, drugs, and jewels. And that my countrymen may more commodiously rejoice " at this my travel, I have caused it to be printed in this order; and I now present it to thee, gentle and " loving reader, by whom, for the varieties of things herein contained, I hope that it shall be with great delight " received. And thus God of his goodness keep thee!" C. Fredericke, 1593.

* * * * *

" If then my fortunes can delight my friend,
These pages, fruitful in events, attend:
Another's travels may thy ear enjoy,
And distant scenes thy leisure hours employ.
Here let us feast, and to the feast be join'd
Discourse, the sweeter banquet of the mind;
Review the series of our lives, and taste
The melancholy joy of dangers past!" Homer's Odyssey.

Engraved by Bull

JAMES FORBES ESQ[R] F.R.S. F.A.S. &c.

ÆT. 62. — 1811.

——— *Nil non mortale tenemus,*
Pectoris exceptis ingenuique bonis
Ov. Trist. 3. 7

Published by White, Cochrane & Co Fleet street, June 1st 1812

TO

Sir CHARLES WARRE MALET, Bart.

I ENJOY a heartfelt pleasure, and gratify a laudable pride, in dedicating these volumes to a friend with whom I spent my juvenile years in distant climes, and participated in many interesting events related in the following pages. To you these memoirs are indebted for several valuable acquisitions, which you was peculiarly enabled to furnish, from having explored countries little known to Europeans, whilst employed in a public character for the East India Company, and the representative of the British nation at different Asiatic courts—situations filled with honour to yourself, advantage to your employers, and lustre to the name of an Englishman.

Those best acquainted with your talents lament, that on returning to your native country in the prime of life, and the vigour of a superior mind, you should have chosen that private walk which you embellish with all the endearing characteristics of social life; the protector of the poor, and encourager of industry, throughout your extensive influence. On this delightful theme I will not expatiate, but you must allow me to say, that the amiable owners of Wilbury House present a bright example of those days when generosity, urbanity, and hospitality, dignified the character of an English Country Gentleman, and the maternal virtues and charities of life were deemed the most brilliant female ornaments.

Your reasons for preferring *otium cum dignitate* are known to your friends; they also can estimate the public loss from your not occupying a seat in the British senate: because you possess patriotic zeal and virtue worthy of those illustrious ancestors who adorn the history of our country in three of its most distinguished periods—the battle of Hastings, the signing of Magna Charta, and the civil wars during the reign of Charles the First.

Notwithstanding my promise to the National Institute at Paris, and through it to the French government, as mentioned in the ensuing preface; and notwithstanding what I once thought a duty to my friends and country, without your encouragement and kind assistance, I should have been too diffident to publish these volumes. Lavish as you were with the former, I must ever regret that your avocations did not allow me more of the latter. I have now embarked too far to recede; you must be my pilot: whatever may be the imperfection of these memoirs, your name will impress them with the seal of truth.

You need no adulatory expressions to convince you of the sincerity with which I subscribe myself

Your sincere, and affectionate friend,

JAMES FORBES.

STANMORE HILL,
May 1, 1812.

PREFACE.

THESE memoirs are founded on a series of letters written during a long residence in India. A variety of new and interesting matter collected from valuable and accurate sources, has induced me to alter their original form, and present them to the world in the shape of a connected narrative. I consider this explanation necessary, to account for the epistolary style, and occasional repetitions, which will be found to pervade them.

Leaving England before I had attained my sixteenth year, and being, while in India, deprived of a choice of books, I lay no claim to literary merit. I am conscious of numerous defects in a work commenced at that early age, and continued for eighteen years in the India Company's service, when duty stationed me at many of their settlements, and curiosity led me to other places, in the western provinces of Hindostan.

Diffident as I am of this performance, I deem myself, in some degree, pledged to publish it, in consequence of the following correspondence with the National Institute at Paris; which was the immediate cause of procuring the liberation of myself and family from captivity. I also asssign as another reason, that some of my letters at full length, and copious extracts from others, have appeared in several late publications, without being ascribed to their real author.

Translation of a letter to Mons. Carnot, President of the National Institute, at Paris.

"Sir,

In consequence of a letter which I have just received from a member of the Royal Society in England, I take the liberty of enclosing a copy of one sent to him by our worthy President, Sir Joseph Banks; in which he mentions his intention of writing, to entreat your interest, with a view of obtaining an order for my return to England.

"Such an introduction from our President has induced me to trouble you with this address, to inform you of a few particulars respecting my situation; a representation which, I trust, will have some weight with the members of an Institution so justly celebrated for the encouragement of science.

"In the public offices at Paris and Verdun, my name and situation are thus inserted, 'Mr. James Forbes, (Gentilhomme) Fellow of the Royal and Antiquarian Societies in London, and of the Arcadian Society at Rome.'

"I left England before I had attained my sixteenth year; with a little knowledge of drawing, and an ardent desire to explore foreign countries, I travelled and resided upwards of nineteen years in different parts of Asia, Africa, and America; endeavouring to investigate the manners and customs of the inhabitants, to study the natural history, and to delineate the principal places and picturesque scenery in the various regions which I visited: to these I added the costume of the natives, and coloured drawings of the beasts, birds, fishes, insects, fruits, flowers, and vegetables, produced in such infinite variety in those climates. During that time I resided some years amongst the brahmins in Hindostan, at a distance from the European settlements; where I had an opportunity of observing the modes of life, and the peculiar tenets, of that singular people.

"Twenty years are now elapsed since I returned from thence to my native country: never having seen the continent of Europe, I left England a few years ago, in order to view the classical scenes in Italy, the romantic regions of Switzerland, and the varied kingdoms of Germany; the late war prevented me from entering France at that period.

"In April 1803, when peace waved her olive over the contending nations of Europe, I accompanied my wife and daughter to Holland; and from thence, ignorant of the renewal of hostilities, arrived at Paris the day after the English were made prisoners. I was compelled to share the same fate, and am now with my family at Verdun.

"My drawings, and the letters which were written during those travels, occupy fifty-two thousand pages, contained in a hundred and fifty folio volumes; the work of my own hands: these obtained me the honour of being elected a member of the Royal and Antiquarian Societies of London. My friends insisted upon my publishing them; and, previous to leaving England, I had devoted some time to a selection of the most interesting parts, which I was preparing for the press. In that state they now await my return, when I hope to complete the undertaking.

"Not knowing, Sir, that I should enjoy my present fortunate access to you, and having suffered much in my health, on the 11th of Ventose I addressed a letter to General Berthier, minister of war, requesting permission to drink the waters at Baréges; but I have not yet been honoured with an answer. Could you have the goodness to procure me this favour, and, still more, could you second the wishes of the President and members of the Royal Society, by enabling me to return to England before declining years render me incapable of finishing my undertaking, you will confer the greatest obligation on,

"Sir,

"Your obliged and obedient servant,

"JAMES FORBES."

Verdun, 21st Germinal, An 12.
(11th April, 1804).

Copy of the Answer from the Secretary to the National Institute at Paris.

"*A Monsieur James Forbes, Anglais, Membre de la Société Royal, a Verdun, sur Meuse.*

Institut National,

Classe des Sciences, Physiques, et Mathematiques.

Paris, le 19 Floreal,
An 12 de la Republique Française.

"*A Monsieur James Forbes, de la Société Royale, et de celle des Antiquaires de Londres.*

"JE m'émpresse de vous annoncer, Monsieur, que la Classe s'est interressée pour vous auprés du Ministre de la

Guerre; et qu'elle a appuyé votre demande de tous les motifs qu'elle pouvoit puiser, dans votre age, dans vos travaux scientifiques, et surtout dans la réciprocité que méritent les services rendues par le Chevalier Banks, et par la Sociéte Royale, aux Français qui ont été dans le cas de réclamer leur protection. Si les réclamations de la classe ont le même succès que pour M M. Osborne et Ferguson je me hâterai de vous en faire part.

J'ai l'honneur de vous saluer,

G. Cuvier, Sécrétaire.

Copy of a Letter from General Wirion.

Verdun, le 29 Prairial, An 12.

" Commandement Supérièur de la place de Verdun. Exécution de l'arrêté du gouvernement, du 1er Frimaire, An 12. L'Inspecteur de la Gendarmerie, Commandant Superieur à Verdun, à Monsieur Gouthot, Chef de la 5e division du Ministre de la Guerre."

" Monsieur,

" J'ai l'honneur de vous addresser Mr. James Forbes, savant Anglois, qui a obtenu de sa Majesté imperiale l'autorisation de retourner dans sa patrie. Il a choisi le port de Morlaix pour son embarquement. Je vous prie de vouloir bien faire expédier, le plus promptement possible, les ordres nécéssaires pour qu'il n'éprouve aucun obstacle; et s'il en est besoin, veuillez le recommander aux ministre de la marine. Mr. James Forbes voyage avec son épouse et sa fille; il s'est acquis l'estime générale pendant son séjour à Verdun, et c'est à ce tître que je le recommande à votre obligeance. En passant à Paris, Mr. Forbes, a l'intention de remercier les membres de l'Institut, par qu'il a été recommandé à sa majesté impériale. Les sciences, les arts, la peinture, la botanique, forment toutes les occupations de cet estimable etranger. Il vous sera conduit par mon aid-du-camp Ricard.

"J'ai l'honneur de vous saluer avec consideration,

"Wirion."

Á Monsieur Cuvier, Sécrétaire perpétuel de la classe des Sciences Physiques et Mathématiques.

"Monsieur,

"Pendant mon séjour à Verdun, j'ai eû l'honneur de reçevoir votre lettre de la part de l'Institut National. Je prends la liberté de vous prier de vouloir bien-être, auprès de cette respectable et sçavante société, l'interprète de ma reconnoissance, pour la bonté et la promptitude avec lesquelles elle a bien voulu se prêter à la demande de Mr. le Chevalier Banks, président de la Société Royale d'Angleterre, dont j'ai l'honneur d'être membre. Par ses soins, et par l'indulgence de l'empereur, la *liberté* m'est rendue; et bientôt, au sein de ma famille, je jouirai dans ma patrie du bonheur et de la tranquillité. Veuillez bien, Monsieur, assurer les membres de l'Institut que je me souviendrai toujours avec reconnoissance d'une si grande faveur que je dois à leur bienveillance, et que non seulement notre président, mais encore tous ceux à qui je pourrai le communiquer, sçauront que l'Institut National ne doit pas seulement sa juste réputation à l'étendue de ses connoissances, mais à sa générosité, à son humanité, et à toutes les vertus sociales, qu'elle sçait si bien pratiquer.

"J'ai l'honneur, &c. &c.

"JAMES FORBES."

Paris, 11 *Messidor, An* 12.
(*30th June*, 1804.)

The manuscripts from which these volumes are compiled, and the drawings which illustrate them, have formed the principal recreation of my life. The pursuit beguiled the monotony of four India voyages, cheered a solitary residence at Anjengo and Dhuboy, and softened the long period of absence from my native country: it has since mitigated the rigor of captivity, and alleviated domestic sorrow. Drawing to me had the same charm as music to the soul of harmony. In my secluded situation in Guzerat, I I seemed to be blest with another sense. My friends in India were happy to enlarge my collection; the sportsman suspended his career after royal game to procure me a curiosity; the Hindoo often brought a bird or an insect for delineation, knowing it would then regain its liberty; and the brahmin supplied specimens of fruit and flowers from his sacred enclosures.

India formerly was not the resort of artists; when there I had little to excite emulation, and no other instruction than a few friendly hints from Sir Archibald Campbell; who, during a short residence at Bombay in 1768, encouraged my juvenile pursuits.

In the original letters I occasionally introduced a few remarks and quotations from other travellers to illustrate my own observations in India. In arranging them for the press, I have considerably, but I trust not unnecessarily, enlarged these acquisitions. The names of Sir William Jones, Dr. Robertson, Major Rennel, and other respectable writers of whose superior talents I have now availed myself, would add value and authenticity to a work of much greater merit.

I also acknowledge my obligation to another author of acute discrimination and strict veracity, Dr. Fryer, F.R.S. who was appointed physician to Bombay, soon after it was ceded to the English, on the marriage of Charles the Second with the Infanta Catherine of Portugal; and on his return published his letters from India and Persia. Dr. Fryer's travels corroborate and illustrate many seeming improbabilities in the manners and customs of the Hindoos; a people who then were, and still remain, in the same state as when the Greek historians recorded the invasion of Alexander. I shall conclude my own preface in the simple language of that prefixed by this intelligent writer to his own publication.

" As to the method I have taken in this work, it is unconfined, such being the privilege of a traveller; not bounded with the narrow terms of an historian, nor loosely extravagant, like poetical fictions; but suited both to time and place, and agreeable to the nature of the relation; which, though it may make some unevenness in the style, as where the ruggedness of the way interposes, or the subject matter is varied, it must happen; yet the warp quite through is of the same thread; which being the clue to so many and intricate meanders, trodden by a few, I am the more pardonable when I slip; though I do declare my desire is, to shew my diligence in collecting, and sincerity in compiling, what may make the road more easy to the next adventurers, and satisfy the present inquirers."

"Nisi utile est quod facias, stulta est gloria." PHÆD:

Brighthelmstone,
March 1, 1812.

CONTENTS.

CHAPTER I.

CHAPTER II.

CHAPTER III.

CONTENTS.

CHAPTER IV.

CHAPTER V.

CHAPTER VI.

CHAPTER VII.

CHAPTER VIII.

CHAPTER IX.

CHAPTER X.

CHAPTER XI.

CHAPTER XII.

CHAPTER XIII.

CHAPTER XIV.

CHAPTER XV.

CHAPTER I.

A VOYAGE FROM ENGLAND TO BOMBAY,

IN 1765.

CONTAINING REMARKS ON THE ISLAND OF ST. JAGO, THE COAST OF BRAZIL, AND THE SETTLEMENTS ON THE MALABAR COAST.

"Lo! now the ship unfurls her spreading sails,
"Their swelling bosoms catch the rising gales;
"Like distant clouds appears the lessening shore,
"Till the faint prospect can be seen no more:
"Adieu, my friends, my countrymen adieu!"

B

CONTENTS.

The author embarks as a Writer for Bombay—Peak of Teneriffe—Cape de Verd islands—St. Jago briefly described—sail for the Cape of Good Hope—obliged to steer to the coast of Brazil—arrival at Rio de Janeiro—beauty of the country—brilliancy of the birds—Humming-birds described—serpents and reptiles—City of St. Sebastian—inhabitants—provisions—natives of Brazil—gold and diamond mines—departure from South America—Tristan de Cunha—Table land—storms off the Cape of Good Hope—Ocean Fish—dying Dolphin—ship on fire—calms—sea-scurvy—funeral ceremony at sea—public worship on board a large vessel a delightful spectacle—monotony and distress in long calms—discovery of land!—Malabar coast—settlement of Cochin—Calicut—Tellicherry—Mangalore—Goa harbour, and city—arrival at Bombay.

CHAPTER I.

Having obtained the appointment of a writer in the East India company's service at Bombay, I embarked with fourteen other passengers for that settlement, in the month of March 1765, before I had attained my sixteenth year; and at that early age I commenced my descriptive letters, and the drawings which accompany them.

After encountering the boisterous seas in the Bay of Biscay, we entered the warmer latitudes; and had a distant view of the islands of Madeira, Palma, and Ferro: we next saw the Peak of Teneriffe, rearing its majestic head above the clouds, and presenting a scene of infinite grandeur. From thence we steered for St. Jago, the largest of the Cape de Verd islands, for a supply of water and refreshments; and passing by the Isles of Bona-vista, Sal, and Mayo, whose barren and rocky shores are seldom visited by strangers, we arrived at Porto Praya the middle of May: this is the principal sea-port of St. Jago; the city where the governor and bishop reside is situated at some distance inland; but there is so little attraction in the manners of the Portugueze, and so great a scarcity of horses, that the passengers do not often go there. The fortress and principal houses at Porto Praya, are on a rocky eminence near the watering place; but below it is a beautiful valley, which we daily visited. Our youthful party were charmed with its novelty, and regaled on the plantanes, cocoa nuts, and pine-apples, with which it abounded. The lofty cocoa-tree, and waving plantane, were enlivened by monkeys, and a variety of birds; but the weather being extremely hot, and the hills barren, we seldom strolled beyond the limits of the valley.

We remained about a week at St. Jago, and then sailed for the Cape of Good Hope; but on discovering a dangerous leak in the ship, we were obliged to alter our course, and to proceed immediately to Rio de Janeiro, a Portugueze settlement on the coast of Brazil, where we continued from the end of June until the middle of October; while the vessel underwent the necessary repairs.

If I was pleased with St. Jago, I had much greater reason to be delighted with the Brazils: the grandeur of the mountains, the fertility of the vallies, the mildness of the climate, and the general beauty of animal and vegetable nature, render this part of South America very interesting; the variety of trees and plants, the profusion of fruits and flowers, and the brilliancy of the birds and insects, afforded an ample scope for my earliest attempts in natural history. One lovely valley, over which the aqueduct passes which supplies the city of St. Sebastian with water, was my favourite place of resort; and I seldom passed a day without visiting this sweet retreat; there the rose and myrtle mingled their fragrance with the clustering blossoms of the citron and orange trees, bending at the same time, under the weight of their golden produce.

" For here great Spring
" Greens all the year, and fruits and blossoms blush,
" In social sweetness, on the self-same bough." MILTON.

Thousands of nature's choristers, arrayed in all the brilliancy of tropical plumage, enlivened these extensive orange groves; and the humming-bird, the smallest and most lovely of the feathered race, buzzed like the bee, while sipping the nectarious dew from the blossoms and flowers. Nothing can exceed the delicacy of these little beauties; especially of that, which from its minuteness, is called the fly-bird; its bill and legs are not thicker than a pin; its head, tufted with glossy jet, varies with every motion into shades of green and purple; the breast is of a bright flame colour; every feather, when viewed through a microscope, appears as if fringed with silver, and spotted with gold.

The serpents in this part of South America are large and noxious, but often beautifully coloured; the town and country are infested with lizards, scorpions, centipedes, and troublesome insects of various kinds. The wild animals generally keep upon the mountains, and leave the vallies to the cows, sheep, and goats, which were introduced into these colonies by the Portugueze.

St. Sebastian, the capital of Rio de Janeiro, is a large city, with numerous churches, convents, and nunneries; but the manners and customs of the inhabitants are neither pleasing nor interesting: pride, poverty, indolence, and superstition, are the prevailing characteristics of these degenerate Portugueze; and seem to have entirely extinguished the noble virtues of their ancestors: their cruelty to the plantation negroes, and slaves of every description, is excessive: humanity shudders at the constant smack of the whip, and the loud cries for mercy, vainly implored by these poor wretches, from their tyrannic masters, who seem to have lost every sense of that divine attribute.

The splendor of the churches, the pompous ceremonies of the Romish worship, the various dresses of the monks and nuns, and the beauty of the gardens at their convents, were all attractive. I could enlarge on these subjects, as also on the variety of the animal and vegetable productions, which fill many pages in my manuscript volumes; but as I am endeavouring to condense them as much as possible, I shall only further observe, that the coast abounds with excellent fish of different kinds; a profusion of fruit and vegetables supplies the public markets, and the numerous vessels which are constantly arriving in this noble harbour; beef, mutton, pork, and different kinds of poultry, are also plentiful, and at a moderate price.

The native Brazilians are seldom to be seen at Rio de Janeiro; the few who yet remain live at a distance from the Portugueze settlements; and their manners and customs are little known. Neither could I obtain much information about the gold and diamond mines, for which Brazil is celebrated; they are in the interior mountains, far from the capital; and the roads are strictly guarded to prevent all communication. The jewellers shops at St. Sebastian's make a grand display of diamonds, topazes, amethysts, and other precious stones, brought from the mines; a great deal of gold dust is found in the beds of brooks and torrents near the mountains, and eagerly sought for, especially after heavy rains; by means of which a few of the poor African slaves have purchased their liberty, and become masters of a little plantation, where they enjoy the sweets of freedom.

We left Rio de Janeiro on the 12th of October, for the Cape of Good Hope; and about the end of the month saw Tristan de

Cunha, a desolate island in the Atlantic ocean, inhabited only by seals and sea-fowl. On the 15th of November, we had a distant view of the Table mountain at the Cape; the southern boundary of Africa, and for many ages the barrier of navigators from Europe to India, until Vasco de Gama, at the conclusion of the fifteenth century, surmounted every obstacle; and his approving monarch changed its name from the Cape of Storms, to that of Good-Hope.

In those seas we encountered violent tempests; and, for weeks together, passed through such foaming mountains, as baffle all description: indeed it is difficult for a person unaccustomed to such scenes, to form any idea of this immense body of water when agitated by a storm. In those southern latitudes we saw abundance of whales, grampuses, sword-fish, and porpoises; with flocks of albatrosses, and other aquatic birds, usually met with in stormy seas: in the milder climates, the ocean was enlivened by shoals of albicores, bonitos, dolphins, sharks, and flying-fish; which amused the passing hour, furnished variety at table, and afforded me an opportunity of delineating their different characters: the remora, or sucking-fish, which adheres to the body of the shark; the azure pilot-fish, which conducts him to his prey, but is never devoured himself; and the flying-fish, which by means of its long fins, wings its way through another element, and escapes its direful jaws, are all curious and beautiful; but the exquisite colouring of a dying dolphin, surpasses every effort of the pencil. Falconer, in his inimitable poem of the Shipwreck, has happily described it:

"What radiant changes strike the astonish'd sight?
"What glowing hues of mingled shade and light!
"Not equal beauties gild the lucid west,
"With parting beams all o'er profusely drest;
"Not lovelier colours paint the vernal dawn,
"When orient dews impearl th' enamell'd lawn,
"Than from his sides in bright suffusion flow;
"That now with gold empyreal seem to glow;
"Now in pellucid sapphires meet the view,
"And emulate the soft celestial hue;
"Now beam a flaming crimson on the eye,
"And now assume the purple's deeper dye;
"But here description clouds each shining ray,
"What terms of *Art* can *Nature's* powers display?

We were not permitted to touch at the Cape, and therefore bore away for India. Soon after leaving the coast of Africa, we were awoke at break of day by the cry of fire! No situation can be more distressing; every dreadful idea which present danger suggests, or future misery anticipates, rushes on the mind; and most other trials of human fortitude appear light in the comparison: from conflagration on shore there is some prospect of escaping; and we look forward with hope, to the cessation of the severest tempest; or, if shipwrecked on a desolate island, we thank Providence for our preservation, and, like Crusoe or Selkirk, endeavour to make the best of our situation; but to be in flames on the boundless ocean, is a scene fraught with horror! in momentary expectation of the powder taking fire, and blowing the vessel to atoms; or, of gradually burning to the surface of the water, and then foundering: a dreadful alternative! Providentially we did not continue in suspense; the captain and officers acted with a calm intrepidity, and in an hour the flames were extinguished.

On our second approach to the equator, we met with calms and contrary currents, which drove us quite out of our reckoning; fresh provisions and water became scarce, and the men were attacked by the scurvy; a distemper which was then very incidental to mariners in long voyages: it is various in its symptoms and progress; but is generally attended with heaviness, restlessness, swelled limbs, livid spots, and ulcerated gums: the last stage seems to be a total putrefaction; which soon carries off the unhappy sufferer. The scurvy baffles all the art of medicine; but if the patient is taken on shore, to breathe a pure air, and enjoy the refreshment of fruit and vegetables, he generally recovers. Before we experienced this happy change, many of the seamen, and more of the recruits for the army in India, fell a sacrifice to the malady; and we were often called upon to attend the awful ceremony of committing their remains to the deep. There is something peculiarly solemn in a funeral of this kind, where the body is consigned to the fathomless abyss: but Faith anticipates that glorious morn, when the ransomed of the REDEEMER shall hear his voice, and the sea shall give up her dead!

Except at the funeral ceremony, which was now so frequently performed, I never had an opportunity of seeing a ship's company assembled at public worship; it is a fine spectacle; every feeling mind must rejoice to behold the deck of a large vessel covered with her crew, in the humble attitude of devotion: surrounded by the boundless ocean, the foundation of their august temple; and the cerulean expanse of heaven, its magnificent canopy! to see them in the midst of this unstable element, when separated from all their friends, adoring the universal Friend and Father of the creation; who maketh the clouds his chariot, and walketh upon the wings of the wind; who raiseth the tempest; and saith to the raging waves, peace! be still?—I am sorry to observe, that the solemnity of public worship is a duty too little attended to in these floating habitations, these worlds of wonder! Surely, in such a situation, it must be the highest gratification to offer the tribute of prayer and praise to the great JEHOVAH; for the sea is his, and HE made it!

During the calms under the line the sea was smooth as glass; and every floating substance thrown over-board, remaining round the vessel, we were often obliged, in the cool of the evening, to lower the boats, and tow her to some distance. We continued six weeks in these sultry climates, with only now and then a light air to waft us gently on; and when most wanted, our water began to fail: we at last became almost spiritless from the languor occasioned by the enervating heat, and the dull uniformity of this part of our voyage.

At length, after being disappointed by many deceitful appearances of imaginary shores, and when reduced to our last cask of water, the man at the mast-head saw land, and the coast of Malabar was soon discerned through the telescopes on deck: the powers of language fail to express the joy which thrilled in our hearts at this happy prospect; those only who have been in a similar situation can conceive it: favoured by a gentle breeze, we gradually approached the cocoa-nut groves, which seemed to rise from the ocean, on the low sandy shore, near the Dutch settlement of Cochin, where we anchored in the evening. The ship was soon surrounded by boats, laden with cattle, poultry, fruit, and vegetables: this was indeed a most grateful visit to us all: but especially to our poor invalids; who were immediately brought upon deck to enjoy the refreshing gales from the land, and partake of our delicious fare. The town of Cochin is pleasantly situated near the road, at the entrance of a broad river, surrounded by the low lands and cocoa-nut trees just mentioned; beyond them are woody hills, and majestic mountains, forming a noble boundary to the landscape.

We remained only two days at Cochin, and then sailed for Bombay, aided by the land and sea winds, which alternately prevail on the Malabar coast, after the breaking up of the south-west monsoon: the former blows fresh during great part of the night, and gradually declines a few hours after sun-rise; when the western breeze sets in from the ocean, and renders the navigation delightful. As the season advances towards the commencement of the ensuing monsoon, in the months of April and May, the north-west winds blow strong; and the ships sailing to the northward, no longer assisted by the land breezes, are obliged to stand further out to sea, to beat up against their powerful adversaries; and thus the passenger loses the beauties we daily enjoyed in this pleasant part of our voyage.

From Cochin we proceeded along a diversified coast to Calicut; the celebrated emporium where Vasco de Gama landed after his perilous voyage round the Cape of Good Hope, in the first European vessel which ever navigated the Indian seas: it was then a place of great importance, now little more than a Malabar fishing-town, with four European factories. We did not anchor at Calicut, but arrived the next day at Tellicherry, a settlement belonging to the English, in a pleasant and healthy situation. From thence, sailing by a hilly tract of country, we arrived at Mangulore, then a principal sea-port of Hyder Ally Khaun; where, after procuring water and refreshments, we renewed our coasting voyage, and passing Onore, Mirjee, and some other places of little importance, we anchored in the beautiful harbour of Goa; a noble basin, surrounded by woody hills and fertile vallies, enriched by plantations of cocoa-nuts, and fields of rice: the prospect was embellished by numerous churches, convents, and villas; whose white aspect was finely contrasted with the dark mango and tamarind groves which embosomed them. This noble harbour is defended by the fortress of Alguarda; and the city of Goa, situated a few miles up a navigable river, presents some lovely scenery on its hilly shores: Goa was the most magnificent of all the European settlements in India; and the churches, monasteries, and other public structures, indicate the former splendour of the capital of the Portugueze Asiatic establishments, the seat of the inquisition, and the residence of the governor-general, the archbishop, judges, and other principal officers.

This was the last place we touched at on the Malabar coast, and after sailing along the mountainous shores of the Concan, we anchored in Bombay harbour, exactly eleven months from the commencement of our voyage.

> Should Fate command me to the farthest verge
> Of the green earth, to distant barbarous climes,
> Rivers unknown to song; where first the sun
> Gilds India mountains, or his setting beam
> Flames on th' Atlantic isles, 'tis nought to me:
> ——I cannot go where UNIVERSAL LOVE not smiles around!
>
> THOMSON.

HUMMING BIRDS *at the* **BRASILS,**

with the nest on the Orange Tree.

W. Hooker fecit. *Jam. Forbes, 1765*

BLUE BANANA BIRD *at* RIO *de* JANEIRO.

on a Sprig of the GUAVA *Tree*.

Jan. Parkin. 1768.

W. Hooker, fecit.

CHAPTER II.

CONTAINING

A DESCRIPTION OF THE TREES, PLANTS, FRUITS, AND FLOWERS,

ON THE ISLAND OF BOMBAY, AND THE WESTERN PARTS OF HINDOSTAN.

Not content
With every food of life to nourish *Man*,
Thou mak'st all Nature beauty to his eye,
Or music to his ear: well-pleas'd he scans
The goodly prospect; and, with inward smiles
Most sweet, he feels their influence!

Akenside.

CONTENTS.

CHAPTER II.

A RESIDENCE of eighteen years on the island of Bombay, and several of its subordinate settlements, afforded me an opportunity of seeing a great deal of the western part of Hindostan; and I occasionally visited most of the principal places, from Ahmedabad, the capital of the northern province of Guzerat, to Anjengo, the most southern factory on the coast of Malabar.

During that interesting period, I corresponded with a near relation, whose congenial mind wished to share in the novelty I met with in a part of the globe, which is unrivalled in its gratifications for travellers of every description; especially for a youth, to whom all the world was new.

I have already mentioned my arrival at Bombay in 1766; that establishment was then on a smaller scale than at present; especially in the military and revenue departments: the latter was always inadequate to the expenses; but the docks, fortifications, magazines, and storehouses, render it an object of national importance, both in a political and commercial point of view: the harbour is one of the finest in the world, accessible at all seasons, and affording a safe anchorage during the most tempestuous monsoons: the merchants carry on a trade with all the principal sea-ports, and interior cities of the peninsula of India; and extend their commerce to the Persian and Arabian gulphs, the coast of Africa, Malacca, China, and the eastern islands.

Bombay is situated in the latitude of 18° 50′ north, and 73° of east longitude from London: the island does not exceed twenty miles in circumference: and being entirely surrounded by the sea, the heat is seldom oppressive, and the climate in general healthy and pleasant, and the inhabitants are strangers to the hot winds so troublesome on the continent. The surface of the soil is very unequal, consisting of rocks, hills, and plains; except in one part, where a very considerable tract is overflowed by the encroachment of the sea, notwithstanding a very strong wall which was erected at a great expense to prevent it.

From being situated only a few miles from the Mahratta shores, and still nearer the fertile island of Salsette, the markets are daily supplied from thence with all the necessaries of life: for so circumscribed, so rocky, and so unequal is the surface of Bombay itself, that it only produced a sufficiency of grain in one year, to supply its population for six weeks. Yet each spot that will admit of cultivation, and is not occupied by houses, is sown with rice, or planted with cocoa-nut trees; which, in extensive woods, lend their friendly shade to thousands of neat cottages, and form delightful rides, impervious to a tropical sun.

Of all the gifts which Providence has bestowed on the oriental world, the cocoa-nut tree most deserves our notice: in this single production of nature, what blessings are conveyed to man! It grows in a stately column, from thirty to fifty feet in height, crowned by a verdant capital of waving branches, covered with long spiral leaves; under this foliage, bunches of blossoms, clusters of green fruit, and others arrived at maturity, appear in mingled beauty. The trunk, though porous, furnishes beams and rafters for our habitations; and the leaves, when platted together, make an excellent thatch, and common umbrellas, coarse mats for the floor, and brooms; while their finest fibres are woven into very beautiful mats for the rich. The covering of the young fruit is extremely curious, resembling a piece of thick cloth, in a conical form, close and firm as if it came from the loom; it expands after the fruit has burst through its inclosure, and then appears of a coarser texture. The nuts contain a delicious milk, and a kernel, sweet as the almond: this, when dried, affords abundance of oil; and when that is expressed, the remains feed cattle and poultry, and make a good manure. The shell of the nut furnishes cups, ladles, and other domestic utensils; while the husk which encloses it is of the utmost importance: it is manufactured into ropes, and cordage of every kind, from the smallest twine to the largest cable, which are far more durable than those of hemp. In the Nicobar islands, the natives build their vessels, make the sails and cordage, supply them with provisions and necessaries, and provide a cargo of arrack, vinegar, oil, jaggree or coarse sugar, cocoa-nuts, coir, cordage, black paint, and several inferior articles for foreign markets, entirely from this tree. Gibbon, the historian, writing of the palm tree, adds, that the Asiatics celebrated, either in verse or prose, the three hundred and sixty uses to which the trunk, the branches, the leaves, the juice, and the fruit, were skilfully applied.

Many of the trees are not permitted to bear fruit; but the embryo bud, from which the blossoms and nuts would spring, is tied up, to prevent its expansion; and a small incision being then made at the end, there oozes in gentle drops a cool pleasant liquor, called Tarce, or Toddy; the palm-wine of the poets. This, when first drawn, is cooling and salutary; but when fermented and distilled, produces an intoxicating spirit. Thus a plantation of cocoa-nut trees yields the proprietor a considerable profit, and generally forms part of the government revenue.

The cocoa-nut tree delights in a flat sandy soil, near the sea, and must be frequently watered; while the palmyras, or brab trees, grow on hills, and rocky mountains. These also abound on our small island, as well as the date-tree; but the fruit of the latter seldom attains perfection. These trees are of the same genus, though differing according to their respective classes; they all produce the palm-wine, and are generally included under the name of Palms, or Palmetos.

Thomson gives a very beautiful description of these oriental groves; whose leaves, I omitted to mention, are used instead of paper, by the natives on the Malabar coast, and the inhabitants of the Carnatic.

"Stretch'd amid these orchards of the sun,
"Where high palmetos lift their graceful shade,
"Give me to drain the cocoa's milky bowl,
"And from the palm to draw its freshening wine;
"More bounteous far than all the frantic juice
"Which Bacchus pours!"

The Banian, or Burr tree (Ficus Indica, Lin.) is equally deserving our attention: from being one of the most curious and beautiful of nature's productions in that genial climate, where she sports with the greatest profusion and variety. Each tree is in itself a grove, and some of them are of an amazing size; as they are continually increasing, and, contrary to most other animal and vegetable productions, seem to be exempted from decay: for every branch from the main body throws out its own roots, at first in small tender fibres, several yards from the ground, which continually grow thicker; until, by a gradual descent they reach its surface; where striking in, they increase to a large trunk, and become a parent tree, throwing out new branches from the top. These in time suspend their roots, and, receiving nourishment from the earth, swell into trunks, and shoot forth other branches; thus continuing in a state of progression so long as the first parent of them all supplies her sustenance.

A banian tree, with many trunks, forms the most beautiful walks, vistas, and cool recesses, that can be imagined. The leaves are large, soft, and of a lively green; the fruit is a small fig, when ripe of a bright scarlet; affording sustenance to monkeys, squirrels, peacocks, and birds of various kinds, which dwell among the branches.

The Hindoos are peculiarly fond of this tree; they consider its long duration, its out-stretching arms, and over-shadowing beneficence, as emblems of the Deity, and almost pay it divine honours. The Brahmins, who thus "find a fane in every sacred grove," spend much of their time in religious solitude under the shade of the banian-tree; they plant it near the dewals, or Hindoo temples, improperly called Pagodas; and in those villages where there is no structure for public worship, they place an image under one

one of these trees, and there perform a morning and evening sacrifice.

These are the trees under which a sect of naked philosophers, called Gymnosophists, assembled in Arrian's days; and this historian of ancient Greece gives us a true picture of the modern Hindoos; " In winter the Gymnosophists enjoy the benefit of the " sun's rays in the open air; and in summer, when the heat be- " comes excessive, they pass their time in cool and moist places, " under large trees; which, according to the accounts of Nearchus, " cover a circumference of five acres, and extend their branches " so far, that ten thousand men may easily find shelter under " them."

There are none of this magnitude at Bombay; but on the banks of the Narbudda I have spent many delightful days with large parties, on rural excursions, under a tree supposed by some persons to be that described by Nearchus, and certainly not at all inferior to it. High floods have at various times swept away a considerable part of this extraordinary tree; but what still remains is near two thousand feet in circumference, measured round the principal stems; the over-hanging branches, not yet struck down, cover a much larger space; and under it grow a number of custard-apple, and other fruit trees. The large trunks of this single tree amount to three hundred and fifty, and the smaller ones exceed three thousand: each of these is constantly sending forth branches and hanging roots, to form other trunks, and become the parents of a future progeny.

This magnificent pavilion affords a shelter to all travellers, particularly the religious tribes of Hindoos; and is generally filled with a variety of birds, snakes, and monkeys: the latter have often diverted me with their antic tricks; especially in their parental affection to their young offspring; by teaching them to select their food, to exert themselves, in jumping from bough to bough, and then in taking more extensive leaps from tree to tree; encouraging them by caresses when timorous, and menacing, and even beating them, when refractory. Knowing by instinct the malignity of the snakes, they are most vigilant in their destruction: they seize them when asleep by the neck, and running to the nearest flat stone, grind down the head by a strong friction on the surface, frequently looking at it, and grinning at their progress. When convinced that the venomous fangs are destroyed, they toss the reptile to their young ones to play with, and seem to rejoice in the destruction of the common enemy.

On a shooting party under this tree, one of my friends killed a female monkey, and carried it to his tent; which was soon surrounded by forty or fifty of the tribe, who made a great noise, and in a menacing posture advanced towards it: on presenting his fowling-piece, they retreated, and appeared irresolute, but one, which from his age and station in the van, seemed the head of the troop, stood his ground, chattering and menacing in a furious manner; nor could any efforts less cruel than firing drive him off: he at length approached the tent door; and when finding his threatenings were of no avail, he began a lamentable moaning, and by every token of grief and supplication, seemed to beg the body of the deceased: on this, it was given to him: with tender sorrow he took it up in his arms, embraced it with conjugal affection, and carried it off with a sort of triumph to his expecting comrades.

The artless behaviour of this poor animal wrought so powerfully on the sportsmen, that they resolved never more to level a gun at one of the monkey race.

The banian tree I am now describing, is called by the Hindoos cubbeer-burr, in memory of a favourite saint, and was much resorted to by the English gentlemen from Baroche. Putnah was then a flourishing chiefship, on the banks of the Nerbuddah, about ten miles from this celebrated tree. The chief was extremely fond of field diversions, and used to encamp under it in a magnificent style; having a saloon, dining-room, drawing-room, bed chambers, bath, kitchen, and every other accommodation, all in separate tents; yet did this noble tree cover the whole; together with his carriages, horses, camels, guards, and attendants. While its spreading branches afforded shady spots for the tents of his friends, with their servants and cattle. And in the march of an army, it has been known to shelter seven thousand men.

Such is the banian tree, the pride of Hindostan, which Milton has thus discriminately and poetically introduced into his Paradise Lost:

> "Then both together went
> "Into the thickest wood; there soon they chose
> "The fig-tree. Not that tree for fruit renown'd,
> "But such, and at this day to Indians known
> "In Malabar or Decan, spreads her arms,
> "Branching so broad and long, that in the ground
> "The bended twigs take root, and daughters grow
> "About the mother tree; a pillar'd shade
> "High over-arch'd, and echoing walks between:
> "There oft the Indian herdsman shunning heat,
> "Shelters in cool, and tends his pasturing herds,
> "At loop-holes cut through thickest shade."

The areca, or betel-nut tree, the areca catechu, Linn. is one of the most beautiful of the palmyra tribe; it grows perfectly straight, with an elegant tuft of plumy branches on its summit, overshadowing the blossoms and fruit which are interspersed among them: there is a peculiar delicacy in the proportion and foliage of this tree, which makes it generally admired: the Indians compare it to an elegantly formed and beautiful woman; and there is the same allusion in Solomon's Song; "How fair, and how pleasant art thou, O my love, for delights! thy stature is like to a palm tree, and thy bosom like clusters of grapes."

The betel-nut, better known by the name of soopāree, is in appearance like a large nutmeg, enclosed in a thick membraneous covering; and is highly esteemed by the Indians of all descriptions as a fine stomachic, and a preservative of the teeth and gums: they cut it into small pieces, and eat it with a hot pungent leaf, called betel, spread over with chunam, or delicate shell lime; which the natives carry in boxes, like tobacco, and chew it at all hours. The betel is also introduced at visits of ceremony, when the nut is cut into slices, mixed with cardamoms and chunam, and folded up in a betel-leaf, fastened by a clove: these are presented on a salver to each guest at the conclusion of a visit, and is generally an indication to take leave. The betel-leaf, properly so called (piper betle, Linn.) is a plant entirely distinct and separate from the areca, or betel-nut tree; and grows in neat regular plantations, like hop-grounds, creeping up the small poles, prepared for their protection.

The groves and gardens on Bombay and the adjacent continent, supply the inhabitants with guavas, plantains, bananas, custard-apples, jacas, tamarinds, cashew-apples, ananas, jamboos, oranges, limes, citrons, grapes, and pomegranates: but the most useful, plentiful, and best fruit, is the mango (mangifera, Linn.) which grows abundantly all over Hindostan, even in the forests and hedge-rows, on trees equal in size to a large English oak, but in appearance and foliage more resembling the Spanish-chesnut: this valuable fruit varies in shape, colour, and flavour, as much as apples do in Europe: the superior kinds are extremely delicious; and in the interior resemble the large yellow peach at Venice, heightened by the flavour of the orange and anana: and so plentiful are mangos, in the hot season, throughout most parts of India, that during my residence in Guzerat, they were sold in the public markets for one rupee the culsey; or six hundred pounds in English weight for half a crown: they are a delicacy to the rich, and a nutritious diet for the poor, who in the mango season require but little other sustenance.

The anana, dignified by Thomson as the " pride of vegetable life," needs no description; nor have I ever tasted pine-apples of a superior flavour in the torrid zone, to some produced in the English conservatories. The custard-apples, of two kinds, are pleasant fruits: the pompelmose, or shadock (malus aurantia, Indica,) is much larger and more estimable than the orange: the jaca (artocarpus integrifolia, Linn.) is of a prodigious size, growing from the trunk and large branches of the tree; the fruit is luscious, and of a powerful smell; with a seed resembling the chesnut: the guava (psidium, Linn.) shaped like a pear, has something of the strawberry flavour: some of the jamboos are palatable, and that species called the jambo-rosa, or rose-apple, has the scent and taste of the rose. The carambola, bilimbing, corinda, halfaluree, and some of the smaller fruits, are pleasant, particularly in tarts and preserves.

Hindostan is celebrated for a variety of flowers and odoriferous plants, much esteemed by the Asiatic ladies, but generally too powerful for Europeans. The champach (michelia champaca, Linn.) which resembles the magnolia glauca, and whose blossoms perfume the air to a great extent, is the most highly prized. The mogree, keurah, oleander, hinna, and several others, whose oriental names and characters it would be uninteresting to detail; together with myrtles, jasmins, and a few Chinese flowers, flourish in the Indian gardens; but two of their principal ornaments are the tube-rose and mhadavi (ipomœa, Linn.) the former, both double and single, are extremely luxuriant; and from their alluring fragrance in the cool of the evening, are called by the Malays, soondul mullam, the intriguer of the night. The mhadavi is a most beautiful creeper, covering our seats and arbours with a small monopetalous flower, divided into five angular segments, like fine crimson velvet, surrounded by a foliage uncommonly delicate: it is introduced in the Hindoo drama of Sacontala, translated by Sir William Jones, with the blooming patalis, the balmy usira, and other flowers highly prized by the Hindoo females. How beautiful is the apostrophe of Sacontala to this her favourite plant, when about to leave the sacred groves, where she had spent her early days in innocence and peace. "O mhadavi! thou lovely creeper, whose red blossoms inflame the grove! O, most radiant of shining plants, receive my embraces, and return them with thy flexible arms! I must, from this day, leave thee! O my beloved father, consider this creeper as myself!"

The double and single Japan-rose (hibiscus rosa sinensis, Linn.) form excellent garden hedges, and the rich crimson of the flowers, contrasted with the vivid verdure of the leaves, add much to our hortensial beauty: but, from being almost scentless, they are less esteemed than the kenna, or mendey (lawsonia spinosa, Linn.) which makes as fine a fence, and perfumes the air with a delicious fragrance; few shrubs are more esteemed throughout India, Persia, and Arabia, than the kenna. The hibiscus mutabilis, or changeable-rose, in its three varieties, of white, rose-colour, and crimson, all blowing at one time on the same plant, is a pretty object in an oriental garden.

Bombay abounds with excellent vegetables, indigenous to the climate, and is not unfavourable to cabbages, lettuce, potatoes, and several others, introduced from Europe and the Cape of Good Hope. The banda (hibiscus esculentus, Linn.) is a nutritious oriental vegetable; so is the bungal, or egg-plant (solanum melongena, Linn.) which grows to a much larger size than in Europe; the yam (dioscorea, Linn.); with the fenugreek (meli trigonella fœnum-græcum, Linn.); the sweet potato, and a variety of calavances, or Indian beans, are much liked at the English tables. The Chili pepper (capsicum), of various sorts, is planted throughout Hindostan, and forms a principal ingredient in curries, and other savory dishes, which the natives are all fond of, whether they eat animal food or not: to the capsicum they generally add the cardamom (amomum-repens, Linn.) a pleasant spice from the Malabar coast;

which, with salt, pepper, and ginger, season their viands, mingled in small quantities with the rice, which is the chief article of food among all the higher classes of Indians: the poor live principally upon juarree (holcus sorghum), bajaree (holcus spicatus), and other inferior grains.

The rice, or batty, is sown in June, at the commencement of the periodical rains; which continue, more or less, until October, when the harvest begins. The rice-grounds are enclosed with mounds of earth, and contain a great deal of water; for rice will not grow in a dry soil; and as it always rises with the water, in Pegu, and some other countries, the harvest is reaped in boats; and many low lands which can be artificially watered, produce two crops of rice in a year, with the addition of a little manure.

During the rainy season, and for a few weeks afterwards, the country in Hindostan is delightful; nothing can exceed its verdure, and general beauty; but the fervour of a tropical sun soon clothes the earth with a russet hue, which continues until the annual fall of rain; in that long interval of eight months not a single shower falls; and the nightly dews, though copious, are insufficient to preserve the grass: yet most of the trees, as in other tropical climates, are ever-greens.

In the temperate climes of Europe, it is difficult to conceive the force and beauty of the eastern language respecting fertilizing streams and refreshing showers: it is not so with the inhabitants of the torrid zone, who look forward with eager expectation to the setting in of the rainy season; when cultivation commences, the seed is sown, and a joyful harvest anticipated. Should these periodical rains be withheld, when the heavens are "as brass, and the earth as iron," the consequences would be fatal. Famine and pestilence, with all their dire attendants, stalk through the land, and spread destruction and despair on every side: as those can testify who beheld the dreadful scenes at Bengal in the year 1770; and others, who have witnessed the sad effects of a failure of the crops in different parts of Hindostan; where thousands are carried off by famine; and, from being deprived of sepulture or cremation, the atmosphere is rendered pestilential. In such a climate, Christians and Mahomedans, Jews and Gentiles, all unite in the hymn of the royal shepherd, when the rains descended on the arid vales of Palestine: " Thou visitest the earth, and blessest it: thou makest it very plenteous: thou waterest her furrows, thou sendest rain into the little valleys thereof: thou makest it soft with the drops of rain, and blessest the increase of it. Thou crownest the year with thy goodness, and thy clouds drop fatness!"

What renders the privation of rain at the expected season more dreadful on the continent, is the effect of the hot winds which then generally prevail, especially at a distance from the sea: they are very little known at Bombay: in the northern provinces of Hindostan, and in the Carnatic, they are felt more or less in the best constructed houses; but are most distressing to travellers from milder climates, when passing through a country where no caravansera, tent, or friendly banian-tree, afford a shelter; the greatest alleviation is a house with thick walls, to resist the heat, and every door and window shut to exclude the air; or if open, to have screens of matted grass hanging before them, kept constantly watered. When these winds prevail, furniture of wood, glass, porcelaine, and metal, exposed to their blasts, although perfectly shaded from the sun, are as hot as if they had been placed before a fierce fire: at the same time, water in guglets from Persia, and jars of porous earth, hung up in the current of wind, is refreshingly cold; and wine, beer, and other liquors, in a cotton wrapper, constantly wetted, exposed in the same manner, a short time before they are brought to table, are like iced wines in Europe

As a contrast to the violence of the monsoon, and the unpleasant effects of the hot winds, there is sometimes a voluptuousness in the climate of India, a stillness in nature, an indescribable softness, which soothes the mind, and gives it up to the most delightful sensations: independent of the effects of opium, champoing, and other luxuries, so much indulged in by the oriental sensualist!

Engraved by J. Shury

HINDOO PEASANT *ascending the* COCOA NUT TREE

to draw the TARI *or* TODDY.

Jam. Forbes. Bombay. 1768.

Engraved by J. Greig.

View of CUBBEER BURR, the celebrated BANIAN TREE on the Banks of the NERBUDDA.

Jam. Forbes, 1778

Published by White, Cochrane & Co. Fleet Street, June 1st 1811

Engraved by Chs. Heath

MONKEYS, *drawn from Nature at* CUBBEER BURR.

Jam. Forbes, 1783.

Published by White, Cochrane & Co. Fleet Street June 1st 1812.

Engraved by J. Storr

THE JAC TREE.

The Man and Fruit in proportion.

Jam Forbes. Bombay 1767

Published by White Cochrane & C.° Fleet Street June 2.nd 1812.

CHAPTER III.

A DESCRIPTION OF THE BEASTS, BIRDS, FISH, REPTILES, AND INSECTS,

WITH OTHER ILLUSTRATIONS OF NATURAL HISTORY, ON THE ISLAND OF BOMBAY, AND OTHER PARTS OF HINDOSTAN.

Pauca hæc vidimus operum Dei, multa abscondita majora his!

Paraphrased extempore by MARY KNOWLES.

But few, though wondrous, are the works we see
That manifest the hidden Deity!
Of his full glory but a glimpse is given,
Nor can we reach the climax of high heaven!
  A germ unfolded is the soul of man,
Unable to contain creation's plan;
But when transplanted in celestial land,
To the eternal sun it will expand!
Will endless flourish, fill'd by rays divine,
And will in everlasting strength and beauty shine!

CONTENTS.

CHAPTER III.

The small island of Bombay does not afford the variety of animated nature found on the adjacent continent: which abounds with tigers, leopards, wild-hogs, antelopes, deer of many kinds, hares, rabbits, and smaller animals; the elephant and the rhinoceros are common in several parts of India. Armadillos, hyenas, porcupines, and others of less note, are to be seen in most places; but jackals, squirrels, and hedgehogs, are the only wild animals on Bombay. Salsette, and the Mahratta shores, supply its markets with plenty of oxen, sheep, goats, kids, poultry, butter, and every other necessary of life.

The mus malabaricus, or bandicoote rat, frequently undermine warehouses, and destroy every kind of merchandize: so that they are a dangerous enemy. The musk-rats, though small, are nearly as destructive, and have a most disagreeable smell; if one of these vermine gets into a chest of wine, every bottle it passes over smells so strong of the animal, and acquires such a disagreeable flavour, that it cannot be drank.

Nor are the ants less obnoxious; they vary in shape, size, and colour; the largest are black, near an inch long, and of great strength; their bite is painful, and blood frequently follows the wound. They march in large armies, and exact heavy contributions, particularly on sugar and preserves; though few eatables come amiss, and in a few hours they commit terrible depredations. But the termites, or white ants, make still greater havoc; they gnaw through the thickest planks, demolish beams and rafters, and entirely destroy books, papers, and bales of goods; which they perforate in a thousand places. These, at a certain season, quit their reptile state, and become a winged insect.

Lizards abound in the houses, fields, and gardens; they are a harmless race, differing in size, form, and colour; and some, like the chamelion, assume different hues. The alligator, which in all respects resembles the Egyptian crocodile, is a terrible animal, seldom seen on Bombay; but they are found in most of the rivers on the continent, from five to twenty feet in length. The guana, a land animal of the lacerta tribe, is the next in size, though seldom exceeding four feet; its colour is a dirty green, and the skin covered with scales; some of the natives eat the flesh, and consider it a dainty; others use it in medicine as a great restorative. India, like most other countries between the tropics, is infested by serpents, scorpions, centipedes, and noxious reptiles of various kinds.

Among the serpents of India the cobra-minelle is the smallest, and most dangerous; the bite occasions a speedy and painful death. They are of a brown colour, speckled with black and white, though at a distance not easily distinguished from the ground on which they move; and happy would it be if they confined themselves to it; but they enter the houses, and creep upon the beds and chairs; I once found four, and at another time five, in my chamber up stairs. Thomson truly defines this dreadful reptile, as

> "The small close-lurking minister of fate:
> "Whose high-concocted venom through the veins
> "A rapid lightning darts, arresting swift
> "The vital current.—Form'd to humble man!
> "This child of vengeful nature!"

The cobra di capello, or hooded-snake (coluber naja), called by the Indians the naāg, or nagao, is a large and beautiful serpent; but one of the most venomous of all the coluber class; its bite generally proves mortal in less than an hour. It is called the hooded snake, from having a curious hood near the head, which it contracts or enlarges at pleasure; the center of this hood is marked in black and white like a pair of spectacles, from whence it is also named the spectacle-snake.

Of this genus are the dancing-snakes, which are carried in baskets throughout Hindostan, and procure a maintenance for a set of people, who play a few simple notes on the flute, with which the snakes seem much delighted, and keep time by a graceful motion of the head; erecting about half their length from the ground, and following the music with gentle curves, like the undulating lines of a swan's neck. It is a well attested fact, that when a house is infested with these snakes, and some others of the coluber genus, which destroy poultry and small domestic animals, as also by the larger serpents of the boa tribe, the musicians are sent for; who by playing on a flagelet, find out their hiding-places, and charm them to destruction: for no sooner do the snakes hear the music, than they come softly from their retreat, and are easily taken. I imagine these musical snakes were known in Palestine, from the Psalmist comparing the ungodly to the deaf adder, which stoppeth her ears, and refuseth to hear the voice of the charmer, charm he never so wisely.

When the music ceases the snakes appear motionless; but if not immediately covered up in the basket, the spectators are liable to fatal accidents. Among my drawings is that of a cobra de capello, which danced for an hour on the table while I painted it; during which I frequently handled it, to observe the beauty of the spots, and especially the spectacles on the hood, not doubting but that its venomous fangs had been previously extracted. But the next morning my upper servant, who was a zealous Mussulman, came to me in great haste, and desired I would instantly retire, and praise the Almighty for my good fortune: not understanding his meaning, I told him that I had already performed my devotions, and had not so many stated prayers as the followers of his prophet. Mahomet then informed me, that while purchasing some fruit in the bazar, he observed the man who had been with me on the preceding evening, entertaining the country people with his dancing snakes; they, according to their usual custom, sat on the ground around him; when, either from the music stopping too suddenly, or from some other cause irritating the vicious reptile which I had so often handled, it darted at the throat of a young woman, and inflicted a wound of which she died in about half an hour. Mahomed once more repeated his advice for praise and thanksgiving to Alla, and recorded me in his calendar as a lucky man.

Dr. Russell, in his valuable treatise on Indian serpents, has distinguished between the venomous and the harmless species, in the three genera of boa, coluber, and anguis: he has given an accurate description, and coloured engravings of forty-three of the most common serpents in Hindostan; experiments on the effects of their bite, and the several remedies applied; with observations on the apparatus provided by nature, for preparing and instilling their poison: he mentions, that a quantity of warm Madeira wine taken internally, with an outward application of eau-de-luce on the punctures, was generally successful in curing the bite of the most venomous species: and that the medicine called the Tanjore-pill seemed to be equally efficacious. Dr. Russell further observes, that " of forty-three serpents examined and described by him, seven only were found with poisonous organs: and upon comparing the effects of the poison of five oriental serpents on brute animals, with those produced by the poison of the rattle-snake, and the European viper, it may in general be remarked, that they all produce morbid symptoms nearly similar; however much they may differ in the degree of their deleterious power, or in the rapidity of its operation. The bite of a rattle-snake in England, killed a dog in two minutes; the bite of the most pernicious snake in India was never observed to kill a dog in less than twenty-seven minutes."

It would be entering on too extensive a field to describe the character and beauty of the papilios, libellulæ, scarabei, cicadæ, cantharides, and other insects, which animate the Indian groves, and gardens throughout the day: and are succeeded by a variety of moths, and nocturnal visitors; but especially the lampyris, or fire-flies, which glitter by thousands in the dark recesses of the banian-tree; and in perpetual motion on the external branches of the spreading tamarind, produce a singular and brilliant effect. The locusts, which are so much dreaded in many parts of Hindostan, are seldom seen on Bombay: but the creeping-leaf, and some others of the mantis class, are extremely curious.

India also abounds with wasps and bees; the latter build their nests in rocky caverns and hollow trees, and produce plenty of wax and honey; but the best is brought from Muscat, and different parts of Arabia. The bees are sometimes very troublesome and dangerous, and often annoyed us in our visits to the caves at Salsette and the Elephanta; where they make their combs in the clefts of the rocks, and in the recesses among the figures, and hang in immense clusters: I have known a whole party put to the rout in the caverns of Salsette, and obliged to return with their curiosity unsatisfied, from having imprudently fired a gun to disperse the bees, who in their rage pursued them to the bottom of the mountains.

I am surprized that commentators on the scriptures have perplexed themselves about the food of John the Baptist in the wilderness; which we are informed consisted of locusts and wild honey; and for which the cassia-fistula, or locust-tree, and many other substitutes have been mentioned: but it is well known that locusts are an article of food in Persia and Arabia, at the present day; they are fried until their wings and legs fall off, and in that state are sold in the markets, and eaten with rice and dates, sometimes flavoured with salt and spices: and the wild honey is found in the clefts of the rocks in Judea, as abundantly as in the caves of Hindostan.

We often read in scripture of the butter of kine, the milk of sheep, and the fat of the kidneys of wheat; with the pure blood of the grape, and honey out of the rock: "I would have fed thee with the finest of the wheat, and with honey out of the stony rock would I have satisfied thee." There can be as little doubt what that honey was, as of the wild honey on which the Baptist fed in the wilderness; some of the greatest delicacies in India are now made from the rolong-flour, which is called the heart, or kidney of the wheat: and most probably the brooks of honey and butter, mentioned by Zophar, in the book of Job, were the liquid honey from the wild bees; and the clarified butter, or ghee, used throughout Hindostan, which pours like oil out of the duppers, or immense leather bottles in which it is transported, as an article of commerce; and is every where preferred by the natives to butter not so prepared.

The continental woods are enlivened with peacocks, partridges, quails, green-pigeons, and other birds of brilliant plumage and excellent flavour; but under my present limitation, I can only describe a small part of Indian ornithology. Vultures, kites, hawks, crows, and a variety of smaller birds, abound in Bombay; and amadavads, and other songsters, are brought thither from Surat, and different countries.

The myneh is a very entertaining bird, hopping about the house, and articulating several words in the manner of the starling; and frequently repeating its own name of myneh; the sharukh, a bird of the same kind, I am not so well acquainted with, but it is said to imitate the human voice in a wonderful manner.

The baya, or bottle-nested sparrow, is remarkable for its pendent nest, brilliant plumage, and uncommon sagacity. These birds are found in most parts of Hindostan; in shape they resemble the sparrow, as also in the brown feathers of the back and wings; the head and breast are of a bright yellow, and in the rays of a tropical sun have a splendid appearance, when flying by thousands in the same grove; they make a chirping noise, but have no song: they associate in large communities; and cover extensive clumps of palmyras, acacias, and date trees, with their nests. These are formed in a very ingenious manner, by long grass woven together in the shape of a bottle, with the neck hanging downwards, and suspended by the other end to the extremity of a flexible branch, the more effectually to secure the eggs and young brood from serpents, monkeys, squirrels, and birds of prey. These nests contain several apartments, appropriated to different purposes: in one the hen performs the office of incubation; another, consisting of a little thatched roof, and covering a perch, without a bottom, is occupied by the male, who with his chirping note cheers the female during her maternal duties. The Hindoos are very fond of these birds, for their docility and sagacity: when young, they teach them to fetch and carry; and at the time the young women resort to the public fountains, their lovers instruct the baya to pluck the tica, or golden ornament, from the forehead of their favourite, and bring it to their expecting master.

Dr. Fryer gives a very pleasant description of the baya, under the name of the toddy-bird, in his entertaining travels. " Nature, in the rainy season at Bombay, affords us a pleasant spectacle, as well as matter for admiration: for here is a bird, that is not only exquisitely curious in the artificial composure of its nest with hay, but furnished with devices and stratagems to secure itself and young ones from its deadly enemy, the squirrel; as likewise from the injury of the weather; which being unable to oppose, it eludes with this artifice, contriving the nest like a steeple-hive, with winding meanders: before which hangs a penthouse for the rain to pass, tying it with so slender a thread to the bough of the tree, that the squirrel dare not venture his body, though his mouth water at the eggs and prey within; yet it is strong enough to bear the hanging habitation of the ingenious contriver, free from all the assaults of its antagonists, and all the accidents of gusts and storms: hundreds of these pendulous nests may be seen on one tree."

Equally curious in the structure of its nest, and far superior in the variety and elegance of its plumage, is the tailor-bird of Hindostan; so called from its instinctive ingenuity in forming its nest: it first selects a plant with large leaves, and then gathers cotton from the shrub, spins it to a thread by means of its long bill and slender feet, and then, as with a needle, sows the leaves neatly together to conceal its nest. The tailor bird (motacilla sutoria, Linn.) resembles some of the humming-birds at the Brazils, in shape and colour: the hen is clothed in brown; but the plumage of the cock displays the varied tints of azure, purple, green, and gold, so common in those American beauties. Often have I watched the progress of an industrious pair of tailor-birds in my garden, from their first choice of a plant, until the completion of the nest, and the enlargement of their young. How applicable are the following lines in the Musæ Seatonianæ, to the nidification of the tailor-bird, and the pensile nest of the baya.

> " Behold a bird's nest!
> " Mark it well, within, without!
> " No tool had he that wrought; no knife to cut,
> " No nail to fix, no bodkin to insert,
> " No glue to join; his little beak was all:
> " And yet how neatly finish'd! What nice hand,
> " With every implement and means of art,
> " Could compass such another?"

Although the last in my collection, yet not the least in favour with all the orientals, is the bulbul, or Persian nightingale; who also call it hazardasitaun, or the " bird of a thousand songs." Its plumage is variegated by shades of brown and white, with a black tuft upon the head, and some feathers of a bright scarlet near the tail: it has a pleasing wild note, but I never heard one that possessed the charming variety of the English nightingale, or serenaded us with its nocturnal melody: whether the Indian bulbul and that of Iran entirely correspond, I have some doubts: the Persian bulbul is celebrated by Hafiz and Khusroo, not only for the plaintive sweetness of its song, but for its passion for the rose; as they allege it is so enamoured with that flower, that if it sees any person pluck a rose from the tree, it laments and cries. I drew a bulbul fluttering over a full-blown rose, as a vignette to a Persian ode, translated by Colonel Woodburne, who presented me with the following copy, which has not before appeared in print.

51

ON THE ABSENCE OF HIS MISTRESS.

Translated from the Persian of Amir Khusroo.

How, sweet nymph, shall I be gay,
Though it be the month of May?
Banish'd from the flower of spring,
How shall the mournful bulbul sing?

Joy, that once inspir'd my lay,
Joy and hope have fled away:
Plaintive notes must tell my woes
In the absence of the rose!

Looks, the language of the eyes,
Tears may speak, and so may sighs;
But the muse must lend her aid
To describe my lovely maid.

Limner, would you paint her fair,
Mark her mien, her gait, her air;
Mark the mischief of her eye,
Where the loves in ambush lie:

Shew the sense, the ease, the grace,
In each feature of her face;
Every feeling of the mind,
Fond, affectionate, refin'd!

Heavens! how swift our joys have past!
Joys, which heav'n might wish to last!
Fancy, bring me back her charms,
Bring them quickly to my arms.

Haste upon the morning gale,
Tell her all my mournful tale;
Tell her how my bosom burns,
How it bleeds till she returns!

Ah! how happy once, and blest,
Panting near thy spotless breast;
Drinking poison from that eye,
Breathing soft the mutual sigh!

Now complaining, now content,
Free from every false restraint;
Pleas'd we spend each happy hour,
Under love's auspicious power.

Shall ambition, wealth, or pride,
Lead me from thy path aside?
No—sweet sovereign of my breast,
Love alone shall make us blest!

Khusroo, cease thy artless strain,
Nor suppose the numbers vain;
If these pearls at random flung,
Please the nymphs for whom they're strung.

The metaphor of stringing the pearls at the conclusion of these stanzas, is a poetical idea, common in the Persian language; and frequently to be met with in the beautiful odes of Hafiz.

Having limited myself so much in the pleasing walk of oriental ornithology, I shall be very brief in its icthyology: the surrounding ocean supplies Bombay with a variety of excellent fish; some of them are similar to those in Europe, others are peculiar to India. The pomfret is not unlike a small turbot, but of a more delicate flavour; and epicures esteem the black pomfret a great dainty: the sable, or salmon-fish, a little resembles the European fish, from whence it is named: the robal, the seir-fish, the grey mullet, and some others, are very good; but the bumbalo, a small fish, extremely nutritive, and caught in immense numbers, is the favourite with the natives, who are allowed by their religion to eat fish: they are dried for home consumption, and furnish a principal article of food for the Lascars, or Indian sailors, on board their vessels; they are also a considerable article of commerce in their dried state. Turtle are sometimes caught at Bombay, and the adjacent islands; as are sea cray-fish, oysters, limpets, and other shell fish.

THE COBRA DE CAPELLO.

Engraved by T. Wageman

DANCING SNAKE *and* MUSICIANS.

From a Drawing taken on the spot by Baron de Montalembert, 1807.

Published by [illegible] Fleet St. June 1st [illegible]

The Baya or Bottle nested Sparrow of India on a branch of the Baubul Tree drawn from nature 1769 Etched on Stone by J. Forbes 1811

TAYLOR BIRDS *and Fruit bearing* CONVOLVULUS.

W. Hooker fecit. *Jam. Forbes, Bombay, 1768.*

BULBUL or INDIAN NIGHTINGALE,

on a Sprig of the CUSTARD APPLE *Tree.*

Jam. Forbes Bombay

CHAPTER IV.

A GENERAL ACCOUNT OF THE HINDOOS,

THE ORIGINAL INHABITANTS OF HINDOSTAN, AND THEIR DIVISION INTO CASTES;

WITH A PARTICULAR DESCRIPTION OF THE BRAHMINS, AND THE MOST PROMINENT FEATURES IN THE OTHER TRIBES.

Homo sum, humani nihil à me alienum puto. TER.

In India a people present themselves to our eyes, clothed in linen garments, somewhat low descending: of a gesture and garb, we may say, maidenly and well nigh effeminate; of a countenance shy and somewhat estranged; yet smiling out a glozed and somewhat bashful familiarity.

LORD'S History of the Persees in 1630.

CONTENTS.

Inhabitants of Bombay—Hindoos—their ancient history—division into castes—the four grand divisions—Brahmins—sacred books—religious tenets—idols in the Hindoo mythology—Brahmah—creation, rebellion of the celestial spirits—origin of the Hindoo metempsychosis—explanation of its system—sublime description of the Deity—extracts from the vedas—Menu's code of laws—Fakeers and Yogecs—their austerity and severe penances—Chandalas—Pariars—general description of the Hindoos—domestic arrangement—dress of the men—delicacy of the women—their character—dress—ornaments—houses—education—Hindoo school—marriages—funerals—cremation of the widows—astrology—comparison with patriarchal manners—hackeree—palankeen—rural feasts—dancing-girls—religious choristers, singing men and women of scripture—sacred groves and lakes—ablutions—hummums—effects of opium—halcarras.

CHAPTER IV.

HAVING briefly mentioned the animal and vegetable productions of Bombay, I shall proceed to describe its inhabitants, commencing with the Hindoos, the aborigines of Hindostan. From the northern mountains of Thibet and Tartary, to the southern promontory of Cape Comorin; and from the western shores of the Indus to the eastern banks of the Ganges, extended the boundaries of the vast empire of the ancient Hindoos; a country comprising nearly as much land as half the continent of Europe, and containing about seventy millions of inhabitants.

The Persians gave it the name of Hindustan, from being the country of the Hindus, or Hindoos; but in more early ages it was called by themselves Bharata, and sometimes Punyabhumi, or the land of virtues: a name expressive of the gentle government, and flourishing condition of a mild and happy people. The Greeks derived the name of India, which has been so generally adopted, from the Persian appellation; and in modern times, India has been used as a general name, not only for the extensive region abovementioned, but the still more eastern tracts of country, with the island of Ceylon, and those in the oriental archipelago.

The origin of the Hindoos, like that of most other nations, buried in obscurity, and lost in fable, has baffled the researches of the ablest investigators. Megasthenes, who was sent ambassador by Seleucus, to Sandracottos, king of Practri, whose dominion now forms the fertile provinces of Bengal, Bahar, and Oude, wrote an account of his embassy, which Arrian has preserved in his history of India; and that narrative, written two thousand years ago, when compared with the modern history of the Hindoos, convinces us how little change they have undergone in that long period: nor have the conquests and cruelties of their Mahomedan invaders, nor their commercial intercourse with the Europeans settled among them, been able to alter the long established manners and customs, so deeply interwoven with their religious tenets.

The Hindoos are divided into four principal tribes; the Brahmin, the Cshatriya, or Ketterree, the Bhyse, and the Sooder; and these chief tribes, or castes, are distinguished as the followers of Vishnoo, and Seeva; called Vishnoo-bukht, and Seeva-bukht.

The Brahmins study religion, astronomy, arts and sciences: they are the instructors of youth, take care of the dewlahs, or temples, and perform every kind of charity. The Cshatriya tribe includes kings, nobles, magistrates, officers, and the superior orders of mankind. The Vursya, or Bhyse, are employed in commerce, agriculture, arms, and the occupation of shepherds and herdsmen. The Sudra, or Sooder, includes manufacturers, mechanics, servants, and all the lower classes of society. Each of these principal tribes is subdivided into a number of classes, or castes, amounting in all to eighty-four; who neither intermarry, nor intimately associate with each other. So that each caste differs in features, dress, and appearance, as much as if they were of different nations; and by laws most strictly observed, they are separated from each other by insurmountable barriers.

The Brahmins are in all respects the first caste among the Hindoos, and by the laws are entitled to very extraordinary privileges; especially in cases of delinquency: no other tribe is admitted to the priesthood; to them are all the mysteries of their religion and sacred knowledge confined: they alone understand the language of the Shastah, or Shastras, those holy volumes which contain the religion and philosophy of the Hindoos; which are divided into four bedes, or vedas, a word signifying science. These books the Brahmins esteem so sacred, that they permit no other caste to read them; and they are written in the Sanscrita language, which is now understood by very few except the Brahmins, and not by all of them: for although there can be no Hindoo priest that is not a Brahmin, yet it by no means implies that all of the Brahmin tribe are priests: on the contrary, they are employed in the political and revenue departments, and appear in various public characters under the governments in India; the great and powerful Mharatta empire, is at this day ruled by a Brahmin sovereign, with the title of Peshwa: others throughout the vast peninsula, pursue a variety of employments in the agricultural and commercial line, and some even cultivate their own lands.

The Hindoo religion admits of no proselytes; and is therefore a principal means of preserving the castes pure and distinct: neither have the Mahomedan conquests and oppressions, nor the intercourse of Europeans with the Hindoos, been able to subvert a system of theology and jurisprudence, founded on a firm basis, and interdicted from all change by the most rigid laws.

This religious and moral system is no doubt of great antiquity; but those who have deeply investigated the ancient and pleasing fictions in the Hindoo mythology, which bears a great resemblance to that of the Greeks, and may perhaps be traced to the same origin, are of opinion, that the religious and civil laws of the Hindoos, called the Institutes of Menu, were compiled about eight hundred and eighty years before the birth of our Saviour; that the Vedas, or sacred volumes, were written three hundred years prior to the Institutes; and that preceding this period, every thing being handed down by oral tradition, the account was obscure and fabulous.

But divested of extraneous matter, there appears to be a great degree of purity and sublimity in the genuine principles of the Hindoo religion, though now obscured by superstitious rites and ceremonies, and blended with gross idolatry: in their original simplicity, they teach that there is one supreme ruler of the universe; who is styled Brahmā, or the Great One: they inculcate also, that this supreme intelligence consists of a triad, or triple divinity, expressed by the mystic word Om; and distinguished by the names of Vishnu, Brahmā, and Sheva; or the creating, preserving, and destructive power of the Almighty. Images of these attributes are placed in their temples; and worship and sacrifices are daily performed before them, and a variety of other statues, representing the different qualities of the Supreme Being: so that it is a complete system of polytheism, and a source of a thousand fables subversive of truth and simplicity.

Yet it ever was, and ever must be difficult, for either Christians or Mahomedans, to convert a Hindoo: for with them theology is so blended with the whole moral and civil obligations of life, that it enters into every habit, and sanctions almost every action.

On withdrawing the veil from the sacred volumes of the Hindoos, we see Brahma, or the supreme deity, represented as absorbed in the contemplation of his own essence, but from an impulse of divine love, resolving to create other beings to partake of his glory, and to be happy to all eternity. He spake the word, and angels rose into existence! He commanded, and the host of heaven were formed! they were created free; and were made partakers of the divine glory, and beatitude, on the easy condition of praising their creator, and acknowledging him for their supreme Lord. But not content with this happy state in the celestial regions, some of the principal spirits rebelled, and drew a number after them; who were all doomed to languish in that scene of horror, so finely described by our sublime poet:

> " Regions of sorrow, doleful shades, where peace
> " And rest can never dwell; hope never comes
> " That comes to all; but torture without end,
> " Still urges, and a fiery deluge, fed
> " With ever burning sulphur, unconsum'd!" MILTON.

In process of time, at the intercession of the faithful angels, the fatal doom of these fallen spirits was revoked; and they were released on the conditions of repentance and amendment, in a state of probation. For this purpose a new creation of worlds took place; and mortal bodies were prepared for the apostate angels, which they were to animate for a certain space; there to be subject to natural and moral evils; through which they were doomed to transmigrate under eighty-nine different forms! the last into that of man! when their powers and faculties are enlarged, and a merciful Creator rests his chief expectations of their repentance and restoration to his favour. If they then fail, their punishment is renewed, and they are doomed to begin again their first state of transmigration. In this system we are struck with the intermixture of truth with error, and false traditions, bearing in many particulars a resemblance to the sacred truths of divine revelation.

On this hypothesis, it appears that one principal reason for the Hindoos regarding the cow with such religious veneration, is, that they believe the soul transmigrates into this animal immediately preceding its assumption of the human form. No Hindoo, even of the lowest caste, will kill a cow, or taste its flesh; they will die with perfect resignation, rather than violate this tenet; as has been frequently experienced on board the vessels in the Indian seas, when all the provisions except salt-beef has been expended. But I am not certain respecting the first principle of the Hindoo's veneration for the cow; since many conjecture the command to have originated in the preservation of an animal so useful to mankind: and it is well known, that the Egyptians, Phœnicians, and other ancient nations, have equally venerated this valuable animal.

The Hindoos estimate the delinquency of these apostate spirits, by the class of mortal forms which they are doomed to inhabit; thus all voracious and unclean animals, whether inhabitants of earth, air, or water, as well as men whose lives and actions are publicly and atrociously wicked, are supposed to contain a malignant spirit; on the contrary, those animals which subsist on vegetables, and do not prey upon each other, are pronounced favoured of the Almighty.

That every animal form is endued with cogitation, memory, and reflection, is one of the established tenets of the Brahmins; indeed it must necessarily follow, from the supposed metempsychosis of the apostate spirits through these mortal forms: they also believe that every distinct species of the animal creation have a comprehensive mode of communicating their ideas, peculiar to themselves; and that the metempsychosis of the delinquent spirits extends through every organized body, even to the smallest insect and reptile. They highly venerate the bee, and some species of the ant; and conceive the spirits animating these forms to be favoured by God, and that the intellectual faculties are more enlarged under them than in most others.

With such tenets we cannot be surprized at their unwillingness to take away the life of any creature whatever; as they must suppose them to possess still more acute sensations than our dramatic poet describes:

> " The smallest beetle that we tread upon,
> " In corporal suffering feels a pang as great
> " As when a giant dies!" SHAKESPEARE.

The devotion of the Hindoos to the Supreme Being, and the inferior deities, consists in a regular attendance at the dewals, or temples, especially at the solemn festivals; in performing particular religious ceremonies in their own houses; in prayers, ablutions, fastings, and penances; but especially in oblations, which consist chiefly of spices, incense, rice, fruits, and flowers; and although they have been in former times accused of offering human sacrifices, it is certain they now very rarely shed even the blood of an animal in their religious services.

I shall not dwell particularly on the religious books of the Hindoos, but it would be injustice to omit the following sublime description of the Supreme Being, from the writings of Governor Holwell; who was an early investigator of those subjects, before the field of oriental literature so laudably engaged the attention of the English.

" GOD is ONE! Creator of all that is! God is like a perfect sphere, without beginning, and without end! GOD rules and governs all creation by a general providence, resulting from first determined and fixed principles. Thou shalt not make inquiry into the essence of the ETERNAL ONE, nor by what laws he governs. An inquiry into either is vain and criminal. It is enough, that day by day, and night by night, thou seest in his works, his wisdom, his power, and his mercy:—Benefit thereby!"

As applicable to this subject, I shall transcribe a few passages from the Vedas of the Hindoos, translated by Sir William Jones; to whose invaluable works we are indebted for so many acquisitions in oriental literature.

" By one Supreme Ruler is this universe pervaded; even every world in the whole circle of nature. Enjoy pure delight, O man! by abandoning all thoughts of this perishable world; and covet not the wealth of any creature existing."

" To those regions where evil spirits dwell, and which utter darkness involves, all such men surely go after death, as destroy the purity of their own souls."

"Unveil, O Thou who givest sustenance to the world, that face of the true sun, which is now hidden by a vase of golden light! so that we may see the truth, and know our whole duty!"

"O Thou who givest sustenance to the world, thou sole mover of all, thou who restrainest sinners, who pervadest yon great luminary, who appearest as the son of the creator! hide thy dazzling beams, and expand thy spiritual brightness, that I may view thy most auspicious, most glorious, real form."

"Let my soul return to the immortal spirit of God! and then, let my body, which ends in ashes, return to dust!"

"O Spirit, who pervadest fire, lead us in a straight path to the riches of beatitude! remove each foul taint from our souls; who approach thee with the highest praise, and the most fervid adoration!"

"God, who is perfect wisdom, and perfect happiness, is the final refuge of the man who has liberally bestowed his wealth, who has been firm in virtue, and who knows and adores that Great One!"

"Remember me, O Om, Thou divine Spirit!"

In Sir William Jones's institutes of the Hindoo laws, after stating some blemishes, and a few absurdities in the system, that excellent orientalist observes, "nevertheless a spirit of sublime devotion, of benevolence to mankind, and of amiable tenderness to all sentient creatures, pervades the whole work: the style of it has a certain austere majesty, that sounds like the language of legislation, and extorts a respectful awe; the sentiments of independence on all beings but God, and the harsh admonitions, even to kings, are truly noble; and the many panegyrics on the Gâyatri, the mother, as it is called, of the Vedas, prove the author to have adored (not the visible material sun, but) that divine and incomparably greater light, to use the words of the most venerable text in the Indian scripture, which illumines all, delights all, from which all proceed, to which all must return, and which alone can irradiate (not our visual organs merely, but our souls, and) our intellects. Whatever opinion, in short, may be formed of Menu and his laws, in a country happily enlightened by sound philosophy, and the only true revelation, it must be remembered, that those laws are actually revered as the word of the Most High, by nations of great importance to the political and commercial interests of Europe, and particularly by many millions of Hindoo subjects, whose well directed industry adds largely to the wealth of Britain, and who ask no more in return than protection for their persons and places of abode, justice in their temporal concerns, indulgence to the prejudice of their own religion, and the benefit of those laws which they have been taught to believe sacred, and which alone they can possibly comprehend."

The fakeers, or yogees, of the Senassee tribe, are a set of mendicant philosophers, who travel all over Hindostan, and live on the charity of the other castes of Hindoos. They are generally entirely naked, most of them robust handsome men: they admit proselytes from the other tribes, especially youth of bright parts, and take great pains to instruct them in their mysteries. These Gymnosophists often unite in large armed bodies, and perform pilgrimages to the sacred rivers and celebrated temples; but they are more like an army marching through a province, than an assembly of saints in procession to a temple; and often lay the countries through which they pass under contribution.

Many yogees, and similar professors, are devotees of the strictest order, carrying their superstition and enthusiasm far beyond any thing we are acquainted with in Europe: even the austerities of La Trappe are light in comparison with the voluntary penances of these philosophers; who reside in holes and caves, or remain under the banian trees near the temples. They imagine the expiation of their own sins, and sometimes those of others, consists in the most rigorous penances and mortifications. Some of them enter into a solemn vow to continue for life in one unvaried posture; others undertake to carry a cumbrous load, or drag a heavy chain; some crawl on their hands and knees, for years, around an extensive empire; and others roll their bodies on the earth, from the shores of the Indus to the banks of the Ganges, and in that humiliating posture, collect money to enable them either to build a temple, to dig a well, or to atone for some particular sin. Some swing during their whole life, in this torrid clime, before a slow fire; others suspend themselves, with their heads downwards, for a certain time, over the fiercest flames.

I have seen a man who had made a vow to hold up his arms in a perpendicular manner above his head, and never to suspend them; at length he totally lost the power of moving them at all. He was one of the Gymnosophists, who wear no kind of covering, and seemed more like a wild beast than a man: his arms, from having been so long in one posture, were become withered, and dried up; while his outstretched fingers, with long nails of twenty years growth, gave them the appearance of extraordinary horns: his hair, full of dust, and never combed, hung over him in a savage manner; and, except in his erect posture, there appeared nothing human about him. This man was travelling throughout Hindostan, and being unable to help himself with food, women of distinction among the Hindoos contended for the honour of feeding this holy person wherever he appeared.

I saw another of these devotees, who was one of the phallic worshippers of Seeva; and who, not content with wearing or adoring the symbol of that deity, had made a vow to fix every year a large iron ring into the most tender part of his body, and thereto to suspend a heavy chain, many yards long, to drag on the ground. I saw this extraordinary saint, in the seventh year of his penance, when he had just put in the seventh ring; and the wound was then so recent and painful, that he was obliged to carry the chain upon his shoulder, until the orifice became more callous.

I could recite many other facts; with a variety of superstitious as well as indecent rites and painful ceremonies, which these mistaken votaries practise, in hopes of appeasing the deity. Such austerities ought to make us more highly prize the pure and holy tenets of the Christian religion; and should fill our hearts with love and gratitude to HIM who brought life and immortality to light through his gospel; and offered Himself as a complete atonement for the sins of a fallen world!

The Brahmins at the Hindoo temples seldom wear a turban, and the upper part of their body is generally naked; but they never appear without the zennar, or sacred string, passing over them from the left shoulder; and a piece of fine cotton is tied round the waist, and falls in graceful folds below the knee. Their simple diet consists of milk, rice, fruit, and vegetables; they abstain from every thing that either had or could enjoy life, and use spices to flavour the rice, which is their principal food; it is also enriched with ghee, or clarified butter.

We cannot but admire the principle which dictates this humanity and self-denial: although, did they through a microscope observe the animalculæ which cover the mango, and compose the bloom of the fig; or perceive the animated myriads that swarm on every vegetable they eat, they must, on their present system, be at a loss for subsistence. Some of the Brahmins carry their austerities to such a length, as never to eat any thing but the grain which has passed through the cow; which being afterwards separated from its accompaniments, is considered by them as the purest of all food; in such veneration is this animal held by the Hindoos.

From the religious order of Brahmins, I descend to the cast of Chandalahs, or Pariars. These people are considered so abject, are employed in the vilest offices, and held in such detestation, that no other tribe will touch them; and those Hindoos who commit enormous crimes are excommunicated into this caste, which is considered to be a punishment worse than death.

But I will dwell no longer on particular castes; being desirous to draw a portrait of the Hindoos, where they bear a more general resemblance with each other: for although each caste, as I have already mentioned, differs something in dress, and has a few peculiar customs, and rules for ceremonial and moral conduct, yet they all agree in the fundamental tenets of their religion, and the principal duties of life.

They are commonly of the middle stature, slight and well proportioned, with regular and expressive features, black eyes, and a serene countenance. Among the virtues of the Hindoos are, piety, obedience to superiors, resignation in misfortune, charity and hospitality: filial, parental, and conjugal affection, are among their distinguishing characteristics. They are extremely sober, drinking only water, milk, or sherbet; and none but those of the lowest order are ever seen in a state of intoxication. They eat in the morning and evening; their cooking utensils are simple; their plates and dishes are generally formed from the leaf of the plantain-tree, or the nymphea lotos, that beautiful lily which abounds in every lake; these are never used a second time: the furniture of their houses is equally simple; seldom extending beyond what is absolutely necessary for a people whose wants are very few, when compared with those of the inhabitants in northern climates.

The men, in most of the Hindoo tribes, shave the head and beard, but leave the mustachios on the upper lip, and a small lock of hair on the head. The better sort wear turbans of fine muslin, of different colours; and a jama, or long gown of white calico, which is tied round the middle with a fringed or embroidered sash. Their shoes are of red leather, or English broad-cloth, sometimes ornamented, and always turned up with a long point at the toe. Their ears are bored, and adorned with large gold rings, passing through two pearls, or rubies; and on the arms they wear bracelets of gold or silver. The princes and nobles are adorned with pearl necklaces and golden chains, sustaining clusters of costly gems; their turbans are enriched with diamonds, rubies, and emeralds; and their bracelets composed of gold and precious stones.

The inferior castes are of a darker complexion than the superior

Hindoos; their dress generally consists of a turban, a short cotton vest and drawers; but some wear only a turban, and a cloth round the waist; although the poorest among them usually contrive to purchase a silver bangle, or bracelet, for the arm.

The Hindoo women, when young, are delicate and beautiful; so far as we can reconcile beauty with the olive complexion. They are finely proportioned; their limbs small, their features soft and regular, and their eyes black and languishing: but the bloom of beauty soon decays, and age makes a rapid progress before they have seen thirty years: this may be accounted for, from the heat of the climate, and the customs of the country; as they often are mothers at twelve years of age, and grandmothers at five and twenty. Montesquieu justly remarks, " that women in hot climates, are marriageable at eight, nine, or ten years of age; therefore in those countries infancy and marriage generally go together. They are old at twenty; their reason therefore never accompanies their beauty: when beauty demands the empire, the want of reason forbids the claim; when reason is obtained, beauty is no more!" And he further observes, that " those women ought to be in a state of dependence; for reason cannot procure in old age, that empire, which even youth and beauty could not give."

What superior advantages do my fair countrywomen derive from a liberal education, and a milder climate? the virtues and graces assemble in their train, and form a delightful union of chastity, beauty, elegance, and affability! what influence such women have over our sex, every man of feeling and sensibility must acknowledge.

> " Something than beauty dearer, should we look
> " Or on the mind, or mind illumin'd face;
> " Truth, goodness, honour, harmony, and love,
> " The richest bounty of indulgent heaven!" THOMSON.

No women can be more attentive to cleanliness than the Hindoos: they take every method to render their persons delicate, soft, and attractive: their dress is peculiarly becoming; consisting of a long piece of silk, or cotton, tied round the waist, and hanging in a graceful manner to the feet, it is afterwards brought over the body in negligent folds; under this they cover the bosom with a short waistcoat of satin, but wear no linen. Their long black hair is adorned with jewels, and wreaths of flowers: their ears are bored in many places, and loaded with pearls: a variety of gold chains, strings of pearl, and precious stones, fall from the neck over the bosom; and the arms are covered with bracelets, from the wrist to the elbow; they have also gold and silver chains round the ancles, and abundance of rings on their fingers and toes; among the former is frequently a small mirror. I think the richer the dress, the less becoming it appears; and a Hindoo woman of distinction always seems to be overloaded with finery; while the village nymphs, with fewer ornaments, but in the same elegant drapery, are more captivating: although there are very few women, even of the lowest families, who have not some jewels at their marriage.

In these external decorations consist the pride and pleasure of these uninstructed females; for very few, even in the best families, know how to read or write, or are capable of intellectual enjoyment. We learn from Homer, that the women in ancient Greece always kept in a retired part of the house, employed in embroidery or other feminine occupations; and at this day, the Indian females are never seen by those who visit the master of the family; they know but little of the world, and are not permitted to eat with their husbands or brothers, nor to associate with other men.

After the girls are betrothed, the ends of the fingers and nails are dyed red, with a preparation from the mendey, or hinna shrub, already mentioned as a principal ornament of the Asiatic gardens. They make a black circle round the eyes with the powder of antimony, which adds much to their brilliancy, and heightens the beauty of the eastern ladies.

The houses of the rich Hindoos and Mahometans, are generally built within an inclosure, surrounded by galleries, or verandas, not only for privacy, but to exclude the sun from the apartments. This court is frequently adorned with shrubs and flowers; and a fountain playing before the principal room, where the master receives his guests; which is open in front to the garden, and furnished with carpets and cushions.

Education in general among the Hindoos, is attended with very little trouble: few boys in the subordinate tribes are taught any thing more than to read and write, with the rudiments of the trade or profession, they are intended for; but many of the Brahmin youth are instructed in astronomy, astrology, and physic; and acquire some knowledge of the civil and religious laws. Nothing can be more simple than a Hindoo school; which is usually under a thatched shed open on three sides, with a sanded floor, on which the boys learn to write, and go through the first rules of arithmetic, in which science some of them make a great progress.

The ceremonies of the Hindoos open an ample field, on which I can now make only a few cursory observations. The children are married at the discretion of their parents; the girls at three or four, and the boys at six or eight years of age: the nuptials are very expensive; occasioned by an ostentatious parade, nocturnal processions, feasting for several days, and presents to the numerous guests. The bride afterwards sees her husband as a play-fellow, she is taught to place her affection on this object, and never thinks of any other; until, when about eleven years old, she is conducted with some ceremony to his house, and commences the duties of a wife, and the mistress of a family. But should the boy die during that interval, the girl must remain a widow for life, have her head shaved, be divested of every ornament, and perform many menial offices. One delicate attention which most of the Hindoo women voluntarily pay to their husband, is, that when he is absent from home for any length of time, they seldom wear their jewels, or decorate themselves with ornaments; since the object they most wished to please is no longer in their presence. No widow is permitted to marry a second time; but a man may have a succession of wives: polygamy is allowed by the Hindoo law, though not generally practised, except when the first wife proves barren. Every Hindoo must marry into his own caste; but among the lower classes at Bombay, I have known this ordinance evaded. And in several parts of India, especially in Mysore and Malabar, the ryots, or cultivators of the land, take as many wives as they can maintain, as the women there are extremely useful in different branches of husbandry, and are not expensive to their husbands.

Most of the Hindoos burn their dead. The funeral piles of the rich are mingled with sandal-wood, and fed by aromatic oils; while the poor are consumed with humble faggots. Some put the bodies of their deceased friends into rivers, especially those they deem holy streams; and there are particular castes in Bengal, who, when they think the sick past recovery, expose them on the banks of the Ganges, fill their mouths with sacred mud, and leave them at high-water mark, to be carried away by the tide.

Throughout the greater part of Hindostan, when all hopes of recovery are over, the sick person is taken from the bed, and laid upon the earth, that he may expire on the element from which he was originally formed. After his death, the house is surrounded by widows, hired for the purpose; who make loud lamentations, beat their breasts in a violent manner, and affect every token of grief and despair. The male relations attend the corpse to the funeral pile; which, if possible, is always near the water, and after the body is consumed the ashes are sprinkled with milk and consecrated water, brought from the Ganges, or some other holy stream; and ceremonies are performed for several days.

Although the custom of burning the dead so generally prevails, yet in some districts, on particular occasions, they are interred. The extraordinary custom of the widow burning herself with the body of her deceased husband, is never permitted under the English government, and very seldom by the Mahomedans, but is constantly practised among the Mahrattas, and different castes of Hindoos, under their own princes on the continent.

On the decease of the husband, if his widow resolves to attend him to the world of spirits, a funeral pile is erected, covered with an arbour of dry boughs, where the dead body is placed: the living victim follows, dressed, in her bridal jewels, surrounded by relations, priests, and musicians. After certain prayers and ceremonies, she takes off her jewels, and presenting them with her last blessing to her nearest relative, she ascends the funeral pile, enters the awful bower, and placing herself near the body of her husband, with her own hand generally sets fire to the pile; which being constantly supplied with aromatic oils, the mortal frames are soon consumed: and the Hindoos entertain no doubt of the soul's reunion in purer realms; where, however false the principle, they are taught to believe that such heroic virtue, and approved constancy, will meet with a proportionate reward. During the cremation, the noise of the trumpets, and other musical instruments, overpowers the cries of the self-devoted victim, should her resolution fail her: but those who have attended this solemn sacrifice, assure us, that they always observed, even the youngest widows, to manifest the greatest composure and dignity throughout the awful scene.

The Hindoos are much addicted to astrology, and place such implicit faith in their Brahmins and soothsayers, that they will not make a bargain, enter into a contract, nor suffer a ship to sail, on a day, or an hour, which they pronounce unlucky. They have even lucky minutes, when important business can only be transacted. But Greece and Rome, even in the highest state of civilization and refinement, produced many persons who were equally credulous in omens and auspices, and as much addicted to astrology and augury, as any of the modern Hindoos.

Religious disputes and unavailing controversies, seldom disturb the peace of a Hindoo; contentedly he adopts the rites and ceremonies of his forefathers, believes in their tenets, performs his stated ablutions, and keeps the appointed festivals: nor by free inquiries, and freer opinions, does he disturb the peace of others, or permit them to interrupt his own.

It is not then in Hindostan that we are to look for the perfection of art and science, for eminent statesmen, and sage philosophers: but the Hindoos, who reside at a distance from capital cities, still preserve much of that simplicity of manners fancied by the poets in the golden age: and seem, more than any other people now existing, to realize the innocent and peaceful mode of life, which they ascribe to that happy æra. When I saw the Brahmin women of distinction drawing water at the village wells, and tending their cattle to the lakes and rivers, they recalled the transactions of the patriarchal days. Very often have I witnessed a scene similar to that between Abraham's servant and Rebekah, at the entrance of a Hindoo village in Guzerat. "He made his camels to kneel down "without the city, by a well of water, at the time of the evening, "even the time when the women go out to draw water: and behold "Rebekah came with her pitcher on her shoulder; and the damsel "was very fair to look upon: and she went down, and filled her "pitcher, and came up. And the servant said unto her, Let me "drink, I pray thee: and she said, Drink, and I will give thy camels drink also: and she hasted, and emptied her pitcher into "the trough, and ran again unto the well to draw water, and drew "for all the camels." The Hindoo damsels of the present day live in as much simplicity as those formerly in Mesopotamia; they still descend to the wells, and continue to pour the water into an adjacent trough for the convenience of the cattle.

The natives of the torrid zone are not fond of exercise; walking is by no means considered as a pleasing recreation; they like to ride a good horse, with gentle paces, or to take the air in a hackree, a sort of chariot drawn by white oxen; it is seldom hung on springs, and consists of a conical dome, supported by four pillars, covered with broad cloth, and curtains in front and on each side, to open at pleasure. Officers of government, and men of rank are carried in a palankeen, or more properly a palkee, an Asiatic luxury, as yet unknown in Europe. It is composed of a shell, or frame, about six feet long, and half as broad, fixed to a long bamboo, forming a bold curve in the center, which there rises about four feet from the frame. Over the bamboo is spread a canopy of cloth, or velvet, the length of the shell, adorned with fringes and tassels of gold, silver, or silk; and the frame contains a bed and pillows, covered with silk, and so disposed that you may either sit up or recline, as is most agreeable. The palankeen is carried by four men, who with relays, travel at a great rate; and I think there is not a more cheerful or happy set of people in India, than the generality of the palankeen bearers.

The Asiatics love to retire with their women and children to some cool spot near a river or tank, shaded by the friendly banian tree, or spreading mango; there they enjoy that sort of indolent repose which they are so fond of; and partake of an innocent repast of herbs and fruits, on the verdant carpet.

The wealthy Mahometans, Hindoos, and Parsees, frequently

entertain their friends at their garden houses: but in these mixed companies no women are present, except the dancing-girls, or tolerated courtezans, who are accompanied by musicians, playing on instruments resembling the guittar and violin. These singing-men and singing-women, are hired at festivals and grand solemnities, among all sects and professions in India. Many of the dancing-girls are extremely delicate in their persons, soft and regular in their features, with a form of perfect symmetry; and, although dedicated from infancy to this profession, they in general preserve a decency and modesty in their demeanor, which is more likely to allure, than the shameless effrontery of similar characters in other countries. Their dances require great attention, from the dancer's feet being hung with small bells, which act in concert with the music. Two girls usually perform at the same time; their steps are not so mazy or active as ours, but much more interesting; as the song, the music, and the motions of the dance, combine to express love, hope, jealousy, despair, and the passions so well known to lovers, and very easily to be understood by those who are ignorant of other languages. The Indians are extremely fond of this entertainment, and lavish large sums on their favourites.

Another kind of dancing-girls are dedicated to the principal Hindoo temples; these are supplied by their parents, who are taught, that the presentation of a beautiful daughter to the deity is highly acceptable: they dance and sing at the festivals, but are not considered in the character of the vestal virgins in ancient Rome, or of those we read of among the Peruvians; for if we investigate the brahminical mysteries, we shall find that these damsels are not only dedicated to the principal idols, but to the pleasure of the priests. They seldom leave the place of their initiation, looking upon themselves as wedded to the deities: but as they frequently have children, who partake more of a terrestrial than a celestial origin, the boys are taught to play on musical instruments, and the girls are early instructed in the profession of their mothers.

All the large cities in Hindostan contain sets of musicians and dancing-girls, under the care of their respective duennas, who are always ready to attend for hire at weddings, and other festivities; or to finish the evening entertainment of the Europeans and natives; and many of them accompany the Asiatic armies to the field.

The singing-men and singing-women mentioned by the aged Barzillai, and the daughters of music that we read of in the sacred pages, as well as in the ancient poets, resembled these characters in Hindostan. The women of Israel came out to meet David and Saul, dancing to instruments of music, and complimenting Saul with having slain his thousands, and David his ten thousands. The choristers of Palestine resembled those in India; who now celebrate a prince, or general, in the same manner at a public festival.

It is not only the introduction of dancing-girls and musicians, but a variety of other customs, which remind us of similar scenes among the ancients. The Greeks and other nations kept their religious festivals among consecrated groves, gloomy forests, and sacred fountains. The Hindoos do the same, and have done so from the remotest antiquity. The Druids had their solemn oaks, their awful shades, and holy retreats; the Brahmins have their venerable trees, favourite tanks, and consecrated rivers; to which, at appointed seasons, they repair with their followers, to perform ablutions, to drink of the hallowed stream, and deck the banks with flowery oblations. There is something awful in the gloomy shade; it naturally inspires religious reflections; and therefore the Druids, and pagan priests, always held them in veneration: but nothing in this respect equals the banian-tree, that rural fane, which is so fully described in a former chapter.

The Hindoo religion requires frequent ablution, which is a custom wisely introduced in a warm climate, where cleanliness is very conducive to health: these ablutions are performed in the consecrated tanks near the temples; but in most of the principal cities are hummums, or public baths; and people of fortune, especially among the Moguls, have these conveniences in their own houses. Bathing sumptuously was a great luxury among the Greeks and Romans; and the buildings appropriated to this purpose, constitute some of the most magnificent remains of antiquity. The hummum, or warm-bath, is equally the delight of the Asiatics; as is the subsequent anointing with aromatic oils. The Hindoo women perfume their hair with oil of cloves, cinnamon, sandal, mogrees, and other sweet-scented flowers; and those who can afford it, use the oil, or ottar of roses: this delicate and costly perfume is made in Persia, and the northern provinces of Hindostan: it is the pure essential oil of roses, rising in small particles on the surface of newly-distilled rose-water. In Persia, whole fields are covered with the Damascus-rose, or the scripture rose of

Sharon: but it requires many gallons of rose-water to furnish only a few drops of this delicious essence.

The Hindoos, as well as the Mahometans, are forbidden the use of wine and spirituous liquors; and I believe most of the higher classes attend strictly to the prohibition; the lower classes are less abstemious: but rich and poor, especially officers in the army, and soldiers, are addicted to the use of opium, which they take in large quantities, and enjoy the pleasing delirium it occasions. In battle it inspires a false courage, and sometimes produces a phrenzy, which lasts only for a short time; leaving those who swallow this pernicious drug in a state of languor and imbecility, until a renewal of the dose revives the spirits: but its frequent use enfeebles the constitution, and shortens the lives of its deluded votaries.

Opium is used to a better purpose by the halcarras, who are a set of people employed as messengers, spies, and letter carriers. An halcarra takes a letter, wraps it up in some secret fold of his shabby garment, and with a little opium, some rice, and a small pot to draw water from the wells of the charitable, he undertakes a journey of several hundred miles, and receives his reward on delivering the letter.

Engraved by T. Wageman.

A YOUNG HINDOO *among the Secular* BRAHMINS *of distinction.*

Jam. Forbes 1780.

Published by White Cochrane & Co Fleet street June 2d 1812

Engraved by J. Shury

A HINDOO FAMILY, *of the* BANIAN CAST.

Jam. Forbes, Bombay 1769.

Published by White, [illegible] Fleet Street June 1st 1812.

Engraved by Chas Heath.

DANCING GIRLS (and MUSICIANS.

Jam Forbes del. 1781

Published by White, Cochrane & Co. Fleet Street June 1st 1812

Manner of Travelling in a PALANKEEN *in India!*

An INDIAN HACKEREE, *drawn by* GUZERAT OXEN,
with the Costume of different Casts in Hindostan.
from a Drawing by Baron de Montalembert, 1807.

Published by White, Cochrane & Co. Fleet Street, June 1st 1812.

CHAPTER V.

THE INVASION OF THE AFGHANS IN HINDOSTAN,

WITH THE CONQUESTS AND ESTABLISHMENT
OF THE MAHOMEDANS,
IN DIFFERENT PARTS OF THE HINDOO EMPIRE:
A GENERAL DESCRIPTION OF THE FOLLOWERS OF THE
ARABIAN PROPHET,
AND PARTICULARLY OF THOSE SETTLED ON THE
ISLAND OF BOMBAY.

"Every writer of travels should consider, that like all other authors, he undertakes either "to instruct or please; or to mingle pleasure with instruction. He that instructs, must offer "to the mind something to be imitated, or something to be avoided; he that pleases, must "offer new images to his reader, and enable him to form a tacit comparison of his own state "with that of others." DR. JOHNSON.

CONTENTS.

CHAPTER V.

The rich and fertile kingdoms of Hindostan were inhabited entirely by the Hindoos, until the year 976 of the Christian æra, when the Islamites, or Mahomedans, commenced their conquests in the northern provinces, and formed the empire of Ghizni. These invaders were Tartars, from the northern parts of Asia, who brought with them the most bigotted attachment to the Mahomedan faith; and under a pretence of converting the Hindoos to the tenets of the Koran, they destroyed their temples, and plundered them of the wealth which had been accumulating for ages. The treasures of gold and jewels found in some of those sacred repositories, appear almost incredible. History informs us, that the Sultaun Moaz-ul-Dien, who made nine expeditions into Hindostan, left behind him in diamonds alone, of various sizes, five hundred maunds in weight, which is little less than twenty thousand pounds in avoirdupois: and the avarice and cruelty of Mahmood, the first sultaun of Ghizni, in consequence of an impious vow, are too shocking to relate. These invaders at length reduced all the northern kingdoms; the Mahomedan religion was established, and followed by the most horrid massacres and devastations during the reign of eighteen princes: a period which presents a sanguinary picture of war and famine, desolation and despair! arising from the frequent but ineffectual struggles of the wretched Hindoos, for their civil and religious liberties.

At the end of the fourteenth century, Timur Bec, or Tamerlane, a prince descended from Zingis Khan, chief of the Mogul Tartars, invaded the empire, established by the former Mahomedan conquerors, and with atrocious cruelty plundered not only the Hindoos, but the followers of the prophet; although the Mogul empire was not completely founded until the sixteenth century; when Baber, a descendant of Timur, got possession of Delhi, and made it the capital of his dominions. Most of the southern districts were shortly after subdued, and the tenets of the Koran adopted by numbers; the converts entirely relinquished the Hindoo manners and dress, and lost the name.

After these Mogul sovereigns were firmly established on the imperial throne, they permitted their Hindoo subjects the free enjoyment of their religion; and although, from foreign wars, and intestine commotions, the picture of the times too often presented a scene of blood and cruelty, yet the blessings of peace sometimes prevailed: during those happy intervals, poetry, history, and music, raised their dejected heads, and with many useful arts and sciences, assumed a short-lived smile; convincing us they only wanted the aid of milder governments, and less tumultuous times, to flourish in the realms of Hindostan, as well as in Grecian or Italian climes.

> "Can misery bid the imagination glow,
> "Or genius ripen, midst domestic woe?
> "Sad sits the bard amidst his country's tears,
> "And sighs, regardless of the wreath he wears.
> "Did ever want or famine sweetly sing?
> "The fetter'd hand uncouthly strikes the string."

Among the sovereigns of Hindostan, the imperial Akber merits particular notice; and, did my limits permit, gladly should I attempt a theme, on which poets and historians have dwelt with fond delight. Akber succeeded his father Humaioon, the eldest son of sultaun Baber, in the fourteenth year of his age; and from that early period, during a long reign of fifty years, shone a bright example of wisdom, clemency, and justice. He was supreme monarch over all the provinces of Hindostan, from the Indus to the Ganges; and by his mildness and equanimity diffused happiness throughout his extensive dominions: the Hindoos enjoyed their religious privileges without molestation; no distant governor was suffered to be guilty of the smallest oppression; agriculture and commerce flourished; the elegant arts were cherished, and a princely encouragement was given to literature and science. The Ayen Akbery, or institutes, compiled by Abul Fazel, the secretary and historian of Akber, remain a lasting monument of the justice, prudence, and unwearied assiduity, of this great prince, for the true interest of his subjects. He reigned from 1556 to 1605.

The Mogul empire continued to flourish from the reign of Akber until the death of Aurungzebe, in the beginning of the eighteenth century; soon after that event, the nawabs, or governors of the distant provinces, began to shake off their allegiance to the court of Delhi, and establish themselves as independent princes; by which means the power of the emperors gradually declined, and instead of one Mahomedan despot, a number of inferior sovereigns, styled nabobs, or nawabs, arose in different parts of the empire; so that there is now hardly a place of note in Hindostan, where the followers of the Arabian prophet are not found; being tolerated under the Hindoo rajahs, and protected by all the European governments.

It is unnecessary to discuss the tenets of the Koran, which is the standard of the Mussulmaun faith; its rules for religious and moral conduct, are as much attended to in Hindostan, as in other countries professing the same religion. This book, which was composed by Mahomed, a native of Mecca, in Arabia, assisted by a monk, named Sergius, is a most extraordinary instance of imposture.

Mahomed, the only son of Abdallah, a prince of Mecca, was born in that city in the year of Christ 571, and died at Medina in 631. At the age of forty, he publicly assumed the character of a prophet sent by God to establish in its purity the religion of the patriarchs. Being desirous of superseding the missions of the Jewish and Christian law-givers, he admitted their divine origin; but from having proved ineffectual to accomplish their intended purpose, the artful Arabian announced himself to be the Paraclete promised by Jesus Christ, and asserted that the Almighty had sent him with more ample powers; and had especially commissioned him to compel those by force, who resisted gentler means, to embrace the doctrines of the Koran, which had been revealed to him from heaven by the angel Gabriel. By his uncommon art and address, and by the temporal power which he had acquired in Arabia, Mahomed not only spread his religion in that country, but throughout Egypt, Syria, and Persia: his posterity were looked upon as holy, and reigned over some of the most considerable kingdoms in Asia.

About ten years after the commencement of his religious career, some of his more enlightened countrymen, who had known the prophet from his youth, but neither approved of his life or doctrine, resolved to destroy him, and deliver the world from such an impostor: Mahomed, apprized of their design, fled from Mecca to Medina, where the fame of his sanctity procured him a favourable reception. This event, which happened in the six hundred and twenty-second year of the Chrisian æra, is called the hegirah, or flight; and from this period the Mahomedans compute their time, dating every thing from the first year of the hegirah.

Mahomed not only distributed to his followers the spoils of the earth, as a reward for their faithfulness in propagating his doctrines, but promised them a paradise in the world to come, so luxurious, that it wrought powerfully on their minds, and worked them up to a high degree of enthusiasm. A description of this sensual Eden has been given by an English poet, with as much delicacy as the subject admits of.

> " There, in the gardens of eternal spring,
> " While birds of paradise around you sing,
> " Each with his blooming beauty by his side,
> " Shall drink rich wines that in full rivers glide;
> " Breathe fragrant gales o'er fields of spice that blow,
> " And gather fruits immortal as they grow:
> " Ecstatic bliss shall your whole powers employ,
> " And every sense be lost in every joy!"
>
> HUGHES.

The complexion of the Mahomedans in India, is much the same as that of the Hindoos; a clear olive brown: their dress is in many respects similar; especially in the turban, the long white gown, sash, and shoes; but in addition, the Mussulmauns wear full long drawers, generally of a satin, called kincob, with gold and silver flowers; and a catarra, or short dagger, in their girdle. The warriors have a broad sword, with spears, lances, and fire-arms; and some of the bravest troops in Hindostan are Mahomedans, from Arabia, Candahar, Scindy, and the provinces bordering on Persia. Their religion permits the use of all animal food, except pork; and as they secretly indulge in wine and spirits, they are more robust and hardy than the disciples of Brahma: avarice, indolence, and effeminacy, mark the character of the Hindoo; and if, to the two former, we unite ambition, valour, and jealousy, we shall have a tolerably correct outline of the Mogul.

The Mahomedan women in India enjoy less liberty than the Hindoos; but in complexion, manners, and behaviour, are not unlike them. They adorn themselves with a variety of jewels, worn over a close gown of muslin, with long sleeves and a short waist; silk or satin drawers reach to the ancles, and a transparent veil covers the head: the education of these women, like that of the Hindoos, is very confined; the men do not seem to wish them to be rational companions, and purposely keep them in a state of ignorance. I believe music is prohibited by the Koran; but the Mahomedans have dancing girls among them; and hire vocal and instrumental music at weddings, and other entertainments where a mixed company is invited.

The Moguls, Persians, Arabians, and the generality of the

Asiatics, believe in genii, angels, and supernatural agents of various denominations, and degrees of existence; their histories, tales, and romances, abound with such imagery. Some are the friends and guardians of the human race; others, called the evil genii, are in a constant state of warfare with the benevolent spirits. On this account, talismans, amulets, and charms, esteemed for their latent virtues, and mysterious powers, are worn by the inhabitants of India; who believe that such cabalistical preparations are effectual against witchcraft, fascination, and all the operations of the malevolent genii: they serve also as guards and protectors of hidden treasures, which are frequently buried under the earth, to conceal them from the avarice of Asiatic despots.

The Greeks and Romans were not exempt from these prejudices, nor is it long since they have subsided in England. Acts of parliament on this subject, were passed so late as the reign of James the First. In the age of chivalry, enchantment and divination prevailed throughout Europe; and in the oath administered by the constable to the combatants in a duel, are these expressions;

" Ye shall sweare that ye shall have no stone of virtue, nor
" hearbe of virtue; nor charm, nor experiment, nor none other
" enchauntment by you; and that ye trust in none other thinge
" properly, but in God, and your body, and your brave quarrel."

I constantly wear one of these talismanic stones, it having been left to me by an invaluable friend: it consists of a convex oval emerald, as taken from the mine; uncut and unpolished by art: it is set in plain gold, and shines in native beauty without any extraneous ornament. I pretend not to investigate the antiquity and legendary tales of this ring during the time of its oriental proprietors, which gave it an imaginary value, far exceeding its real worth: but the English gentleman who possessed it fifty years ago, fully appreciated those virtues. He had from his early youth been much with the Hindoos; and although a Christian in principle, and possessing the amiable and benevolent characteristics of that divine dispensation, yet he believed also in lucky and unlucky days, omens, and spells, so universally accredited by the Hindoos.

This gentleman had often been at Poonah, the capital of the Mahratta empire, and had resided much among the Brahmins: when a member of the council at Bombay, about forty years ago, he was appointed ambassador to the Mahratta government, on an affair of great importance to the East India Company, and the English nation: the business was so urgent, that he left Bombay in the middle of the rainy season to ascend the Gaut mountains, and reach the Mahratta capital on a day which the Hindoo astrologers had marked as peculiarly auspicious. Being in a public character, he travelled with a considerable retinue; there being no choultries, or caravansaries, on that road, they generally pitched their tents where they found the convenience of shade and water; for in the rainy season, on the western side of the Indian peninsula, a series of fair weather often holds for several weeks together, when those accommodations are as desirable to travellers as during the fine months.

On the second evening of the journey, the encampment was formed under a friendly banian tree, on the margin of a lake: on retiring to his sleeping-tent, the ambassador missed his ring; but

but could not recollect whether he had taken it off when he washed his hands after supper: the strictest search was immediately made for it without success: it was not merely the loss of the ring which now troubled the owner; he annexed certain ideas to the event, which I shall not attempt to explain; and, notwithstanding the urgency of the embassy, and the implied necessity of being at the Mahratta durbar on the auspicious hour already mentioned, he remained the next day at the encampment, in search of this precious gem, and offered a large reward for its discovery; but in vain: and the following morning he proceeded on his journey, under very unpleasant sensations. The embassy continued about thirteen months; at which period, during the ensuing rainy season, the gentleman and his suite returned to Bombay.

The advantage of shade and water induced them to occupy the ground of their former little encampments, and the tents were again pitched upon the same spot where the ambassador had lost his ring: it had rained hard in the day, but the evening was remarkably fine, and the moon at the full: while sitting at his tent-door after supper, reviewing his late negociations at Poonah, and by an association of ideas, reverting to the loss of his ring in that very place, he perceived the dark side of the grove illuminated by thousands of fire-flies, flitting among the branches, with a brilliancy, of which the faint light of the European glow-worm gives but little idea. Those who have travelled in Italy during the summer months, and have there seen the lampyris, or lucciola, although not so numerous as in the Asiatic woods, can easily conceive the nocturnal splendour of these insects in the torrid zone. I have seen them produce a fine effect in the dark recesses of the majestic coliseum, and illumine the gardens of the Villa Medici at Rome; on the banks of the Arno, they add much to the beauty of the Tuscan evening; and the Italian and the English poets are fond of celebrating the "*emerald-light*" of the lucciola and the glow-worm.

While the ambassador was amusing himself with the splendid appearance of these insects in the surrounding shades, he observed one of them settled among the grass, which was always stationary and motionless, although shining with equal lustre. Having remarked it for a considerable time, curiosity led him to approach it: the moon shone on the spot; he stooped to seize the insect; and took up his ring. We must first enter into his peculiar feelings respecting omens, talismans, and charms, and then conceive his surprize and joy at this auspicious event. It had most probably been shook from the table cloth thirteen months before, and remained on that spot the whole time, unobserved by other travellers: during the fair season it was probably covered with dust; but now a heavy shower combined with Cynthia's beam to produce the brilliant effect on the convex face of the emerald, and to restore the lucky ring to its owner; who having so highly prized it before the adventure, it is needless to say how much it was now advanced in his estimation.

My most intimate friend was not only the public assistant, but the confidential friend of this gentleman; he was always his agent during his absence, and left the sole executor to his will: he had an only son then in England for his education; and knowing that he would not appreciate the ring as his father did, he promised it to my friend at his death; but omitted to mention it in his will.

Being absent at a distant settlement when that event happened, I was commissioned to sell the effects of the deceased, and to purchase the ring at any price: a number of Europeans and natives, some attracted by its real value, but more by its imaginary virtue, attended the sale; and as I had not mentioned my commission when the ring was put up, it was already advanced far beyond the price of such a jewel, either for its size or lustre; when, as the gentleman had died worth a considerable fortune, and had only one child to enjoy it, I thought it proper to declare my friend's resolution to purchase it at all events. The company were only hurt at my having kept silence so long, and unanimously declared that he only ought to have the ring, for whom it was intended by its late owner: too soon, alas! it came into my possession, as a testamentary legacy from one of the best of men, and dearest of friends; and has been ever since my constant companion.

The three divisions of Arabia were conquered and commanded by Mahomed himself: Abubekir, his immediate successor, assumed the title of caliph, or vicar to the prophet; which continued in that line for several generations. In Europe, and among the Asiatic Christians, his disciples were generally called Saracens; and, under that appellation, in less than a century from the decease of the successful impostor, they spread his religion from the Atlantic ocean to India and Tartary; and his successors reigned in Syria, Persia, Egypt, Africa, and Spain.

The establishment of the religion of Abraham and Ishmael, the great progenitors of the Arabians, was no doubt the principal design of Mahomed, as I have already mentioned; he wished, at the same time, to extend the commerce, and increase the wealth of his native country. The Ishmaelites had always been famous merchants, as well as warriors: in a very early state of their tribe, they travelled with their camels to Egypt, laden with spicery, balm, and myrrh; neither had they any objection to deal in slaves, as the history of Joseph exemplifies.

It would be foreign to my purpose to enter into a detail of oriental commerce from that transaction, until the time that " Solomon made a navy of ships at Ezion-geber, which is beside Eloth, on the shore of the Red Sea, in the land of Edom: and Hiram put in the navy his servants, shipmen that had knowledge of the sea, with the servants of Solomon; and they came to Ophir, and fetched from thence gold, four hundred and twenty talents; and plenty of Algum trees, and precious stones: and they had at sea a navy of Tharshish, with the navy of Hiram; once in three years came the navy of Tharshish, bringing gold and silver, and ivory, and apes, and peacocks."

It is not yet decided whether the island of Ceylon was the Ophir of Solomon, as well as the Serendib of the Persians and Arabians, or whether the vessels of Hiram traded to other parts of India: but from that period the commerce of the East has been a most interesting and productive source of wealth. When refinement and luxury had made a rapid progress in their extensive empire, the Romans were supplied with the most costly productions from all parts of the known world; and received by different channels, a variety of articles from India and China; but there was little maritime intercourse on these seas, until after the promulgation of the Koran; when the Arabians, with a boldness unknown to former navigators, and never exceeded by any, until the discovery of the magnet, were urged by their enthusiastic zeal to spread their new religion on the shores of the Indian continent, and its remotest islands: they were for some time established in the city of Canton, subject to their own laws, and enjoying many privileges: they indeed only resided there as merchants, the cautious policy of the Chinese not permitting them to colonize. In most other places they not only planted their religion, but increased their trade, and returned to their own country with a variety of valuable articles. Thus was the oriental commerce enlarged; and numerous converts, from the Red Sea to the remotest of the eastern islands, were added to the Mahomedan faith.

I shall conclude this account of the Mahomedans in Hindostan, with a summary of their general character, from the writings of an intelligent officer, who travelled through the Nizam's country in 1791, and communicated his observations in the first volume of the oriental collections. I am not acquainted with his name; but as far as my knowledge extends, I have found all his remarks extremely correct and satisfactory.

"What is most surprising to an European, is the decorum, gravity, and elegance of the Moorish children. They are, for the most part, handsomer at this age than when fully grown; and with all that is infantine and engaging, they can upon cases of ceremony assume the unaffected steadiness of an old courtier. By paying attention to what was said to these children by their tutors, and by observing the most admired and popular characters among the men, I endeavoured to acquire some insight into what style of manners was held in greatest repute among the Moors; and I found the leading principle of external behaviour to be a majestic and martial deportment, a serene and steady countenance, which should remain calm and unaltered amidst the greatest events; neither manifesting signs of depression nor exaltation, but capable of that pliability which softens the countenance to the reception of friends, and accompanies good offices with a benignant smile. This frequently borders upon dissimulation, since condemned persons of rank have often been dismissed from the presence to execution, without threats or menaces, but with every mark of politeness. Having discoursed upon this subject with the Moors, reminding them of similar circumstances in history, they have replied, those instances were marks of collected firmness in the prince; since whatever the cause might be, he should never derogate from his own dignity, nor forget the attentions due to a man of rank, whatever his situation or conduct might be. They are extremely careful not to interrupt one another in discourse; and generally possess a natural eloquence, which they utter with fluency, in a soft, but audible tone; and are peculiarly graceful in their action, which is so expressive, as often to forestall what they are about to deliver."

The same observant traveller makes a remark on the seclusion of the Mahomedan women from the society of the men, which I believe to have great weight in the general opinion of the Orientals. "On combining together the inclinations of Mahomed with his policy, we shall find the seclusion of women from the society of men, gives to the latter all those hours, which, in Europe, are generally employed by men to please the object of their wishes;

leaving them at full leisure to pursue, without distractions of jealousy, the business of the day. It also prevents those bitter feuds and lasting animosities, which poison the minds of contending rivals, otherwise formed for mutual esteem and friendship. It preserves the marriage-bed not only from pollution, but also from the dread of it: and it secures women from those delusions and temptations, which irritate the mind with fleeting joys, leaving behind the permanent sting of bitter remorse! while never having tasted the universal triumph and dominion which beauty gives in the circles of Europe, the loss of power is not added to the painful sensation of fading charms."

Engraved by J. Shury.

A MAHOMEDAN YOUTH of Distinction.

Jam. Forbes. 1769

Published by White, Cochrane & Co. Fleet Street June 1st 1812.

Engraved by T. Wageman.

A MAHOMEDAN of Distinction, with a DERVISE on his Pilgrimage.

Jam. Forbes, 1768.

CHAPTER VI.

THE EMIGRATION OF THE PARSEES,

THE DISCIPLES OF ZOROASTER, AND THE ANCIENT MAGI, FROM PERSIA;

AND THEIR ESTABLISHMENT IN HINDOSTAN: WITH A PARTICULAR DESCRIPTION OF THE PARSEES SETTLED AT BOMBAY.

He that would travel for the entertainment of others, should remember that the great object of remark is human life. Every nation has something particular in its manufactures, its works of genius, its medicines, its agriculture, its customs, and its policy. He only is a useful traveller, who brings home something by which his country may be benefited; who procures some supply of want, or some mitigation of evil, which may enable his readers to compare their condition with that of others; to improve it whenever it is worse; and whenever it is better to enjoy it.

Dr. Johnson.

CONTENTS.

Parsees, or Guebres—under the Mahomedan persecutions, emigrate to Ormuz, and from thence to Hindostan—land near Surat—arrangements with the Hindoo Rajàh—dispersion in India—worshippers of fire—everlasting fire near Baku, in Persia—manners and customs of the Parsees—treatment of their dead—women—ancient Persians—religion of Zoroaster and the ancient Magi.

CHAPTER VI.

The Parsees, or Guebres, are a people whom the Mahomedan persecutions drove from Persia, their native country, in the eighth century of the Christian æra. They are descended from the ancient Persians, followers of Zoroaster; to whose religious tenets and moral laws, they still profess to adhere.

While the Mahomedan religion was established in Persia under the system of terror, these people emigrated to the isle of Ormuz, and continued there fifteen years; they then embarked in small vessels for India; bringing with them the autus-byram, or sacred fire, which they preserved with the greatest care. After a dreadful voyage, they landed at Diu, on the south-west point of the Cambay gulph, a settlement now belonging to the Portugueze. They continued at this place for some time, and then crossing the gulph, landed at Suzan, near Nunsarrée, which is a little to the southward of Surat. Here these unhappy Persians implored the protection of the Hindoo rajah; and pathetically related their religious persecutions, their flight from their native land, and all their subsequent misfortunes. Astonished at the appearance of so many armed strangers, the rajah was doubtful how he should receive them: at length humanity prevailed; he granted them permission to settle in his dominions, and to build a temple for their sacred fire, on their compliance with certain conditions; particularly, that they should never put an ox or a cow to death, nor on any consideration taste the flesh; a covenant, which both themselves and their descendants have kept inviolable to this day.

As their families increased, the Parsees dispersed, and settled at Bombay, Surat, Baroche, and other northern towns on the western coast of India. Active and industrious, they applied themselves to domestic and foreign commerce; and many of the principal merchants and owners of ships at Bombay and Surat, are Parsees: others learned the mechanic arts, and engaged in the varied manufactures of the loom: the best carpenters and shipwrights in India are of this tribe.

Their number at Bombay is considerable, and at Surat they amount to twenty thousand families: hitherto they have not attempted to establish a government of their own; and an unfortunate schism in their religious tenets has divided them into two separate factions.

The Parsees are all worshippers of fire; and in every temple is a sacred flame, lighted at first from that originally brought from Persia, which is still preserved with great reverence at Oodwarra, near Nunsarree. These fires are attended day and night by the andaroos, or priests, and are never permitted to expire. They are preserved in a large chafing-dish, carefully supplied with fuel, perfumed by a small quantity of sandal-wood, or other aromatics. The vulgar and illiterate worship this sacred flame, as also the sun, moon, and stars, without regard to the invisible Creator; but the learned and judicious adore only the Almighty Fountain of Light, the author and disposer of all things, under the symbol of fire. Zoroaster, and the ancient magi, whose memories they revere, and whose works they are said to preserve, never taught them to consider the sun as any thing more than a creature of the Great Creator of the universe: they were to revere it as his best and fairest image, and for the numberless blessings it diffuses on the earth; the sacred flame was intended only as a perpetual monitor to preserve their purity; of which this element is so expressive a symbol. But superstition and fable have, through a lapse of ages, corrupted the stream of their religious system, which in its source was pure and sublime.

Some of the Parsee tribe still reside in Persia, near the city of Baku, on the shores of the Caspian sea, about ten miles from the everlasting fire which they hold in such veneration. This fire issues from the cleft of a rock, five or six feet in length, and three in breadth, appearing like the clear flame over burning spirits; sometimes it rises to the height of several yards, at others only a few inches above the aperture. It has continued thus for ages without intermission, and the rock is said not to be in the least affected, either by the fire consuming its substance, or changing its colour. Travellers mention, that if a hollow tube is put a few inches into the ground, for some hundred yards around this rocky opening, a similar flame issues through the orifice: the poorer people, who live in the neighbourhood, frequently cook their victuals over the flame. What the cause may be I know not, but the effects of subterraneous fire, which I observed at Solfaterra, near Naples, greatly resemble those on the border of the Caspian.

In their nuptial ceremonies, and many other particulars, the modern Parsees have adopted the customs of the Hindoos; but their mode of treating the dead, seems to be peculiar to themselves. At Bombay, soon after the decease, the body is conveyed to Malabar Hill, an eminence about three miles from the town; where are two large cemeteries, fifty or sixty feet in diameter, surrounded by circular walls, twenty feet high. Within this enclosure is a smooth pavement, sloping gradually from the side of the wall to the center, where it terminates in a deep pit, the bodies are laid on this pavement, which is divided into three distinct parts, for men, women, and children; they are exposed naked, to be devoured by vultures and birds of prey, which generally hover over them: a person is appointed to watch which of the eyes they first pluck out; as they annex some superstitious idea, respecting the happines or misery of the departed spirit from this circumstance: and the bones are afterwards deposited in the pit, to make room for others in this extraordinary mausoleum. When they are carrying the corpse to the tomb, which is a duty belonging to a particular set of people, they must neither speak, nor touch wood; for which reason the body is laid upon an iron bier, and the drawbridges at the town-gates, when they pass over them, are covered, either with sheets of copper, or with fresh earth.

The Parsees are generally a tall comely race, athletic and well formed, and much fairer than the natives of Hindostan; the women are celebrated more for chastity than cleanliness; the girls are delicate and pleasing, but the bloom of youth soon decays; before twenty they grow coarse and masculine, in a far greater degree than either the Hindoos or Mahomedans.

Wherever the Parsees settle throughout Hindostan, they build a temple for their sacred fire, and construct a cemetery: whether there is any particular mode of consecrating either of these, I cannot say: the sacred fire must be lighted at that originally brought from Persia; and never suffered to go out: this was also positively enjoined to the Levites, and was adopted by the Greeks and Romans, under all their governments. Quintus Curtius tells us, that the eternal fire was carried before the army of Darius, on silver altars, followed by the magi singing hymns, and by three hundred and sixty-five youths clothed in scarlet, amounting to the number of days in the year.

I am almost led to suppose, that the worship of fire originated at the mountain of Baku. An ancient hisorian* mentions, that the Persians relate a story concerning Zoroaster, whose love of wisdom and virtue leading him to a solitary life upon a mountain, he found it one day all in a flame, shining with celestial fire; from the midst of which he came without any harm, and instituted certain sacrifices to God, who, he declared, had appeared to him.

Herodotus says, that the ancient Persians venerated fire as a divinity, and the magi, who detested the adoration of images, worshipped the Almighty only by this element; at the same time they admitted two principles, one which was the cause of all good, the other that of all evil; the former was called Oramasdes, the latter Ahriman; the one represented by light, the other by darkness. This was the system of Zoroaster, and the Magi; and under various modifications, inculcated with their moral system, is supposed to form the contents of the Zend-Avesta, or sacred books of the modern Parsees. It is well authenticated, that for a long

* Dion Chrysostom.

time the ancient magi retained the exclusive privilege of having their bodies left as a prey to carnivorous animals; and that afterwards the Persians exposed all the dead bodies of their friends indiscriminately, to be devoured by birds and beasts of prey; a custom, which is still in some measure adhered to by their posterity in India, and by the Guebres in Persia, although so very repugnant to the feelings of almost every other civilized nation.

From my own knowledge and observation, I can assert nothing more respecting the Parsees, who are certainly an industrious and increasing people, and a valuable class of subjects in the Company's settlements: but, in addition to this chapter, which was originally written in 1769, the following extract from Butler's Horæ Biblicæ, will prove extremely satisfactory to those who may not have met with that interesting and entertaining work.

" To the exertions of Mons. Anquitel du Perron, we are indebted for our first knowledge of the Zend-Avesta, containing the doctrines of Zoroaster and the ancient magi; his translation of that interesting work are deposited with his other manuscripts, in the national library at Paris. From them we learn, that under the name of Zerouane, or time, without bounds or beginning, the followers of Zoroaster recognized a first and original Being: that by him, and in him, they believed the universe to exist, appears sufficiently clear: but they seem to have considered him rather as a principle, giving motion to a machine, or an impulse of fate, than a real object, possessed of wisdom, independence, and energy. From him Ormuzd and Ahriman proceeded; each independent of each other; each possessed of the power of creation. Ormuzd is the being absorbed in excellence, living in primeval light, good in his essence, and the cause of all good. Ahriman was originally good, but from envy against Ormuzd became wicked; was hurled into darkness, is evil, and the cause of all evil. Ormuzd formed mankind for virtue and happiness; the malice of Ahriman plunges them in vice and misery: whatever is good in the moral or physical world, is the production of Ormuzd; all that is bad is the production of Ahriman.

" The morality of the Zend-Avesta is entitled to praise: purity of word, action, and thought, is repeatedly inculcated; an attention to truth is likewise particularly enforced. To multiply the human species, increase its happiness, and prevent evil, are the general duties inculcated by Zoroaster to his disciples; agriculture and the multiplication of useful animals, are particularly recommended to them. " He," says Zoroaster, " who sows the ground " with diligence, acquires a greater stock of religious merit, than " he could gain by ten thousand prayers." The disciple of Zoroaster is enjoined to pardon injuries; to honour his parents and the king, whose rights are derived from Ormuzd; to respect old age; to observe a general gentleness of manners, and to practise universal benevolence. Fasting and celibacy are forbidden to the men; and as far as may depend on themselves, the latter is discouraged in women: if a man's wife be not barren, one wife only is allowed to him: a marriage with his cousin-german is recommended to him as an act particularly pleasing to heaven.

" Fire was considered by Zoroaster as the purest symbol of the divinity; and the original element from which Ormuzd produced all beings: he therefore enjoined his disciples to keep up a perpetual fire, and to perform other devotional exercises in the presence of fire; and every supposed corruption of fire is forbidden under the severest penalties. To every act of devotion purity of heart is necessary; and to purity of heart, Zoroaster supposes purity of body greatly contributes. Every thing which related to religion, or its concerns, is placed under their priests; they were formed into a regular hierarchy, not unlike the hierarchy of the Christian church.

"From the reign of Artaxerxes, who summoned a general meeting of the magi, amounting to eighty thousand, until its conquest by the Mahomedans, the whole kingdom of Persia was faithful to the doctrine of Zoroaster. The Mahomedans destroyed the fire temples of the Parsees, and insulted the magi; they afterwards allowed them the enjoyment of their places of worship, on their paying tribute."

Engraved by I. Wageman.

PARSEES *at* BOMBAY.

Jam. Forbes 1769

Publish'd by White Cochrane & Co. Fleet street June 1st 1812

CHAPTER VII.

AN ACCOUNT OF THE PORTUGUEZE, ARMENIANS, AND OTHER INHABITANTS OF BOMBAY:

WITH A VIEW OF THE BRAHMINICAL RELIGION, IN ITS CONFIRMATION OF THE TRUTH OF THE SACRED HISTORY, AND ITS INFLUENCE ON THE MORAL CHARACTER.

No hypothesis can be lightly esteemed, which has for its object the confirmation of revealed truth; nor can the philosophy of that man ever be useless, which brings him nearer to God; which either strengthens his faith, or animates his piety. It has for its reward what is far more valuable than the praise of men; that reward which shall remain when tongues shall cease, and knowledge shall vanish; which indeed can only receive its full accomplishment when our present limited attainments shall be ripened into perfection, when hope shall be recompensed by enjoyment, and when our capacities shall be fitted for the comprehension of infinite truth.

CARWITHEN.

CONTENTS.

CHAPTER VII.

Such as I have endeavoured to describe, in the preceding chapters, was the state of Hindostan, and such the character of its inhabitants at the close of the fifteenth century, when the passage to India, round the Cape of Good Hope, was discovered by Vasco de Gama, the celebrated Portugueze navigator. That nation soon extended her commerce to its remotest shores, and established settlements in different regions, especially on the Malabar coast, and island of Ceylon: the excellent harbour at Bombay caused it to become one of the principal ports: it continued under their government until it was ceded to the English, on the marriage of the Infanta Catherine to Charles the Second. The Portugueze have left numerous descendants there, who live under the protection of the English laws, and enjoy the free exercise of their religion: they are generally styled Portugueze, retain their European names and dress, and speak their original language, although greatly corrupted; but from their intermarriages with the natives of inferior tribes, their complexion is darker than the high castes of Hindoos, and their education is very contracted.

The proselytes made by the Romish missionaries in the East are generally among the lowest tribes of the Hindoos; or such whose misconduct having caused them to lose their caste, are glad to embrace Christianity, as a religion which is open to all. But whenever the Hindoos or Mahomedans are baptized into the Christian faith, the women lay aside their becoming eastern drapery, and put on a jacket and petticoat; and the men wear as much of the European apparel as their circumstances will admit of: a coat and stockings seldom form part of their dress, except on a religious festival, or some particular occasion.

Many respectable Armenian merchants, with their families, reside at Bombay and other British settlements in India; they carry on an extensive trade, and are valuable subjects, conforming to the laws, and enjoying the exercise of their religion, which is that of the Greek church: their complexion is as fair as that of the southern Europeans; and their conversation and manners are grave and polite. The dress of both sexes, in many respects, resembles that of the Turks; except that the men, instead of a turban, wear a high cap of black velvet, and the women conceal the mouth with a muslin handkerchief.

A few Persians, Turks, Arabians, and Jews, occasionally reside at Bombay; but the Hindoos, Mahomedans, and Parsees, form the great mass of the inhabitants. Fearful of prolixity, I have, in the foregoing pages, omitted many things inserted in my original letters; but I have endeavoured to give a faithful portrait of these interesting people; every thing I have asserted was dictated by as impartial a judgment as I was enabled to form, during a long residence among them: I viewed them with an unprejudiced mind, and wherever I went, I sought for knowledge at the best sources of information among the natives themselves: but in that respect I find my own opinion confirmed by an intelligent observer, that "to whatever country of Europe the traveller directs his steps, he meets with people ready to give him information, and proud to display their knowledge; in Asia the reverse occurs; the natives are difficult of access, averse to strangers, and reserved in their manners: slaves to their own customs, they hold those of other nations in contempt. Ever desirous to preserve their own dignity, they are too apt to consider the unstudied manners and familiarity of the English, as marks of disrespect; and will never conceive we dare to conduct ourselves in like manner to our own superiors."

Since my return to Europe, the researches into Asiatic history, the investigation of oriental manners and customs, and especially an inquiry into the moral and religious system of the Hindoos, have engaged general attention: much valuable information has been given to the public within these few years, by those who made their observations in Hindostan, or by literati, who derived their knowledge from physical and philosophical studies at home; who have compared the transactions of remote ages, with the occurrences of the present day; and from the stores of sacred and profane history, have produced such documents and proofs in favour of the former, as must satisfy every candid and unprejudiced mind. I shall therefore close this subject with some interesting extracts from recent publications; and especially from Butler's Horæ Biblicæ, and the Bamptonian lectures at Oxford, by Mr. Carwithen, on a view of the Brahminical religion, in its confirmation of the truth of the sacred history, and its influence on the moral character. From these sources I can illustrate and finish my own general character of the Hindoos with satisfaction; the extracts are necessarily unconnected; and if not entirely conclusive to every reader, they will not, I trust, be deemed irrelevant to the general tendency of these volumes.

It is remarked in the Horæ Biblicæ, that "Sir William Jones traces the foundation of the Indian empire above 3800 years from the present time; the highest age of the Yajur Veda to 1580 years before the birth of Christ, or 100 years before the birth of Moses; and the highest age of the Institutes of Menu, to 1280 years before the birth of our Saviour."

"The Vedas contain one hundred thousand stanzas, of four lines each; they treat of divination, astronomy, natural philosophy, the creation of the world, religious ceremonies, prayers, morality, and piety; and include hymns in praise of the Supreme Being, and in honour of subaltern intelligences."

"The geography of the Brahmins is admitted by all to be fanciful and absurd in the extreme: now, if the Brahmins could give so much loose to their imaginations in the severest of all sciences; if they could be so grossly ignorant in things which lay perpetually before them, how much more extravagance and error must be expected from them in the sciences of astronomy and chronology, as loosely as all those sciences have ever been treated in India?"

"Considering Hindostan, in the very largest sense in which that word is used, it answers to the India infra Gangem of the ancients; or the country bounded on the north by the Tartarian and Thibetian mountains, on the south by the sea, on the west by the Indus, and on the east by a supposed line extending to the north from the Ganges. The country bordering on the eastern side of the Indus made a part of one of the satrapies of Darius

Hystaspes; but, speaking generally, the Indus was the easternmost boundary of the Persian empire, and all the country beyond it was divided into a number of kingdoms and states."

"About a hundred and sixty years after the reign of Darius Hystaspes, Alexander the Great advanced with his army into India; that point of the Hyphasis, or Beeyah, where it receives the Setlege, or Setooder, was the scene of the memorable refusal of Alexander's army to follow him. On his death, Seleucus made himself master of the Persian empire; and turning his attention to India, sent Megasthenes in the character of ambassador to Palibothra, the capital of the Prasii; or the country watered by the confluence of the Jumna and Ganges."

I shall make no further quotations from the Horæ Biblicæ, as the Bamptonian lectures offer a rich mine of information.

"In the countries of the East, where the serenity of the climate is peculiarly favourable to the observation of the celestial luminaries, we might naturally expect to discover an early attention to their magnitude and their motions. It was by their periodical revolutions, indeed, that the necessary concerns of human life were formerly regulated: the constellations were not only in after times rendered subservient to the purposes of a blind and trembling superstition; they were not only regarded with emotions of fear or transport, as they were supposed to bear an aspect malignant or auspicious to the interests of man; but they were originally instrumental to more useful and noble ends: they directed the course of agricultural labours, and of maritime adventure. Astronomy, instead of being the offspring of solitude, leisure, and contemplation, may be termed more properly the child of necessity

ninth century their chronology was as complete, or perhaps entirely the same, as we find it at present."

"The supposition has been hazarded, that as India can now indisputably assert her title to the invention of the numerical figures, which had once been attributed to an Arabian origin, she will hereafter be found to have formed the first zodiac, which is generally supposed to have proceeded from Egypt."

"The facts stated in the second lecture tend to establish the following important conclusions: that the strongest presumption arises, both from the testimonies of ancient authors, as far as they can be collected, as well as from internal evidence, that the chronological system of the Brahmins has suffered a material change, and that their present scheme is of comparatively modern invention; that, in earlier times, this system had some obvious and striking similarity to that of the Mosaical history; that even if the reality of the æra from which their present age commences, and which is now generally supposed to be founded on retrograde calculation, were established, this admission could not, in any degree, affect the truth of the sacred writings; and that the only probable origin, which can be assigned to the invention of the primeval zodiac, expressly contradicts the unwarrantable assumption of an Egyptian sphere, formed at the immense distance of sixteen thousand years before the present time."

The author then naturally asks, to what cause it can be assigned, that in all the historical documents which have hitherto been brought to light, they should ascend to nearly the same point of time, and then become enveloped in obscurity, and degenerate into fable? whence happens it, that these fables, in nations, the most distant and dissimilar, however they may be disguised by difference of language, however incumbered by the adhesion of foreign circumstances, which the diversity of national character may have engrafted on them, should still retain such an evident similarity as to be clearly traced to the same source? what cause can be assigned, that the whole fabric of pagan mythology, whether surrounded by the gaudy, but mishapen ornaments of eastern magnificence, or rising in the graceful elegance and exact symmetry of Grecian taste, or frowning terrors in the ponderous and massive grandeur of northern architecture, should be raised on the same foundation, however the superstructure may be modelled or varied, by the influence of national manners? If this globe had been inhabited by nations of a separate and independent origin, could this uniformity in their traditions possibly have existed? If mankind had reached that perfection, both in science and refinement, which is pretended, would there not have occurred some distinct and diversified events, which would have clearly characterized these periods, and would have found their way to future generations?"

" From every investigation it clearly appears, that no computations have been able to invalidate the only historical narrative, which, independently of the stamp of divine authority, presents a rational account of the formation of the universe, of the creation of man, and of the infant state of the world; which, in accuracy of description, not less than in sublimity of language, stands unrivalled. In vain have they been applied to invalidate that everlasting covenant, which was established before the foundations of the world were laid, before ' the morning stars sang together, and all the sons of God shouted for joy.' In vain have they been applied to invalidate that covenant, which, as it had a retrospect to the period before creation existed, shall receive its full and glorious accomplishment when creation shall be no more; when the sun shall be darkened, and the moon shall withdraw her shining, and the stars shall fall from heaven: for thus its Almighty author has declared concerning it; 'Heaven and earth shall pass away, but my words shall not pass away.'

"The variety of fables to which the awful event of the deluge has been accommodated, the diversities in the narrative, adapted to local prejudices or to theological opinions, prove that they are taken from uncommunicated fragments of some original tradition. The incident is recorded, not by construction of philosophical theories, but by simple narrators of facts. It is also observable, that the accounts of a deluge still to be found among the more eastern nations, are as strongly marked by truth, and are equally conformable to the history of Moses, as those which are preserved in Egypt."

"But although the concurrent voice of antiquity thus loudly responds to the testimony of the Hebrew historian; though the memorials of an event, so interesting to the early world, must have been treasured up with care, and recollected with sentiments of awe and gratitude; though they have been recorded on the tablet of the skies, and shadowed out in hieroglyphic sculpture in monuments on the earth; though the combined powers of fancy and erudition have been successfully employed, in referring, to this source, many of the pagan symbols and devotional ceremonies; yet vague and unsatisfactory would all these evidences appear, if they had not been illustrated and confirmed by that narrative, of which all other records are but faint adumbrations. If all the solitary fragments scattered throughout the voluminous mass of oriental mythology, joined with those which the nations of the west have retained, were collected and concentrated, their united testimony would be insufficient to establish the reality of this calamitous prodigy. It is not on the exact coincidence of sacred and profane history, that we attempt to prove the truth, and assume the superiority of the former; but that the one is perspicuous and full, where the other is obscure and defective: the one is concise where amplification would be unnecessary, or would tend to no other purpose than the gratification of a vain curiosity; the other, by those additions which the artifice or conceit of man has interwoven, has sometimes suppressed the truth by concealment, and sometimes weakened it by expansion."

"In common with other nations, the Hindoos attribute the creation of all visible things in six distinct periods, the successive formation of all terrestrial animals, and finally of man, to one Supreme God. In common with all other nations, they have also preserved some indistinct remembrance of the antediluvian generations, and the antediluvian personages mentioned in the Jewish scriptures. But the first great and important event, which they attest, clearly and unequivocally, is the awful catastrophe of the general destruction of the world by a flood; and therefore it is from that point, that the monuments of profane antiquity are properly called in, to confirm the truth of the sacred history."

"Distinguished as the whole recital of the deluge is in the Hindoo Purana, by that mixture of the puerile and sublime, which so eminently characterizes the exuberant fertility of an oriental fancy; yet we cannot fail to discover in it evident traces of the more simple and succinct account transmitted to us in the Mosaical history. The cause of this signal display of divine vengeance; the number of persons who were miraculously preserved from this convulsion of nature; the manner by which Omnipotence interposed to effect their deliverance, are all clearly defined; and remarkably correspond with what we are accustomed to consider, as the words of inspired truth."

"As has been now shewn, we can clearly prove the reality of an universal deluge, not from the Jewish oracles, which relate the event in its connection with their national history; not from the phænomena of the natural world, which are in harmony with those oracles; not from the nations of Arabia and Tartary, who have preserved many of the facts related in the sacred history, but who also retain a veneration for the Jewish law-giver; but from the arrogant and presumptuous Brahmin, who disclaims all kindred with the less favoured nations of the earth; who regards his own country as the spot on which the Divinity has displayed a peculiar manifestation of his presence, as the centre of terrestrial creation, and the 'land of virtues;' and who views, with a consciousness of superior sanctity, the professors of that faith which his own records have shewn to be historically true."

The civil history of mankind, contained in the remaining fragments of the earliest annalist, agrees with the narrative of Moses. They concur in placing the theatre of the first memorable events that befel the human race, within the limits of Irán, understood in its true and extended signification, between the Oxus and the Euphrates, the Armenian mountains and the borders of India.

What, however, is still more decisive, and confirms the accuracy of the Hebrew historian, is, that the literature of India, lately explored, records the establishment of the Brahminical religion in Irán, previously to its adoption in Hindostan. We are informed, that a mode of faith and worship, essentially different from that of Zoroaster, was anciently professed in Persia, and continued to be secretly entertained by many eminent men, long after the general predominance of the latter.

" That Irán, understood in its true and enlarged signification, was the country from which the three original and distinct races of men first separated, is rendered still more probable, from its central situation. It was from this part of the globe, that the adventurous progeny of Japhet could best transport themselves to those countries, which, on account of their being separated from Judea by the sea, are emphatically styled in the writings of Moses, ' the isles of the Gentiles;' in contradistinction to Asia, which to Palestine was strictly continental. It was nearest to this quarter that the peaceful descendants of Shem settled themselves in Arabia, where so many of their names may now be discovered; and it was from this quarter, that the Ammonian race, so famed for daring exploits, subdued the vast and fertile countries of India, Ethiopia, and the countries situated on the Nile; where they have left so many vestiges of their scientific excellence, and of their martial prowess."

" From an accurate survey of the Brahminical religion, as we find it established in India, it is impossible not to perceive its essential identity with that of the Egyptians, and therefore that both must have emanated from a common origin. Both nations were distinguished by a division into various orders, of which the philosophers were the most honourable. Each tribe adhered to the profession of its family, and never invaded the department of another. The fundamental principles of their astronomical systems, would also incline us to suppose, that their sciences were derived from the same source."

"From a comparison of different facts, the following will appear to be the result: at the time of the general dispersion of mankind, some tribes migrated towards the East to India; while others diverged towards the West to Egypt; and some still remained in their original settlements in Chaldæa. Egypt, therefore, we might expect to find the source of knowledge for the western, and India for the eastern parts of the globe. The few general traditions which they had received from their ancestors, it is reasonable to imagine, would find a place in the religious systems of all. These traditions would remain unaltered, chiefly in countries like India, insulated from the rest of the world by continued and almost impregnable barriers. From the unrestrained intercourse which so long subsisted between India and Egypt, it is probable, that a communication might have taken place on subjects of religion and science; that we have the strongest reason to conclude that large bodies of Hindoos have settled themselves in Egypt; but that there is no reason to imagine, that the Brahminical system was transported, at a recent period, from Egypt into India."

" We find, that the most common method of accounting for the origin of evil is the degeneracy of man from a state of purity to a state of corruption: a doctrine which has retained a place in the popular creed of every nation. Of Brahminism, it may be almost said to form the basis. It is this idea which has regulated its elaborate scheme of chronology; it is this idea, which causes its followers to submit to the most excruciating penances, in order to purge the soul from the stains which she has contracted during her abode in this polluted body. They have indeed corrupted and obscured this doctrine; they have engrafted on it additions which do not properly belong to it; they have carried it so far, as to inspire them with a hatred of life, and a dereliction of every worldly enjoyment; they have continually placed before their eyes the accomplishment of that melancholy period, when a total decay of bodily strength, as well as an entire degeneracy of morals, shall increase the sum of present misery; but these deviations from the truth could never have happened, unless they had truth itself for a foundation. These are phantoms of the imagination, which would never have existed, if they had not been derived from some correspondent reality."

" From the fall of man, we are naturally led to the consideration of a positive ordinance immediately connected with it, and springing out of it; THE CUSTOM OF SACRIFICIAL OBLATIONS, AS AN EXPIATION FOR SIN. In whatever point of view this custom may be regarded, whether as eucharistical or propitiatory, whether originating in the idea that it was a proper mode of expressing sentiments of gratitude to the Deity, for the enjoyment of the bounties of nature, or as a proper atonement for guilt; still a rite so peculiar, and so universal, must have received its sanction from some positive command, and could never have been the dictate of natural reason."

"The Vedas themselves, on some occasions, enjoin the oblations of men, as well as animals; and that the sacrifices of the latter were anciently practised, we have the authority of Strabo and Arrian. It is also well known, that one of the incarnations of Vishnû, that of Buddha himself, is described by the Brahmins, as having taken place for the purpose of abolishing the sacrifices enjoined in the Vedas; and whatever difference of opinion may be entertained concerning the time, or the genuineness of this descent, it is a decided proof, that the custom of sacrificial offering must have been universally prevalent."

"In the Brahminical religion, we behold a system, subsisting at the present time in the same form, by which it has been known since the earliest period of authentic history. We have taken a review of its doctrines, from a comparison of foreign testimony with its own sacred records; and these have afforded mutual illustration; and the one proves the veracity of the other. We have seen the regal government, which was established under this religion, long since overthrown; we have seen its hierarchy partaking in the same destruction; but even in this disjoined state, retaining those inherent seeds of vitality which have preserved its dominion over a vast and refined population. We have, in the first place, shewn on what a baseless foundation those claims to unfathomable antiquity, which its professors assume, must at length rest; that there is the strongest reason to suppose, that their chronological scheme, in its pure state, was not widely different from the moderate computation which the Mosaic writings give concerning the age of the world; that before this limited period, we see nothing but cycles of artificial construction, and an immense space of unoccupied vacuity. We have seen, that the first event, which its records clearly and unequivocally attest, is the renovation of the present world from destruction by a flood; and that the modern Hindoos, however solicitous to conceal or deny the fact, can never rationally explain many of their fables, but by an allusion to this catastrophe. In the sequel of our researches, a striking coincidence has been discovered, between the geography of the Puranas, and the Mosaical account of the origin and settlement of nations, branching from three different stocks: and the geography of the Puranas, however disfigured by wild allegory, is in many instances, strikingly confirmed by the Grecian historians and geographers. In the last place, we have attempted to shew, that man was never left by his Creator without some revelation to direct his steps; and what that revelation was, what promises it unfolded, and what doctrines it was designed to inculcate, may be collected from the concise information contained in the history of Moses, compared with those traditions, which are yet to be discovered in all the mythologies of the ancient world."

"In contemplating the moral character of the Hindoos, as taking its complexion from their religion, we observe, that as their superstitious ritual presents a strange mixture of images, sanguinary and voluptuous, an intimate union between obscene mirth and austere devotion; so the manners of its followers have been actuated by contending and contradictory principles; a circumstance which has excited much wonder, and given birth to much erroneous and unprofitable speculation. While, on the one hand, the native of Hindostan has been represented as shuddering at the sight of human blood, as carrying this terror to the most troublesome excess; to an excess, which prevents him from destroying the most noxious animals, or of partaking of such as were designed for the use of man; and while he has been represented as sunk in the most degrading inactivity; on the other hand, the same character is distinguished by such acts of deliberate cruelty, of undaunted resolution, and of painful and continued exertion, as sometimes astonish, and sometimes disgust; such acts as surpass all credibility, and even exceed description. This union, so unnatural and discordant, can never be distinctly explained nor understood, but by tracing the steps which led to its formation; by shewing in what manner the different kinds of superstition have been so blended with each other, as, at length, to compose one confused whole."

"The facts which have been adduced, will contribute to decide how far the national character may be influenced by climate; and and how far the power of religious enthusiasm may exclude climate from any share in its formation. We here behold a people, living under a temperature favourable to voluptuousness, and, in some measure, taking the complexion of their national character from its influence: living in that state of oscitancy, which arises from natural imbecility, or oppressed by that lassitude which proceeds from intemperate gratification. But we also see the same people, when the force of religious impressions stimulates their natural indolence, displaying instances of self-denial, of laborious and painful exertion, which almost exceed belief."

" We may behold the native of Hindostan, whose form is naturally of a tender texture, and whose body is enfeebled by age, patient of fatigue, careless of danger, taking his long and painful journey from the Ganges to the Volga, to offer up a prayer at the shrine of his god. We may behold him at another time, relinquishing every worldly connection, subduing every feeling of self-love, and all the sympathies of social life, " motionless as a tree, and fixing his eyes on the solar orb" until exhausted nature sinks, or despair prompts him to devote himself to the fury of the flood or fire."

" In a country, where the superior orders have repressed every hope, and precluded even the possibility of advancement in those below them; where indolence may be indulged without any call to activity, and where tyranny may be exercised without fear of resistance; it is impossible that there should not be, on the one hand, capricious rigour, and, on the other hand, ignorance and servility. Though such a variety of opinion on religious subjects is prevalent throughout Hindostan, and though even the Brahminical hierarchy itself is, at the present time, nothing more than an oligarchical form of government, yet its power is not less arbitrary because its operations are desultory and partial. Its influence is felt in a greater or less degree throughout India; and wherever it is felt it is converted into an instrument of evading just demand, or of enforcing immoderate exactions."

" Happy then are they, who live under the benign influence of a religion, in which the Deity is represented, not as a stern and inflexible tyrant, delighting in the sufferings of his slaves; but as a kind and compassionate parent, who rejoices in the happiness of his offspring; in which human life is represented, not as a state of servitude, but as a state of discipline; in which the Almighty does not address himself to man in the accents of terror, but speaks to him in the same consolatory voice in which he once proclaimed himself to his chosen people of old, "The Lord, the Lord God, merciful and gracious, long suffering, abundant in goodness and truth."*

These illustrations form an excellent answer to the queries put, thirty years ago, by Bishop Watson, when Archdeacon of Ely, to the clergy of that diocese; and seem such a fulfilment to the almost prophetical spirit in which he then delivered the following part of his charge, as must afford a high gratification to that venerable prelate, whose life has been preserved to witness the light of truth dispelling pagan darkness; and withdrawing the veil from the traditional fables, and erroneous data of the Hindoo chronology.

"To men whose minds are chained to the earth by the sordid pursuits of wealth, or the empty ones of ambition; who are debilitated by sensual pleasure, or rendered torpid to every arduous exertion, by habitual inactivity; who, unconscious of its importance, fritter away this short period of existence in a frivolous attention to trivial concerns; in a slavish subserviency to the uniform

* Carwithen's Lectures.

prejudices of the age or country in which they happen to be born; to men of this complexion every attempt to investigate the nature of this earth, or the history of its inhabitants, will appear a chimerical undertaking, originating in idle speculation, and terminating in useless conjecture. But notwithstanding the indifference which many men feel respecting every intellectual accomplishment, which happens not to fall in with their particular mode of study, or apprehension, I doubt not but there are many of a contrary turn, who would zealously sacrifice their health, riches, and repose, in support of any liberal and enlarged plan, which might be concerted for bringing us acquainted with the general history of our species.

"Concerning the various colonies, which, in process of time, after the deluge, traversed the plains of Asia, from the Indus to the Ganges, from the Ganges to the extremity of China, Tartary, and Japan, profane history is wholly silent, or speaks with extreme diffidence and uncertainty. There can no possible reason, I think, be assigned, why the descendants of Noah should have all gone in one direction; for the part of the globe to the east of the settlement of Noah and his family, after the flood, was peopled in all likelihood as soon as that to the west. Arts and sciences have been as successfully cultivated, and the contest for power may have been as sharp, and may have produced as many great monarchies amongst the inhabitants of the eastern portion of the globe, as we know they did in the western.

——" Medus ademit
" Assyrio, Medoque tulit moderamina Perses.
" Subjecit Persen Macedo: cessurus et ipse,
" Romanis."

These lines of Claudian contain a compendium of all the ancient history, which the Greeks and Romans, and we, through them, have had any account of: but we have good reason to believe, that could the synchronous histories of Hindostan, Thibet, Siam, and China, be obtained, they would be well worthy of our attention. For if a skill in manufactures be a sign of civilization, we know from various authorities, that the Indians and Chinese were as much superior to the most ancient nations of the western world, in the arts of dying, japanning, weaving of silk, and linen, and other trades, as they are at present to us. And if we may be allowed to draw any conclusions from the immense buildings now existing, and from the little of the inscriptions which can be interpreted on several of the choultries and pagodas, I think it may safely be pronounced, that no part of the world has more marks of antiquity for arts, sciences, and civilization, than the peninsula of India, from the Ganges to Cape Comorin.

" We yet know nothing, or next to nothing, of the treasures of eastern learning; but, from what we do know, there is no reason why we should be deterred from endeavouring to know more. Proverbs and poems have their graces and their uses: but from eastern learning we derive more substantial benefits than what can be expected from such compositions. We owe algebra entirely to the Indians, or Arabians: chemistry, medicine, natural history, geography, and many of the abstract sciences are indebted to the Arabians, if not for their birth, at least for their support and protection, when they were abandoned by all the states of Europe.

"The writings of Moses have hitherto been considered as the oldest in the world; but in the preface to the Code of Gentoo Laws, we are told of a curious history of India composed four thousand years ago, and from thence tracing mankind upwards, through several millions of years. This, and all the rest that is delivered concerning the great antiquity of the annals of India, you and I may probably be disposed to consider as a mere fable; but there are many, neither profligate in their manners, nor destitute of talents, who have not the same veneration for the writings of Moses that we have; and they may consider the Indian annals delivered down by the ancient Brahmins, to be as authentic as those of the Bible; at least they will be perplexed with an uneasy scepticism, from which nothing but a further examination into the Indian writings can free them. God forbid, that the search of truth should be discouraged for fear of its consequences! The consequences of truth may be subversive of systems of superstition; but they never can be injurious to the rights, or well founded expectations of the human race. We believe the Scriptures, and our hopes of eternal life are built on their truth; but we trust, that no faith can be acceptable to God which is not grounded on reason; and as reasonable beings, we wish not to entertain any hopes, the foundations of which can be shaken by the most rigid inquiry into the history of mankind.

"But the antiquity of the Indian annals is not the only circumstance which seems to militate against the Mosaic history: we are told, that the Gentoo scriptures make no mention of the deluge; and that the Bramins affirm, that the deluge never took place in Hindostan. Now, I look upon the deluge to be a circumstance of such a singular nature, that, supposing it to have happened, the memory of it could never have been extinguished amongst the generality of the nations which inhabit the earth. It is not, according to the most received chronology, much above four thousand years since that great event took place; and if any individual had the means of tracing back his pedigree through less, perhaps, than an hundred and forty generations, he would find either Shem, Ham, or Japhet, to have been his great progenitor. It is very possible for a tradition, which has passed through so many hands, to have been much altered; yet the tradition of so signal a calamity as the destruction of the human race by a deluge, could not, I conceive, have been wholly lost, except perhaps amongst a few nations utterly buried in barbarism. And, in fact, learned men have abundantly proved, that a tradition concerning a deluge has prevailed in every quarter of the globe; not only amongst the Romans, Grecians, Egyptians, Babylonians, Persians, Scythians; but amongst the Iroquoix, Mexicans, Brazilians, Peruvians, and other nations of America; and I have been informed by one of the navigators to the southern hemisphere, that the inhabitants of Otaheite being asked concerning their origin, simply answered, that their supreme God, a long time ago, being angry, dragged the earth through the sea, and their island, being broken off, was preserved. Now if a tradition concerning a deluge has prevailed in almost every part of the globe, except in India, may it not be reasonable for us to hesitate a little, till we know more of that country, before we positively affirm that they have no such tradition, especially when there is a diversity of testimony upon the subject?

"If, therefore, we should be able to find in the history of the eastern nations, as certain traditions concerning a deluge, and as certain proofs of the invalidity of their pretensions to any great antiquity, as are confessedly to be met with in every other quarter of the globe, should we not have great reason to acquiesce in the account given by Moses of the deluge, and the subsequent spreading of the descendants of Noah over all the earth, notwithstanding the difficulties which may attend our endeavours to explain the manner in which the deluge was effected, or the doubts which some have suggested concerning its ever having taken place, from their not being able to discover any vestiges of it on the surface of the earth."

Happily since this learned Prelate delivered his excellent charge to the clergy of Ely, Sir William Jones, and many other gentlemen of taste and judgment, have made deep researches into the sacred books of the Hindoos, and have solved all these difficulties: and, as is clearly stated in the preceding extracts from a view of the Brahminical religion (of which I hope to be excused the repetition of a few words), it is proved, "that in common with all other na-"tions, the Hindoos have preserved some indistinct remembrance "of the antediluvian generations, and the antediluvian personages "mentioned in the Jewish scriptures. But the first great and im-"portant event which they attest *clearly* and *unequivocally*, *is the* "*awful catastrophe of the general destruction of the world by a flood;*

" and therefore it is from that point, that the monuments of profane " antiquity are properly called in, to confirm the truth of the " sacred history."

CHAPTER VIII.

A VIEW OF THE SOCIETY AND MANNERS OF THE ENGLISH IN INDIA;

AND PARTICULARLY IN THE ISLAND OF BOMBAY.

Quietò et puré atque eleganter actæ ætatis placida ac lenis recordatio.

The soothing and calm remembrance of a life passed with quiet, innocence, and elegance.

CICERO.

In all my wandering round this world of care,
In all my griefs—and GOD has given my share,
I still had hopes, my latest hours to crown,
In ALBION's happy isle to lay me down:
My anxious day to husband near the close,
And keep life's flame from wasting, by repose:
I cherish'd hopes, for pride attends us still,
Amidst my *English friends* to shew my skill;
Around my fire an evening group to draw,
And tell of all I felt, and all I saw.

GOLDSMITH, *altered.*

CONTENTS.

CHAPTER VIII.

I SHALL conclude my letters on Bombay with a short account of the European inhabitants, and their mode of living at that settlement. The principal town takes its name from that of the island, and is situated near the harbour, at the southern extremity; on the north side is a smaller town, called Mahim, and several villages in different parts of the country.

The town of Bombay is about two miles in circumference, surrounded by modern fortifications; with a fosse, draw-bridges, three principal gates, and several sally-ports; but the works having been constructed under different engineers, without any regular plan, cannot boast of the strength or uniformity which would otherwise have characterized them.

The harbour is large, and secure from the storms and hurricanes which are very frequent and destructive at Surat bar, and on the Malabar coast: near it were three excellent docks, which I believe are since increased in number; and a spacious marine-yard, amply supplied with naval stores of every description: here they build vessels of all sizes, from a ship of the line, to the smallest grabs and gallivats, employed in the Company's service: the timber used is chiefly teak (Tectona grandis), the most valuable of the oriental forest-woods, and more durable than the oak: the master-builders and shipwrights of the Parsee tribe, are very skilful, and exact imitators of the best models from Europe.

When I left Bombay, the generality of the public buildings were more useful than elegant: the government-house, custom-house, marine-house, barracks, mint, treasury, theatre, and prison, included the chief of these structures; there were also three large hospitals, one within the gates for Europeans; another on the esplanade for the sepoys, or native troops in the Company's service; and a third, on an adjacent island, for convalescents.

The only Protestant church on the island stood near the centre of the town; a large and commodious building, with a neat tower: there was also a charity school for boys, and a fund for the poor, belonging to the church of England: there were seldom more than two chaplains belonging to the Bombay establishment when I was in India; the one resided at the Presidency; the other, alternately at Surat and Baroche, where were considerable European garrisons. The Roman Catholics had several churches and chapels in different parts of the island; and enjoyed every indulgence from the English government.

The English houses at Bombay, though neither so large nor elegant as those at Calcutta and Madrass, were comfortable and well furnished; they were built in the European style of architecture, as much as the climate would admit of; but lost something of that appearance by the addition of verandas, or covered piazzas, to shade those apartments most exposed to the sun; when illuminated, and filled with social parties in the evening, these verandas gave the town a very cheerful appearance: but since I left India, the town-houses have been almost deserted by the English, who reside entirely at their country villas; the gentlemen only go to the fort in the morning, to transact their business; devoting the evening to domestic pleasure, and convivial meetings at their garden-houses.

The large bazar, or the street in the black-town, within the fortress, contained many good Asiatic houses, and shops stood with merchandize from all parts of the world, for the Europeans and natives. These shops were generally kept by the Indians, especially the Parsees; who, after paying the established import customs, were exempted from other duties.

Bombay was then one of the first marts in India, and employed a great number of vessels in its extensive commerce; Bussorah, Muscat, Ormuz, and other ports in the Persian Gulph, furnished its merchants with pearls, raw-silk, Carmenia wool, dates, dried fruits, rose water, ottar of roses, and several other productions. Arabia supplied them with coffee, gold, drugs, and honey. A number of ships annually freighted with cotton and bullion to China, returned laden with tea, sugar, porcelain, wrought silks, nankeens, and a variety of useful and ornamental articles. From Java, Malacca, Sumatra, and the eastern islands, they brought spices, ambergris, perfumes, arrack, and sugar: the cargoes from Madagascar, the Comorro isles, Mosambique, and other ports on the eastern coast of Africa, consisted chiefly of ivory, slaves, and drugs: while the different parts of India produced cotton, silk, muslin, pearls, diamonds, and every precious gem; together with ivory, sandal-wood, pepper, cassia, cinnamon, and other luxuries. This valuable commerce was carried on by vessels belonging to the European and native merchants settled at Bombay; totally independent and unconnected with the trade of the East India Company. The exports consisted of English woollen-cloths of every description; with copper, iron, lead, and other European staples, purchased at the Company's sales by the native merchants, both at Bombay, and from the continent. A great deal of cotton, imported in boats from Surat, Baroche, Ahmood, and Jamboseer, was shipped in large vessels at Bombay for Madras, Bengal, and China. The Portuguese from Goa, Damaun, and Europe, carried on a trifling trade with Bombay; but the French, Dutch, and Danish ships seldom touched there; the American intercourse with India was then in its infancy.

The government of Bombay, in its civil and military departments, courts of justice, and other arrangements, was established by the East India Company under the royal charter; but the system has of late years been so often changed, that I decline entering upon the subject. During my residence there, a simple and regular system in the different establishments seemed to answer all the necessary purposes of government, and every thing was conducted with order and propriety.

I never visited Bengal or Madras, but I have been at all the settlements subordinate to Bombay, from Ahmed-abad to Anjengo; and I can assert, that the character of the English in India is an honour to their country: in private life, they are generous, kind, and hospitable; in their public situations, when called forth to arduous enterprize, they conduct themselves with skill and magnanimity: and, whether presiding at the helm of the political and commercial department, or spreading the glory of the British arms, with courage, moderation, and clemency, the annals of Hindostan will transmit to future ages names dear to fame, and deserving the applause of Europe. As husbands, fathers, masters, they cannot easily be excelled; and in private friendship, they act with true nobility of soul. Friendship, illustrated in its more general sense, by unostentatious acts of humanity and benevolence, shines in India with conspicuous lustre; distress never pleads in vain, and the milk of human kindness flows in ample streams. How often have the sons and daughters of misfortune experienced the blessed effects of oriental benevolence! how often have the ruined merchant, the disconsolate widow, and the helpless orphan, been relieved by the delicate and silent subscription, amounting in a few hours to several thousand pounds, without the child of sorrow knowing its benefactors! And here, with all the milder virtues belonging to their sex, my amiable countrywomen are entitled to their full share of applause. This is no fulsome panegyric; it is a tribute of truth and affection, to those worthy characters with whom I so long associated. It will be confirmed by all who have resided in India; and Mr. Budworth, in his pleasant Ramble to the Lakes, mentioning the kindness of Colonel Duff, and several of his brother officers, during his distresses in Bengal, justly observes, that " similar instances are not unusual in India: the heart expands in proportion to the distance from their native country, and the frequent warfare they are engaged in; and war ever brings home the soldier's feelings to the noblest effects. A systematic cold-blooded Indian is almost a phænomenon in their armies."

I have not the smallest intention of praising the Anglo-Indians at the expense of my countrymen at home: the seeds of philanthropy and benevolence, which every where adorn the English character, impregnated in their native soil, flourish vigorously when transplanted in a foreign country, where fortunes are generally more easily obtained than in Europe; where a distressed individual, separated from parents, friends, and every natural source of redress, seems to have a double claim upon the compassion of his more fortunate comrades; and where an annual increase of wealth admits of more unrestrained bounty than a limited income. During my abode in India, there were no arts or sciences to patronize; no literary or charitable institutions to support; and neither hospitals nor infirmaries to call forth private benevolence; the Company provide for the Europeans, and the natives in general, take care of their own poor: the chief expenses of the English are therefore confined to convivial pleasures, and domestic arrangements: whereas, in Britain's favoured isle, how abundant are the channels for an ample fortune; and how numerous the worthies who appropriate a very considerable portion of their income to relieve the distresses of their fellow creatures!

As far as the climate admits, the English fashion in houses, equipage, and dress, is generally adopted: very few ladies or gentlemen kept European servants; the former were better served by young female Malabars, trained by themselves; and by negro, or Malabar boys, who were our favourite personal attendants; while the upper servants were usually Mahomedans and Parsees; men of character and family, in most respects preferable to Europeans, and less expensive. Our clerks and writers were mostly Hindoos, who from being liable to so many religious and ceremonial pollutions, were seldom domestic servants; these writers at

Bombay are generally called Purvoes; a faithful diligent class, much attached to their employer, careful of his interest, accurate in their accounts, and very often such exact imitators of his hand-writing, that it is impossible in a long letter to discriminate the fac-simile from the autograph: such an amanuensis is peculiarly useful in a country where the conveyance of letters was then so precarious, that both in public and private dispatches, it was necessary to send duplicate and triplicate copies.

When I resided at Bombay, early hours prevailed throughout the presidency and its subordinate settlements: these are now altered to the more fashionable routine of England. The morning was then dedicated to business; every body dined at one o'clock; on breaking up, the company went to their respective houses to enjoy a siesta, and return after a walk or ride in the country, to pass the remainder of the evening, and sup where they had dined. Our rural excursions in that climate are early in the morning, or after the sun declines: the twilight, so near the equator, is short; but the mildness and serenity of the moonlight nights render them peculiarly delightful: there indeed we behold the nocturnal luminary " walking in her brightness," without a vapour to dim the " sweet influences of the Pleiades, or veil the bands of Orion." Such a spectacle naturally disposes the mind to solemn musings; and, while enjoying the western breeze on the flat roofs of the oriental houses, and beholding the celestial canopy so gloriously adorned, it is impossible not to meditate with pious awe on the Great Parent of the universe,

" Who gives its lustre to the insect's wing,
" And fills with glory the celestial world!"

Having now given an account of the natural history of Bombay, and of its native and European inhabitants, towards the conclusion of the eighteenth century, it may not be uninteresting to contrast it with a few particulars respecting that island about an hundred years before, from the letters of Dr. Fryer, who went there in 1673, ten years after it had been ceded to the English, as part of the marriage portion of Catharine of Portugal.

" On the English taking possession of Bombay in 1664, they found a pretty well seated, but ill fortified house; four brass guns being the whole defence of the island; unless a few chambers housed in small towers in convenient places, to scour the Malabars, who heretofore have been more insolent than of late; adventuring not only to seize their cattle, but depopulate whole villages by their outrages; either destroying them by fire and sword, or compelling to a worse fate, eternal and intolerable slavery.

" About the house was a large garden, voiced to be the pleasantest in India, intended rather for wanton dalliance, love's artillery, than to make resistance against an invading foe: for, the Portugals generally forgetting their pristine virtue, lust, riot, and rapine, the ensuing consequences of a long undisturbed peace, where wealth abounds, are the only remarkable reliques of their ancient worth; their courages being so much effeminated, that it is a wonder to most how they keep any thing; if it were not that they have lived among mean-spirited neighbours. But to return to this garden of Eden, or place of terrestrial happiness, it would put the searchers upon as hard an inquest as the other has done its posterity. The walks which before were covered with nature's verdant awning, and lightly pressed by soft delights, are now open to the sun, and loaded with hardy cannon: the bowers dedicated to rest and ease, are turned into bold rampires for the watchful centinel to look out on; every tree that the airy choristers made their charming choir, trembles, and is extirpated at the rebounding echo of the alarming drum; and those slender fences, only designed to oppose the sylvan herd, are thrown down, to erect others of a more warlike force.

" Not far from the fort lies the town, about a mile in length; the houses are low, and thatched with olas of the cocoa-nut trees; all but a few the Portugals left, and some few the Company have built; the custom-house and warehouses are tiled or plaistered; and instead of glass, they use panes of oyster-shells for their windows; which, as they are cut in squares, and polished, look gracefully enough. There is also a reasonable handsome bazar.

" At the end of the town, looking into the field, where cows and buffaloes graze, the Portugals have a pretty house and church, with orchards of Indian fruit adjoining. The English have only a burying-place, called Mendam's Point, from the first man's name there interred, where are some few tombs that make a pretty shew at entering the harbour; but neither church nor hospital, both which are mightily to be desired. There are no fresh-water rivers, nor falling streams of living water: that usually drank is rain-water preserved in tanks; which decaying, they are forced to dig wells, into which it is strained, hardly leaving its brackish taste; so that the better sort have it brought from Massagon, where there is only one fresh spring.

" In the gardens of India, are gourds of all sorts for stews and pottage, herbs for salad, and some flowers, as jasmin, for beauty and delight; there also flourish pleasant tops of plantains; cocoas; guavas, which are a kind of pear; jacs, with a coat of armour over it like a hedge-hog's, to guard its weighty fruit, oval without from the space of a span, within in fashion like unto squills parted; mangos, the delight of India, a plum; pomegranates; bananas, which are a sort of plantain, though less, yet much more grateful; betel, which must not be slipped by in silence; it rises out of the ground twelve or fourteen feet in heighth, the body of it green and slender, jointed like a cane, the boughs flaggy and spreading; under whose arms it brings forth from its pregnant womb, which bursts when her month is come, a cluster of green nuts, like walnuts in green shells, but different in the fruit, which is hard when dried, and looks like a nutmeg.

" Near the towns of Bombaim and Mahim, are woods of cocoas; these hortoes being the greatest purchase and estates on the island, for some miles together. Up the bay a mile lies Massagon, a great fishing town, peculiarly notable for a fish called bumbalo, the sustenance of the poorer sort: here the Portugals have another church, and religious house, belonging to the Franciscans. Beyond it is Parell, where they have another church, and demesnes belonging to the Jesuits, to which appertain Siam, or Sion, upon a hill. Under these uplands the washes of the sea produce a lunary tribute of salt, left in pans or pits, made on purpose at spring tides, for the overflowing; and when they are full, are incrustated by the heat of the sun. At Mahim the Portugals have another complete church and house; the English a pretty custom-house and guard-house: the Moors have also a tomb in great veneration for a peon, or prophet, instrumental in quenching the flames that were approaching their prophet Mahomet's tomb at Mecca, by the fervency of his prayers, he being at that time at Mahim, in the island of Bombay. At Salvesong, the furthest part of this inlet, the Franciscans enjoy another church and convent; this side is all covered with trees of cocoas, jacs, and mangos: in the middle lies Verulee, where the English have a watch. On the other side of the great inlet, to the sea, is a great point abutting against Old Woman's island, and is called Malabar-hill, a rocky woody mountain, yet sends forth long grass. A-top of all is a Parsee tomb, lately reared; on its declivity towards the sea, the remains of a stupendous pagod, near a tank of fresh water, which the Malabars visit it mostly for.

" The President has a large commission, and is vice-regis; he has a council here also, and a guard when he walks or rides abroad, accompanied by a party of horse: he has his chaplain, physician, chyrurgeons, and domestics; his linguist and mint-master: at meals he has his trumpets usher in his courses, and soft music at his table: if he moves out of his chamber, the silver staves wait on him; if down stairs, the guard receives him; if he go abroad, the Bandarines and Moors, under two standards, march before him: he goes sometimes in his coach, drawn by large milk-white oxen, sometimes on horseback, and at other times in a palankeen; always having a sumbrero of state carried over him: and those of the English inferior to him, have a suitable train. But for all this gallantry, I reckon they walk but in charnel-houses, the climate being extremely unhealthy."

" Happy then are those, and only those, brought hither in their nonage, before they have a gust of our Albion; or next to them, such as intoxicate themselves with Lethe, and remember not their former condition. When it is expostulated, is this the reward of an harsh and severe pupilage? Is this the elysium after a tedious waftage! For this will any thirst, will any contend, will any forsake the pleasures of his native soil, in his vigorous age, to bury himself alive here? Yet this abroad and unknown is the ready choice of those to whom poverty threatens contempt at home: what else could urge this wretched remedy? For these are untrodden paths for knowledge, little improvement being to be expected from barbarity. Custom and tradition are only venerable here; and it is heresy to be wiser than their forefathers;—whereby society and communication, the characteristic of man, is wholly lost. What then is to be expected here, where sordid thrift is the only science? After which, notwithstanding there is so general an inquest, few there be acquire it: for in five hundred, one hundred survive not; of that one hundred, one quarter get no estates; of those that do, it has not been recorded, above one in ten years has seen his country."

I will not make any further extracts from Dr. Fryer's interesting letters; nor particularize the numerous diseases, inconveniences, and unpleasant manners and customs which then prevailed among the European inhabitants of Bombay. When I arrived there, most things were on a pleasant medium between the evils of that period, and the present refined and luxurious mode of living: comfort, hospitality, and urbanity, then characterized the settlement: some of the younger classes thought there was rather too much subordination and economy: no government can exist without a proper degree of the former, and there was no alternative between living with the greatest economy, or contracting debts; which, at the common interest of nine per cent. annually compounded, soon swelled the amount to an enormous sum, and involved the borrower in distress and difficulty for many years. The small salaries then allowed by the Company to their junior servants, occasioned much inconvenience and anxiety to those who had no other resources for their maintenance; and caused us, at different times, to address two letters upon the subject, to the government of Bombay; which will hardly be credited by the young gentlemen who now occupy the same situation in the Company's service: I introduce them in evidence of these assertions, and to convince the English reader, that those who dedicate their best years in the torrid zone, in the service of their country, are not to be envied their independence when they return to their native land: and it must also be remembered, that very few, comparatively, ever enjoy that blessing: how many of that fortunate class may now be reckoned, I am not competent to decide; but thirty or forty years ago, the average of the calculations at the India House, respecting those of every description who went to the different settlements in India, including the Company's recruits, and of those who returned home, was, I am informed, in the proportion of eighty-three to one.

To the Honourable THOMAS HODGES, *Esquire, President and Governor, &c. Council on Bombay.*

HONOURABLE SIR, AND GENTLEMEN,

WE the undersigned, who have the honour to be employed as writers on this establishment, to the Honourable East India Company, do humbly beg leave to prefer to your Honour, &c. a request, which we assure ourselves will not be deemed unreasonable.

The Honourable Company have been generously pleased to allow an ample increase of pay to their servants, military and marine, by which they are enabled decently to support themselves; and with their usual and known goodness, have at the same time, unsolicited, thought proper to grant us an increase of salary of ten pounds per annum; for which our warmest acknowledgements are due; and we take this opportunity of expressing our liveliest sentiments of gratitude; and animated by a proper sense of their kind indulgence, shall make due return, by constant and punctual obedience to their orders, and perseverance with steady and unremitting application to business.

Fearful, lest it might be construed into an abuse of our Honourable masters' generosity, it is with peculiar reluctance we do at such a time, take the liberty of assuring your Honour, &c. that their generous and free donation, added to our former pittance, managed with the strictest economy, is not nearly adequate to the expenses we are necessarily and unavoidably subject to: we think it needless to remind your Honour, &c. of the dearness of every kind of provision and necessaries, and that their rates are daily enhancing; as you cannot but be thoroughly sensible of the same; we are therefore under the necessity of troubling your Honour, &c. with this address; most earnestly entreating you will be pleased to give us such farther provision as to your Honour, &c. shall seem meet.

We cannot help observing, that we deem it peculiarly hard that an ensign on this establishment, shall receive sixty, nay, many of them who have double posts, one hundred and twenty rupees per month, while the generality of us have only thirty; that a subaltern officer shall enjoy such an income as will enable him to live genteelly, while too many of us are obliged to run in debt, merely to subsist: and flattering ourselves that we are (at least conscious of having endeavoured to render ourselves), equally deserving of encouragement, are emboldened to trouble you with the above request; relying on your conviction of the justness of it, we beg leave to subscribe ourselves,

Honourable Sir, and Gentlemen,

Your most obedient and faithful servants, &c.

Signed by myself, and sixteen other writers.

Dated Bombay,
1st November, 1768.

I am sorry to observe, that although the preceding letter was strongly recommended by the Governor and Council of Bombay to the Court of Directors, they took no notice of it at home, nor did we obtain any redress. At that time, I can safely affirm, I lived in the most sparing manner, a writer's income altogether not exceeding sixty-five pounds per annum. I never drank wine at my own table, and often went supperless to bed when the day closed, because I could not afford either supper or candle: as the dinner hour was one o'clock, and a writer's age generally between sixteen and twenty-one, the abstinence was not occasioned by a want of appetite. During the bright moonlight evenings, I indulged myself in reading on the flat roof of the writer's apartments at the bunder; where, through the medium of a cloudless atmosphere, I could peruse the smallest edition of Shakespeare without inconvenience.

Those to whom these details may be uninteresting, will have the goodness to pass over a few of the following pages: to many, the next representation made by the civil servants at Bombay, and the remarks accompanying it, will be gratifying: they will there see a candid statement of the civil establishment at that presidency, and a faithful account of the insolvencies, deaths, and fortune, of those gentlemen who devoted themselves to the service of their employers at Bombay, and its subordinate settlements, during a series of more than twenty years: most families are now interested in the affairs of India, and have some endeared connexion in that part of the world: although the general system of the Company's service may, in some respects, be altered, most of the facts stated in the following representation, respecting the civil servants at the different settlements in India, are analogous to the curtailments and deprivations of the present day.

Having received no satisfactory answer to the letters, or representations, repeatedly made by the civil servants at Bombay, as to the inadequacy of their salary, to the unavoidable expenses they were liable to, on the 8th of October, 1777, the senior-merchants at the Presidency, addressed the following letter to the Governor and Council:

To the Honourable WILLIAM HORNBY, *Esquire, President and Governor, &c. Council on Bombay.*

HONOURABE SIR, AND GENTLEMEN,

THE justice and necessity of appointments to the civil servants of the Company in general, more adequate to their real wants of life, have been already so frequently and so feelingly represented by you to the Honourable the Court of Directors, that we should have remained longer silent on this subject, in hopes of relief from them; but as it is now four years since the last reference was made, and not a line yet received in answer, we imagine more material affairs have so engrossed their attention, that your representations have utterly escaped their memory. For this reason, and because our real necessities press so hard on several of us, as to require instant relief; we have made bold to trouble you to apply some immediate remedy to the peculiar hardship of our present situation, which is that of senior-merchants; most of us out of employ, and, of course, from the nature of the service, without means of subsistence from the Company, in the least adequate to the common and indispensable necessaries of life.

Obvious as the hardship we complain of must be to every

member of your Honourable Board; yet as they may not so forcibly strike every person, we think it would be wanting in justice, both to ourselves and to the other servants of the Company, who in their turn must fall into our situation, if we let pass by this opportunity of pointing out very clearly the nature and cause of the peculiar hardship of it; that the Honourable the Court of Directors may feel the justice and humanity of approving and continuing the means, which we trust you will be pleased to apply for the remedy of them.

To explain this matter clearly, it will be necessary to recur to what we conceive to have been, and still to be, the spirit and meaning of the Honourable Company in their appointments in the civil line of their service.

From the ideas we ourselves set out to this country with, and from those we find to be generally entertained both here and in Europe, we conceive that the term of the first station in which the civil servants of the Company are introduced into their service, is meant as a term of probation; a kind of apprenticeship, to qualify them for the future conduct and charge of affairs. The orders of the Company justify this description; as by those orders, a writer cannot be entrusted with any office where there is a responsibility; nor is he admitted of council at any of the subordinates; or even joined with a resident.

Pursuant to this idea, we conceive the Company regulated their appointment to them of thirty rupees per month; which to every member of your Honourable Board must appear rather meant as a token of their servitude, than as an adequate means of subsistence: indeed we have better authority to ground our supposition on than these speculations, relative to the meaning of the Company; there is hardly a writer sent out, but what the individual gentlemen of the Direction, friends to their parents, recommend those parents to send some money with their children; and to make them some allowances, because of the insufficiency of the appointments of the Company during their writership, to the real necessities of life here. We can speak for a certainty as to ourselves: and there are of us, who can affirm, that having mentioned to gentlemen of the Direction this insufficiency, the answer confirmed the ideas above attributed to the Company in their appointments: it was, that the writership was esteemed as an apprenticeship in Europe; and that, conformable to the practice there, young men must look to their friends for assistance during that period.

It may at first appear strange, and even absurd, that this allowance to a writer, not held adequate even to his subsistence, should yet continue the same through every gradation of the service, even until they arrive in council: to explain this, it is again necessary to have recourse to the ideas entertained of the Company's service, and of the advantages arising from it.

It is almost needless to remind you, Gentlemen, that, after the expiration of his writership, a servant of the Company becomes by their orders capable of trust; that in consequence of this he is admitted to be of the council at subordinates, where he of course holds some office of trust: that from the emoluments of these offices a senior servant of the Company could acquire a decent maintenance until his arrival at council, when he would be enabled to acquire that independent means of subsistence in the latter part of life, and in our native country; the hope of which brings us all to this.

These we believe are the ideas generally entertained of the Company's service: for had not the Court of Directors understood, and even allowed, the emoluments their servants become possessed of, in course from their arrival at the rank of factors, progressively increasing, till their arrival at council; we repeat, that had they not supposed these things, it seems impossible that they should have given into the most palpable contradiction to the nature of all other services, and even of their own, in every other branch but the civil, by not increasing the allowances of their servants. The pay of the military keeps increasing, from a cadet to an ensign, to a lieutenant, to a captain, a major, a lieutenant-colonel, a full colonel, to a general, proportionally as they advance in rank. The marine does the same through every gradation; and even with that exactness, that a ship of a lesser or greater rate occasions a material difference of pay: whilst, by a contradiction to common sense, without the supposition above alluded to, the subsistence of a civil servant continues the same through every rank, whether a writer or a senior merchant; whether he has served the Company one hour or one and twenty years; whether he is fresh arrived, and without acquaintance, or whether his first wants are increased by a climate-worn constitution, a decent regard of appearances, and a degree of conformity to the manners of the place, requisite to preserve acquaintance, and the good opinion of the world; whether married or single; in short, whatever may be his situation, this diet money, which was never thought of as an adequate subsistence, and is below the salary of the lowest clerks of the offices in England, these thirty rupees per month, and this trifling salary, are to be the sole dependance of an unemployed civilian for all the necessaries of life. In this statement we have omitted the allowance you were pleased to make for house rent, to those who could not be furnished with apartments by the Company, because it is rather a deduction than an increase: as you must well know, Gentlemen, there are no habitable houses to be hired at so small a rent as forty rupees per month.

It would be necessary to apologize to your Honourable Board for the detail we have been led into on this occasion, had not the reason for it been before assigned. From what has been advanced, one evident conclusion, we think, may be drawn, viz. that, in common with other gentlemen in their service, the Honourable Company always meant and understood, that their civil servants should possess adequate means of subsistence, proportionably to the rank they bore by the course of the service; it was so formerly: but by the number of servants, and the late contraction of the system here, speculation and fact are in this case at variance; and we who now address you, after having laboured in the service of the Company from twelve to upwards of fourteen years, are worse than expelled from it, as to the present; for we are left without adequate means of subsistence from our employers; and precluded from benefitting by the opportunities that offer to those who are not in their service.

We beg leave to observe here, that the Honourable the Court of Directors foresaw the distress that many of their servants would infallibly be involved in, by the new modelling of this presidency. That from a feeling for this distress, they pointed out what appeared to them a mode of relief; by permitting five and twenty of their servants at this presidency to be removed to the Bengal establishment as writers of the year 1773. We humbly conceive that they saw some advantages to us in this offer, that would amply compensate for the sacrifice of those rewards which every servant has a right to look to, after a course of fifteen or sixteen years faithfully devoted to their service, in an unpropitious climate, and banished from our country and our friends; or common humanity would not have permitted them to address those servants in the language their letter by the Gatton in fact amounts to. "You have served us twenty years, we cannot but say irre- "proachably: by the reduction of our system you are thrown out "of employ, and of course out of bread. We cannot help it: "there is no remedy: but if you choose it, you may begin a fresh "course of service in another quarter." We conceive, that without the supposition above alluded to, their humanity would have conferred on us some rank more proportioned to the length of our services: it might have been a hardship to some of their servants at Bengal, but in strictness, we conceive it could not have been an injustice: it would not have been strangers to the Company, who, by mere force of private interest, robbed them of their covenanted rights; but servants of the same masters; equally, though less beneficial, labourers with themselves; whom the necessities of those masters compelled to provide for in a different line of service; and therefore they might have borne this without just cause of complaint, in the same manner that every person connected with the Honourable Company must in some shape participate in all their distresses.

If what we have learnt of the opinions expressed by some in England of the general refusal of this offer be true, our surmises are perfectly just: we have heard that this refusal has been attributed to mere motives of pride; and inferences drawn from our neglect of the benefit that must arise by a removal to Bengal; that there are some secret advantages in the service here, which render it not so unprofitable as it is represented to be. We hope there is no just ground for this report. But in justice to ourselves, we think it requisite to endeavour to remove opinions that may hereafter prove prejudicial to us, should an opening be afforded to better our situation by a removal to one of the other presidencies.

As to the first cause assigned for our refusal, we beg leave to observe, that the distinguished character which the Honourable Company maintain in this part of the globe, renders their servants an object of attention to the first men of it; quite inconceivable to those who have never been in the way to observe that attention. It is also notorious, and easily accounted for, that this attention increases in proportion as they advance to power: it cannot then be longer wondered at, that under such flattering circumstances, a secret pride of rank should grow in the servants of the Company, in proportion also to the years they have numbered in their service: but, in our opinion, it is a pride that the Company ought to cherish: for you will allow us, Gentlemen, that the attentions which give rise to it are also greatly proportioned to the character and conduct of the servants themselves: for it is well known, that there have been men on whom rank could confer no respect, and who have passed equally despised through almost every station of the service. On this ground, which is the true one, we confess our pride; and we must acknowledge for ourselves, that the proposition of the Company conveyed to us an idea so degrading, that nothing but some immediate assurance of completing the great object we all bear in mind, could have overcome our repugnance to it. We cannot better express our sense of it, than by supposing the case possible, of an officer of rank in his Majesty's army, on his regiment being effectually reformed, a proposition to recommence his service in another regiment under the youngest ensign of it.

But, Gentlemen, it was not this pride alone that occasioned our non-acceptance. We have learnt, that to very junior servants, without a very prevalent interest, Bengal does not afford those great advantages which were to compensate for our loss of rank: from our informations, the service there is so overloaded in the junior part of it, that a person ranking only from 1773, cannot reasonably hope in the present state of things to attain the higher offices by course of service in less than thirty-five years. It is our misfortune that we had not an interest to surmount those impediments: and as to the advantages that were to result to a servant of fourteen or fifteen years standing, who must then of course be past thirty, life is so uncertain in this country, and the period so remote, that we could not reasonably hope ever to enjoy the benefits of them: even at this place also, a servant can hardly hope to arrive in council from his first entrance in less than thirty years: yet, unpromising as they are, we thought the prospects of a senior or junior merchant still better by continuing with his rank in the present line of service.

These were the reasons which induced our non-acceptance of the offers of the Honourable the Court of Directors, and which we believe were the cause that only one of their servants of the rank of factor accepted them; and he was well assured of the patronage of Mr. Francis, now lives with him, and we suppose, by such powerful interest, will soon receive the reward of his sacrifices.

As to the second assertion, that there are some secret benefits in the service, which render it not so unprofitable as it is represented to be, we wish to God, Gentlemen, we could discover this to be true: to cut short the matter, we beg leave to present the Honourable the Court of Directors with a list of their servants for these twenty-two years past, and how disposed of: the true inference will then strike them, viz. that there is a want at this settlement of just and legal opportunities to acquire an independence; unless they suppose (which they have no right to do), that the servants of this settlement have wanted parts and industry to embrace them: but if the Honourable the Court of Directors will but please to examine the accounts from this place, they will not be surprised at it: for they will at once perceive the few offices at this presidency that yield any emolument to their servants; and to the misfortune of those who have no interest in England, even these emoluments can no longer be reckoned in the general estimate of their service; for the attentions that have been paid to some of the junior servants, secure to them, during their rise to council, the best provision in the under part of the service, to the exclusion of all others, whatever may be their ability or deserts.

It is foreign, Gentlemen, to our subject to animadvert on the bad effects of this, in destroying a leading motive with every junior servant to signalize himself to you by industry, and by an attention to the Company's affairs; but we hope to stand excused, if we observe here, that this practice seems to us an infringement of our original compact, by which we always understood that we were to have enjoyed the common benefits of the service as we advance in rank: until of very late years, it is well known, that the common chance for these emoluments formed one of those benefits it was stipulated we should enjoy.

Besides the emoluments of the service there is no certain mode in this country of acquiring a rupee; for as to trade, Gentlemen, we believe you will allow, from the observation of many years, that it is in general a much more probable mode of sinking a fortune than of acquiring one: the road that has led nine men to ruin and one to fortune, is not a road that a prudent man will fall into; and we believe, Gentlemen, that this may justly be said of merchandizing, from the general experience of it: it is not our business to point out the causes of it; nor should we have touched thus lightly on the subject, but that it is well known the free liberty of trade in any part of the Company's limits is held out as a great object: now you must well know, Gentlemen, that however advantageous what is called the free liberty of trade may have proved to some of the crowd of free merchants, free mariners, and unlicensed interlopers, whose profits, it must be observed, have chiefly arisen from their commission as factors, from which we are chiefly precluded by the uncertainty of our residence; we repeat, that whatever this free liberty of trade may have been to those persons, it is notorious that, to the servants of the Company, restricted in their residence, and liable at every moment to be ordered away from their private concerns, it has proved only a free liberty to ruin themselves, which too many have unfortunately embraced.

We must again apologize to you, Gentlemen, for this long digression, and return to our subject: we repeat, that from what we have advanced one conclusion may be drawn, that in common with other gentlemen in their service, the Honourable Company always meant and understood, that their civil servants should possess adequate means of subsistence proportionably to the rank they bear. It is evident to you, Gentlemen, that our receipts from the Company will not supply the most common wants of life: it is a truth notorious to the whole settlement, that our necessities press very hard upon us; that we have not a rupee more than what we receive from the Company, nor the means to acquire one: as to those whose better fortunes in former times have placed them in such a state that their present situation is not a case of absolute distress, they still feel it as cruelly hard and unjust, that their little savings should be wasting away to administer to those necessities which they have certainly a right to expect should be supplied by their employers.

In this situation, Gentlemen, we have no other resource but in your justice and humanity; which we hope you will be pleased to afford us, by granting us for the present such allowances as you may deem adequate to the real wants of life here. We feel, with its due force, the repugnance that every gentleman in station must have to innovations tending to increase the expenses of the Company; nor would we have put you on the disagreeable task, if we saw any hopes of relief from any other mode, or even from time itself: for the continual appointments of the Honourable Company to the subordinate stations in the service, cut us off from any assurance of employment in any reasonable time.

Although you have been unfortunately prevented from placing the Company in such a situation, that the relief we request would hardly have been perceived in their expenses, yet we hope you will also bear in mind the present prosperous state of the Company's affairs, in the general system, of which this presidency is a necessary part; and though unfortunately not profitable in itself, yet, as it contributes to the safety and defence of the other two, the individuals who compose this part of the general system, should be considered as contributing to the general prosperity; and not reduced to a situation of distress from a partial view of the state of affairs. From these circumstances we hope, Gentlemen, you will consider, that if, on one side, to grant our request is an innovation, yet on the other, with every man of humanity, the distress of our situation will warrant it.

We remain, with the greatest respect,
Honourable Sir, and Gentlemen,
Your most obedient, and very humble servants,

(Signed) BENJAMIN HOLLAMBY.
WILLIAM GAMUL FARMER.
RICHARD PRICE.
WILLIAM ARDEN.
GEORGE STEVENSON.
JAMES FORBES.
JOHN GRIFFITH.
PATRICK CRAWFURD BRUCE.
JOHN DALTON.

Bombay,
8th October, 1777.

To the preceding letter was annexed a particular statement of the Company's civil servants, from 1755 to 1777, amounting together to 187; which it is unnecessary to insert: not so the following remarks which were annexed to the melancholy catalogue presented to the Governor and Council.

"In the course of twenty-two years, from February 1755 to the present period, three gentlemen have gone to England with fortunes acquired in the service; of the seventy-five gentlemen that belonged to the establishment in 1755, forty-eight have died in India: of these, eight had acquired, or had a prospect of fortunes; but twenty-five died positive bankrupts; and amongst these, were those who had served the Company from twenty-four to thirty-three years, and were of the council at Bombay: the remaining fifteen died possessed of very little more than was sufficient to defray their burial charges, although many of them had been from twelve to twenty years in the service.

Previous to the year 1755, and until the year 1767, the general rise to council was from eleven to fifteen years: from that period it has become more tedious; the two gentlemen who are at present next to council, have been twenty-two years in the Company's service; and those who entered the service of late years have little prospect of gaining that station under thirty years."

On reading the preceding letter, the list of the Company's servants, and remarks annexed, the Honourable William Hornby, Esquire, President and Governor, made the following minute; viz.

"On perusal of the address from sundry of the senior merchants, the following reflections arise to me:

"That the conclusion they have drawn regarding the intentions of the Company, seems a very just one, and warrantable both from common justice, and the former state of the service: for it is certainly but reasonable to think, that in common with other gentlemen in their service, the Honourable Company always meant and understood, that their civil servants should possess adequate means of subsistence, proportionably to the rank they bear. I must also agree with them in another point, that by the course of the service it was in general so formerly.

"I think also, that the gentlemen have been very moderate in confining their request merely to a sufficiency for the real wants of life: the situation of the senior civil servants seems to me very hard, and so very disproportionate to that of the gentlemen on the other establishments, and even in the other lines of their service here, that common justice moves me to enter on this subject, and to point out some certain fact, which, by tending to convince the Honourable the Court of Directors of the truth of this, will at least induce their acquiescence to the relief we may now think fit to administer to the senior merchants, and I hope to some further consideration.

"There are only two methods by which a civil servant of the Company can possibly be imagined to benefit. I mean by the emoluments he receives from the Company, and by commerce: as to the latter, the list produced with the address, and our general knowledge, so strongly confirm the truth of their observations, 'that to a servant of the Company this is rather a road to ruin than to fortune,' that it renders any comment needless. And in the estimate of the service, I shall confine myself solely to their hopes from the benefit of it.

" Throughout the service, under Council, there are not more than ten or twelve appointments, which, by local advantages and the emoluments of office, will yield any thing more than a maintenance; and these, I must concur with the address before me, cannot now justly be reckoned in the general estimate of the service; for, by the special appointment of the Court of Directors to them, they are no longer a common chance. It follows then, that in general the servants of the Company have nothing but their immediate pay to depend on, and the trifling advantages of the few offices on the island; which are not more than adequate to their common expenses, without being in the least extravagant. If then a decent competence to retire with to their native country is but what every man who enters the service of the Company may justly look to, how hard is their situation; for it is but too presumable, that, in the present state of things, they must be thirty years rising to council, and then they must wait for some time before the most reasonable wishes in point of fortune can be gratified.

" The whole system here is on so different a scale from what it is at Bengal, that I would not be thought, with such a deficiency of means, to wish to place the senior servants in the situation they are there: yet I cannot help remarking the liberality of the Company to their servants at that presidency in the common article of salary: the mere salaries of the provincial councils of revenue, I am informed, are as follow; the chief, 1200 rupees per month; the second and third, 800 each; and the fourth and fifth, 700 rupees each: these councils, I am also informed, are composed of senior and junior merchants.

" But we have within ourselves a striking instance of disparity. I mean in the military line: in the mode established by Lord Clive in the distribution of the profits of salt, senior merchants rank with lieutenant-colonels; and considering the years they may have served, I think that in point of emolument this parity is but a just one: in this view we shall perceive the striking difference betwixt the civil and military lines.

	Rupees.		£.	s.
A lieutenant-colonel is in the annual receipt of	8994	or	£.1124	5
A major .... do .... do	6455	or	806	18
A senior merchant, unemployed ...... do	1080	or	135	—

" Besides these certain and constant receipts, the field officers have a batta in the field in proportion to their increased expenses; the chance of prize money; and are equally at liberty with every other person to accumulate their savings, either at respondentia or common interest.

" I am very far from wishing to infer, that the appointments of these gentlemen are more than adequate to the rank they bear, or to the utility of able and experienced field officers: but as appointments in every service should bear some proportion to the length of the service of individuals, it strikes me as very inadequate, that, whilst these gentlemen are receiving from 800 to 1100 pounds a year, a civil servant, who may have served the Company upwards of twenty years, should receive only 135 pounds per annum: which is precisely the receipt of the senior merchants who sign the present address.

" To return to the main subject of this letter, viz. the relief requested by the subscribers of it from their present distress. In reflecting on the mode of effecting this, it occurs to me, that of the share of the Dewannee revenue, with which the Honourable Company have been pleased to favour the members of the board and the field officers, there remains now unappropriated the sum of seventy thousand rupees; it seems but just and reasonable, that the unappropriated part of a sum intended for the benefit of their servants at Bombay, should be applied to the relief of the gentlemen who have now requested relief from us. I therefore propose, that from the first of this month they receive an equal share of the Dewannee from this unappropriated fund with a lieutenant-colonel; which, considering all things, will render their receipts but adequate to their expenses.

" It becomes not me to dictate to my Honourable employers the degree of bounty they should confer on their civil servants; but I cannot help observing, that, by the contraction of the system here, there must at all times be some senior servants at the presidency, who will have only their stated receipts from the Company to depend on: and that these receipts should (as in other cases) bear some proportion to their time of service, considering also that senior merchants of from twenty to thirty years standing in the Company's service may be in this predicament; and that the proposed addition will render their receipts no more than adequate to their real wants, it seems to me but just and reasonable, that all such as may hereafter be in the situation of the present gentlemen, and are found deserving, should at least be entitled to this relief: particularly as some of them, but for the reduction of the number of the members of council, might have been strictly entitled to this share of the Dewannee.

"I therefore propose that this point shall be strictly recommended to the Honourable Company; and I do it with the greater confidence, because from the present amount of the unappropriated fund, and the savings that will constantly arise from the sum now appointed, by the réduction of the members to share in it, the further sum to be occasionally granted from the Dewannee will be very trifling; and, being from Bengal, will not be perceived in the superabundant means they possess of administering to their own charges, and to the Company's investment there.

WILLIAM HORNBY,

President and Governor."

On a due consideration of the preceding address, and accompanying statement, with the minute made by the governor, when they were read in council, the board unanimously agreed to allow the senior merchants who signed the address, a share in the Dewannee-fund from Bengal, equal to that of a lieutenant-colonel, being about 3600 rupees per annum; and they resolved also, that the same allowance should be made to the chaplain, secretary, and deputy-accomptant, in addition to their other salaries. This rendered our situation comfortable, until we obtained an appointment at a subordinate settlement, and enjoyed the emoluments annexed to such a situation.

View of **BOMBAY** *in 1773.*

Jam Forbes

Published by White, Cochrane & Co. Fleet Street, June 1st 1812

A View of BOMBAY, from Malabar Hill,

with the Island of CARANJAH and part of the INDIAN CONTINENT in the Distance.

Jam Forbes 1771

VIEW OF BOMBAY GREEN.

Jam. Forbes, 1768

[illegible]

CHAPTER IX.

FORT VICTORIA,

THE HOT WELLS AT DAZAGON,

AND A DESCRIPTION OF THE ADJACENT COUNTRY

IN THE CONCAN:

A JOURNEY FROM THENCE TO BOMBAY;

WITH SKETCHES OF THE GOVERNMENT, MANNERS, AND CUSTOMS

OF THE MAHRATTAS.

1771.

I conceive every traveller does well to submit to his country observations which have arisen from local knowledge; since out of much dross it is possible some pure gold may be extracted; and by whatever customs or prejudices mankind are enslaved, that very circumstance renders the knowledge of importance. ANON.

CONTENTS.

English settlement of Fort Victoria—adjoining country—Brahmin village of Harrasar, beauty of the women, simplicity of their manners—hot wells at Dazagon—effect of the waters—voyage thither from Fort Victoria—prospect from Dazagon—extreme heat—hot winds—wild beasts, danger from tigers—chamelion of the Concan—serpents—excavations in the mountains—Hindoo devotees, swingers, jugglers, combatants, and vaulters—Marre—religious hermit—Mahratta government—oppression of their subjects—commencement of a journey to Bombay—number of attendants and necessaries—corn ricks—Candhar—caravan of oxen—Vanjarras—Gaut mountains—monsoons—Mahomedan burying ground our dormitory—cultivation, gardens, and produce of the Concan; river fish—grain—corn mills—Guru, Hindoo high-priest—and other religious castes—great respect paid them—value of water in India—charity of digging wells—Mahomedan patriarch at Ram-Rajah—occasional reflections there—reception at Allah Braug—hospitality of the governor—Cotabie—visit from a Mahratta prince—his equipage, dress, and presents—family of Ragojee Angria—generosity to his pundit—beautiful temple and gardens—excellent sentiments of their founder—character of the Hindoos—superiority of Christianity—nymphea lotos—lotophagi—foundation of the Mahratta empire—method of supplying travellers with provisions in Hindostan—conclusion of the journey—reflections—comparison between India and England in their most striking features—oppressions of the oriental governments pervade every class of society—superior blessings of England.

CHAPTER IX.

After residing five years at Bombay, a slight indisposition occasioned me to go for a few weeks to the hot-wells at Dazagon, a village belonging to the Mahrattas, in the Concan, or Cokun, near the English settlement of Fort Victoria; a small fortress sixty miles from Bombay, garrisoned by a company of sepoys, for the protection of a few villages, and a small district in its vicinity: it was then the residence of two gentlemen in the Company's civil service, who collected a trifling revenue, and procured cattle and other articles for Bombay. This settlement was ceded by the Mahrattas in 1756, for Ghereah, a place of far more importance, then lately conquered by Admiral Watson and Lord Clive: during the subsequent wars between the English and Maharattas, it has never been molested.

Fort Victoria is situated on a lofty hill, near the entrance of Bancoote river, where there is also a lower battery: this river was formerly navigable for large ships; but the sand bank at the mouth constantly increasing during the south-west monsoon, it now only admits a passage for small vessels. Its source is among the eastern mountains; at a considerable distance from whence, winding through woody hills and fertile valleys, it receives some tributary streams, affords many delightful prospects, and abounds with a variety of fish and wild fowl.

The western hills near Fort Victoria, from being exposed to the sea wind, are bleak and barren: in the interior the lofty mountains are covered with trees and underwood, which soften their craggy precipices, and exhibit numerous springs, not common in the torrid zone: these not only add considerable beauty to the landscape, but cause an agreeable freshness in the atmosphere, and add to the luxuriance of the cultivated vales, abounding with rice, natchnee, and other Indian grain.

The villages in the Company's districts, generally inhabited by Hindoos, are surrounded by cocoa-nut, tamarind, and mango trees: the houses are small, seldom more than a thatched cottage; but some of the dewals, or temples, situated in deep glens, overshadowed by the burr-tree, have a solemn appearance. These secluded spots are occupied by Brahmins, whose religious ceremonies are strangely contrasted by the antic tricks of the monkeys, which, with green pigeons, bulbuls, and other birds, enliven the surrounding groves.

We sometimes extended our rides for several miles into the Mahratta country, and frequently visited the village of Harrasar, celebrated for the sanctity of its temple, the beauty of the women, and for having been the residence of the ancestors of the Brahmin family who at present govern the Mahratta empire. It is inhabited by a high caste of Brahmins; the women are certainly extremely beautiful, characterized by an elegant form, antelope eyes, and a fairer complexion than the lower classes of Hindoos: their jetty locks are richly adorned with jewels; their garment consists of a long piece of silk, or muslin, put on in graceful folds, falling like the drapery of the Grecian statues.

The simplicity of the patriarchal age was realized in the rural occupations of the women at Harrasar: the pastoral lives of the Mesopotamian damsels, and many customs described by Homer, still exist in the Brahmin villages of the Concan: there women of the first distinction, like Rebeka and Rachel, draw water at the public wells, tend the cattle to pasture, wash their clothes in the tanks, and gather the flowers of the nymphea, for their innocent sacrifice at the dewal, and its foliage for plates and dishes; which are renewed every meal from the lotos, or some other vegetable with a large leaf. The young women washing on the margin of the lakes, resemble Homer's picture of Nausicaa, a Pheacian princess, washing her brother's nuptial garments.

"They seek the cisterns, where Pheacian dames
"Wash their fair garments in the limpid streams;
"Where gathering into depth from falling rills,
"The lucid wave a spacious basin fills:
"Then emulous the royal robes they lave,
"And plunge the vestures in the cleansing waves;
"Then with a short repast relieve their toil,
"And o'er their limbs diffuse ambrosial oil;
"And while the robes imbibe the solar ray,
"O'er the green mead the sportive virgins play." *Homer's Odyssey.*

These delightful recreations soon restored me to health; so that I had little occasion to bathe or drink at the hot-wells, which I afterwards visited, more from curiosity than necessity.

The wells are situated in the Mahratta dominions, thirty miles from Fort Victoria, and two from Dazagon: there are several hot springs, and three baths of different dimensions; varying in heat from 104 to 108 degrees: the cases in which the external and internal use of these waters has been most successful, are visceral obstructions: I am not acquainted with their component parts, or particular classification; being chalybeate and purgative, their general effect in drinking and bathing, is to carry off superfluous bile, create an appetite, and promote perspiration: by relaxing the fibres, without exhausting the strength, they seem peculiarly adapted to invigorate the system, and counteract the languor incident to Europeans in the torrid zone. The Dazagon wells are in essential respects similar to those at Visraboy, in another part of the Concan, nearer to Bombay; and much resorted to by the ladies and gentlemen from thence.

The voyage from Fort Victoria to Dazagon affords an inland navigation of great variety: the river, seldom wider than four or five hundred yards, winds through a chain of hills, stored with timber, or covered with jungle; and the banks are fringed with salt-wood, an ever-green resembling the laurel: an opening valley sometimes presents a view of arable land, villages, and cattle; succeeded by woody mountains, water-falls, and precipices: in the narrow parts the branches unite over the stream, which is enlivened by monkeys, squirrels, and various kinds of birds; all familiar, from being seldom molested: among the halcyon tribes, displaying all the vivid tints of azure, green, and orange, common in other countries, is a black and white king-fisher, with an elegant tuft of the same plumage, not seen at Bombay.

Few prospects exceed that from Dazagon hill, where the English resident of Fort Victoria had a small villa, in which we spent a few days: it commands a view of the river meandering through an extensive valley, and forming a number of islands, clothed with wood, and abounding in villages, cattle, fisheries, and agriculture: this beautiful landscape is bounded by verdant hills and lofty mountains. It was at sun-rise I first beheld this lovely scene, I seated myself under a mango-tree with my sketch-book, wondering how any one could remain in a house, where nature was so lavish of her charms: but short are all rural pleasures between the tropics; situated under the immediate influence of the sun, in less than an hour the sky appeared as in a glow of fire; at that time I had never felt the effects of what are emphatically called the *hot-winds*, nor had I experienced any thing to equal the heat of Dazagon: on the sea-coast the atmosphere is tempered by its breezes; but their refreshing influence does not extend to the interior disstricts of the Concan, or Guzerat, where the hot winds generally prevail from the middle of March until the commencement of the rainy season; and Bombay, from its insular situation, is happily excluded from their effects. These scorching blasts begin about ten o'clock in the morning, and continue till sun-set: by noon, the black wood furniture becomes like heated metal, the water more than tepid, and the atmosphere so parching, that few Europeans could long support it, if the delicious coolness of the nights did not in a great degree alleviate the heat of the day. In the house at Dazagon, Farhenheit's thermometer, at sun-rise, seldom exceeded eighty degrees; at noon on the same day, it often rose to one hundred and twelve. The European convalescents sent from the hospitals at Bombay for the benefit of the hot-wells, complain much of lassitude, diminished appetite, and impaired digestion, since the prevalence of the hot-winds; which seem to counteract the efficacy of the waters: those symptoms, in a greater or lesser degree, affected all our party, after leaving the coast, refreshed by the salubrious breezes from the ocean.

My stay at Dazagon and the hot-wells, afforded me an opportunity of seeing more of Indian farming and agriculture, than the contracted limits of Bombay admitted of. The cultivation in the Concan, and adjoining districts of the Deccan, is similar to what is generally practised in the western parts of Hindostan, at least as far as my knowledge extends. The soil varies considerably in the same tracts; in some places sandy, others marly, and often a rich black earth: sometimes manured with wood-ashes, mixed with horse and cow-dung, which is placed in small parcels over the field, and afterwards worked in by a harrow, consisting of only three or four teeth, like an ordinary rake, drawn by two oxen; the plough, rather an aukward and simple instrument, composed of three or four pieces of wood, is drawn by two or three yoke of oxen, agreeably to the nature of the soil. In other parts of the Concan, they manure with leaves and small branches of trees, spread over the land, and burnt to ashes, mingled, when procurable, with the dung of cattle; but so much of that is made into cakes, dried, and used for fuel by the Hindoos, especially the Brahmins, that not much of it comes to the farmer's share.

The soil, generally shallow, badly ploughed, and slightly harrowed, produces juarree, bajeree, natchnee, and some inferior grains; with various kinds of pulse, melons, cucumbers, gourds, seeds for oil, and indigenous vegetables: but I believe neither cotton nor wheat grow in the southern districts of the Concan.

Fort Victoria is chiefly useful to the Company for furnishing Bombay with oxen; by which the markets are supplied with tolerable beef for the European and Mahomedan inhabitants, and especially the English garrison: a number of buffaloes and horned cattle are bred in this part of India; the latter, though small, are very serviceable in agriculture, and thousands are employed in the mercantile caravans. The sheep of the Concan, as in most of the other provinces, are long, lank, unsightly animals; instead of the snowy wool and silky fleece of the English flocks, they are covered with a coarse brown or grey hair, possessing very few qualities of the wool: in some places they make cameleens, a winter covering and blanket for the poor, from this hair, by twisting it into a thread, and weaving it in a sort of loom: but a considerable manufacture in the Concan, or more properly the Deccan, is the spinning and dying cotton thread, which is sold to the people of Meritch, and wove by them into pieces of cloth called leugra, which forms the principal part of the Hindoo female dress.

In most of the towns and considerable villages is a weekly market, to which the inhabitants of the neighbouring country bring their commodities, either for sale or barter: there is also a collol, or distiller, who pays a duty to government for the privilege of distilling spirits from rice, jagree, mowah, and various other articles: in the Concan there seems to be no prohibition to drinking spirits, except to the Brahmins: it is more generally interdicted in the Deccan, and the decree rigidly enforced. A peculiar species of the brab-tree is thinly scattered on the Concan hills, from which they draw a quantity of nerah, similar to that from the common palmyra; from which this materially differs; the leaves and branches bearing a much greater resemblance to the suparee, or betel-nut tree.

As these hills approach the Deccan mountains, the scenery assumes a sublime aspect: the landscape is varied by stupendous heights, narrow glens, dark woods, and impenetrable jungles; the haunt of beasts of prey, monkeys, and birds: among the latter is the jungle-fowl, or cock of the woods, probably the domestic fowl in a wild state; being of their size and shape, with the head and some plumage of the partridge, which it also resembles in flavour.

The lower part of these mountains is shaded by a variety of trees, and softened by many flowering shrubs; their summits present a curious kind of stones, which are found in much greater abundance on the Deccan mountains, near Poonah, and profusely scattered in other parts of the country; they are stalactical, grow in large masses, and are of a flinty nature: from the upper and lower surface of these stones proceed crystallizations, which denticulate with each other in a very singular manner: in many, from a single base, or bed of pure flint, shoot forth angular chequers of great lustre and beauty; while others consist of a common sort of stone, not very hard, encrusted by a sparry substance: from a close examination, flint appears to be the matrix of the majority; and as the crystallization advances, the flint diminishes.

Most of the jungles, or wild forests of underwood, abound with tigers, hyænas, hogs, deer, and porcupines: the former are as large and ferocious as in other parts of India, and render a solitary excursion dangerous: they approached close to our habitations at the hot-wells, and frequently caused an alarm; the thatched cottages were so close and uncomfortable, that we generally placed our beds under a contiguous mango-grove, until one night a royal tiger, attracted by the smell of a goat which had been recently killed and hung upon a tree, rushed close to my bed, in the road to his prey: the noise awakened us in time to secure a retreat to the cottage before the return of the monster: the moon shone bright, and in a few minutes we saw him pass us with the carcase of the goat: which had he not found, one of our party would most probably have been his prey.

Many natives of the Concan are keen sportsmen, and form hunting parties, with dogs; nothing in appearance like our sporting, but resembling the common pariar dog, except that a few had long hair on the tail and ears. Each man is armed with a stick of hard wood, called *burbur*, which grows in the jungles: the tree bends inwards towards the root, and instead of cutting they break it off, so as to bring away part of the root, to form a head; with this weapon they are admirably dexterous; killing quails, partridges, and pigeons flying; hares running; and breaking the legs of the fleetest deer. A set of these men killed, in this manner, three hares and several quails, in less than an hour. Observing one of the party in a small glen by himself, very intent upon some object, we imagined he saw a hare; on approaching the spot, he warned us by a sign to come on softly, pointing to the root of a milk bush; he then quickened his pace, took up a large stone, and suddenly dropping it on a partridge, instantly killed it, with no small degree of exultation.

Bancoote river abounds with a variety of fish; and is the

nursery of alligators, and other amphibious animals: on the banks are serpents, guanas, chamelions, and the large seroor, or lacerta, commonly called the bloodsucker: some of them, though hideous in shape, are most beautifully coloured: in some the shoulders and dewlap take every intervening shade between the palest yellow and brightest scarlet; in others, the dewlap is of the brightest azure, contrasted by yellow, scarlet, and orange, in other parts of the body.

The greatest curiosity is the chamelion (lacerta chamæleon, Lin.) found in every thicket. I kept one for several weeks; of which, as it differed in many respects from those described in Arabia, and other places, I shall mention a few particulars. The chamelion of the Concan, including the tail, is about nine inches long; the body only half that length, varying in circumference, as it is more or less inflated: the head, like that of a fish, is immoveably fixed to the shoulders; but every inconvenience is removed by the structure of the eyes; which, like spheres rolling on an invisible axis, are placed in deep cavities, projecting from the head: through a small perforation in the exterior convexity appears a bright pupil, surrounded by a yellow iris; which, by the singular formation and motion of the eye, enables the animal to see what passes before, behind, or on either side; and it can give one eye all these motions, while the other remains perfectly still: a hard rising protects these delicate organs; another extends from the forehead to the nostrils: the mouth is large, and furnished with teeth; with a tongue half the length of the body, and hollow like an elephant's trunk, it darts nimbly at flies and other insects, which it seems to prefer to the aerial food generally supposed to be its sustenance.

The legs are longer than usual in the lacerta genus; on the fore-feet are three toes nearest the body, and two without; the hinder exactly the reverse; with these claws it clings fast to the branches, to which it sometimes entwines itself by the tail, and remains suspended: the skin is granulated like shagreen, except a range of hard excrescences, or denticulations, on the ridge of the back, which are always of the same colour as the body; whereas a row of similar projections beneath continue perfectly white, notwith-standing any metamorphosis of the animal.

The general colour of the chamelion so long in my possession was a pleasant green, spotted with pale blue: from this it changed to a bright yellow, dark olive, and a dull green; but never appeared to such advantage as when irritated, or a dog approached it; the body was then considerably inflated, and the skin clouded like tortoise-shell, in shades of yellow, orange, green, and black. A black object always caused an almost instantaneous transformation: the room appropriated for its accommodation was skirted by a board painted black, this the chamelion carefully avoided; but if he accidentally drew near it, or we placed a black hat in his way, he was reduced to a hideous skeleton, and from the most lively tints became black as jet: on removing the cause, the effect as suddenly ceased; the sable hue was succeeded by a brilliant colouring, and the body was again inflated.

The Concan abounds with serpents, similar to those already described: one of the most dangerous is a long snake of a beautiful green; in form resembling the lash of a coach-whip, from whence it is called the whip-snake. This insidious animal conceals itself among the branches of trees, from whence it darts rapidly on the cattle grazing below, generally at the eye. One of them, near the hot-wells, flew at a bull; and wounding him in the eye, threw him into a violent agony; he tore up the ground in a furious manner, and foaming at the mouth, died in about half an hour.

Marre was the nearest Mahratta town of consequence to the hot-wells; by crossing the river, it was within a pleasant walk, and we made frequent excursions to an excavated mountain in its vicinity. Marre is fortified, large, and populous; the governor resided at Poonah, inattentive to the misery of the people, whom his duan, or deputy, oppressed in a cruel manner: indeed the system of the Mahratta government is so uniformly oppressive, that it appears extraordinary to hear of a mild or equitable administration; venality and corruption guide the helm of state, and pervade the departments: if the sovereign requires money, the men in office, and governors of provinces, must supply it; the arbitrary monarch seldom inquires by what means it is procured: this affords them an opportunity of exacting a larger sum from their duans; who fleece the manufacturers and farmers to a still greater amount than they had furnished: thus the country is subjected to a general system of tyranny. From the great chieftains and nobles of the realm, to the humblest peasant in a village, neither the property nor the life of a subject can be called his own; all bow to the iron sceptre; having no law to protect them from oppression, no clement sovereign to redress their grievances. When Providence has blessed the land with the former and the latter rain, and the seed sown produces an hundred fold, the Indian ryot cannot, like an English farmer, behold his ripening crops with joyful eyes; conscious that the harvest may be reaped by other hands: his cattle are in the same predicament; liable to be seized, without a compensation, for warlike service, or any other despotic mandate: money he must not be known to possess; if, by superior talent, or persevering industry, he should have accumulated a little more than his neighbours, he makes no improvements, lives no better than before, and through fear and distrust buries it in the earth, without informing his children of the concealment: this occasions the frequent discoveries of hidden treasure in Hindostan. Often during these excursions in the Mahratta districts did I recollect Lord Lyttelton's patriotic lines,

> "Hail, happy Britain! dear parental land!
> "Where liberty maintains her latest stand!
> "O! while amidst tyrannic realms I rove,
> "Enamour'd, let ~~me pour~~ my filial love
> "Into thy bosom!"

The excavated mountain is about a mile from the town of Marre, of great height, and difficult ascent; like the excavations at Salsette and the Elephanta, there are temples and habitations hewn out of the solid rock, whose origin is lost in fable, and the purposes of such laborious and expensive works are left to vague conjecture. The principal temple is sixty feet long, thirty broad, and ten in height: the roof and sides are not ornamented, but at the termination is a large image, seated on a throne, with a smaller figure on each side, and two mutilated animals under his feet; the light is admitted through a range of pillars, forming a grand entrance.

In one of these caverns I met with an aged Senassee, under very strict vows of abstinence and austerity, which he had observed for many years among those subterraneous regions; with no other companion than a lark and a parroquet: fruit and water were, I believe, the only aliment of the family; nor was the head of it incumbered with furniture, apparel, or any of what are usually deemed the comforts of life: the people of Marre revered him for his sanctity, and religious Hindoos resorted to his cave from a great distance; his most constant visitors were the monkeys, who seemed in possession of all the surrounding territory.

Not far from these sacred caverns, was a spot set apart for swingers, a set of very extraordinary Hindoo fanatics, to be met with in different parts of the country: particular villages are appropriated for this ceremony, where the swingers assemble at stated seasons. In the centre of an area, surrounded by numerous spectators, is erected a pole, from twenty to thirty feet in height, on which is placed a long horizontal beam, with a rope run over a pulley at the extremity: to this rope they fix an iron hook, which being drawn through the integuments of the devoted swinger, he is suspended aloft in the air, amidst the acclamations of the multitude: the longer he is capable of this painful exertion, and the more violently he swings himself round, the greater the merit: from the flesh giving way, the performer sometimes falls from his towering height, and breaks a limb; if he escape that accident, from the usual temperance of the Hindoos the wound soon heals: this penance is generally voluntary, in performance of a religious vow; or inflicted for the expiation of sins committed, either by himself, or some of his family.

In these excursions I saw a variety of tumblers and vaulters of a different description; being in general young Hindoo women, educated for the purpose, who travel in companies throughout Hindostan, and perform surprising feats of agility on the tight rope; turn themselves round with a girdle of drawn swords, on the top of a tall upright bamboo, and exhibit many other spectacles; while the elders of both sexes who accompany them, fill up the interludes by sleight of hand, uncommonly dexterous and entertaining. Sometimes a set of people, more resembling the combatants in an ancient gymnasium, exhibit athletic exercises to the assembled crowds: they generally perform in the large court of a durbar, or some open place selected for the purpose.

At one of these exhibitions in the Concan, where a prodigious number of spectators surrounded the square, four *pelwans*, or combatants, suddenly entered from the left side, with a brisk bounding step, and a shrill yell, or shriek, peculiar to themselves; something like that uttered by the Bheels and wild mountaineers, when they make their sudden attacks, and which in a solitary place would be dreadfully alarming: they were dressed alike in white turbans and short-drawers, with a strong cotton sash, bound tight several times round the loins, and passing between the thighs: their turbans were ornamented with chaplets of mogrees and champahs, and their wrists with bracelets of other fragrant flowers: they were all large full-bodied men, not remarkably tall; after a few manœuvres they made a respectful salam to the company, and retired. Presently after four other men, who, we were informed, were to be their antagonists, came in from the opposite side of the area: these were tall, lank, and bony, with much darker complexions, and a graver deportment than the former. One of each set appeared to be a youth of nineteen, the three others from thirty to forty years of age. These also having made their obeisance, withdrew; and were succeeded by an old man, who it seems was a celebrated teacher of the gymnastic art, and received a pension from the Mahratta government for that purpose: he was received with great respect by the populace, and by a profound reverence from the eight combatants on re-entering the area from their respective portals. The contest, which lasted a long time, consisted of wrestling, boxing, and similar feats: in boxing, one hand was guarded by a case of horn or wood, with a convex protuberance over every knuckle: they commenced the attack by raising the hand unarmed in the attitude of beckoning; with the other they strike desperate blows, particularly at the fingers of their antagonists, when attempting to catch hold of them.

After a few weeks residence at Fort Victoria and the hot-wells, I joined two other gentlemen on a journey from thence to Bombay: I rode on horseback; being invalids, they travelled in palankeens; our retinue consisted of more than fourscore persons, besides horses and pack-bullocks. This number of attendants for only three Europeans, may appear extraordinary to those who have never been in India; but they were all indispensably necessary in a country, where no caravansary, or house of refreshment, is to be met with; a traveller must therefore carry every thing with him, even a bed and kitchen utensils, which renders an Indian journey troublesome and expensive.

The distance from the hot-wells to Mandava, where we embarked for Bombay, was one hundred and thirty miles; yet from necessity it could not be accomplished in less than four days. We commenced our journey at sun-rise, the latter end of May, and after three hours halted at a Mahratta village; unable to procure a house for our accommodation, or to find one shady tree, we sheltered ourselves under a corn rick, which, until the hot-winds blew, was more eligible than a low cottage; as the stacks of corn in the Concan are generally fixed upon a platform of bamboos, supported by strong poles, seven or eight feet from the ground; this being open on all sides underneath, sheltered us from the scorching rays of the sun, and afforded a free circulation of air; which we enjoyed until noon, when the hot-winds set in, and blew violently for many hours: clouds of dust, burning like the ashes of a furnace, continually overwhelmed us; and we were often surrounded by the little whirlwinds called bugulas, or devils; a name not ill applied to their peculiar characteristic of heat, activity, and mischief.

We left that uncomfortable situation early in the afternoon, and travelling through a parched country, reached the village of Candhar, soon after sun-set: here a friendly banian-tree afforded us all ample accommodation; we supped and slept under its verdant canopy, with more comfort than in the best house in the village. Near Candhar the country was well cultivated, and watered by a serpentine river: the stream so late in the season, was narrow and frequently fordable: during the rainy months it fills an ample bed, which was now adorned with a plant called *jewassee*, from which they make the tattas, or screens, fixed in bamboo frames, and placed round the verandas and apartments exposed to the sun: these screens constantly supplied with water trickling in small streams, admit a cool refreshing air, when the exterior atmosphere is in a glow of heat. The beds of many Indian rivers abound with the jewassee, as also with a beautiful shrub named kuseernee, very much resembling a small cypress tree.

Candhar, eighteen miles from the wells, is pleasantly situated on the banks of the river; and a place of considerable trade; being a great thoroughfare from the sea coast to the Gaut mountains. We met there a number of vanjarrahs, or merchants, with large droves of oxen, laden with valuable articles from the interior country to commute for salt on the sea-coast: immense caravans of oxen are employed in the salt trade, in this part of India; where there are no roads for wheel carriages, and all merchandize is transported by these useful animals; especially up the steep ascents and difficult passes of the Gaut mountains, which bound the Concan to the eastward; from whence commences the Deccan, an extent of fertile plains on their summit, containing populous cities, towns, and villages, situated in a fine climate, surrounded by nature's choicest bounties. In some parts this tract is called the Balla-Gaut, or high mountains; to distinguish them from the lower Gaut nearer the sea, and connecting with the Concan.

These Gauts, or Appenines of the East, extend from Cape Comorin to Surat, through thirteen degrees of latitude; in some parts only forty or fifty miles from the sea, in others seventy: their rise is frequently gradual, but all their summits are lofty, and generally visible many leagues at sea. This stupendous barrier occasions the phenomenon of summer and winter, or the wet and dry seasons, to be directly opposite in places exactly in the same latitude, separated only by these mountains, sometimes within a few miles of each other. The diversity of seasons is caused by the monsoons which blow alternately on the coasts of Malabar and Coromandel, collecting the clouds, and carrying them towards these alpine regions; where being arrested in their progress, they become condensed, and refresh the plains with abundant showers, to forward cultivation, and insure a harvest. On the western side of the peninsula, the south-west monsoon continues this blessing, in a greater or less degree, from June to October: the north-east monsoon then commences on the coast of Coromandel, and produces those fructifying rains over the whole country to the east of the Gauts. In Bengal and the northern provinces of Hindostan, where the mountainous regions no longer exist, the south-west monsoon extends its influence, and wafts health and plenty to the "paradise of nations."

Early the next morning we proceeded on our journey by torch-light, and travelled for some hours, through a barren rocky country; after sun-rise we entered a cultivated plain, encircled by verdant hills, forming a pastoral landscape; enlivened by villages, and a busy peasantry. Before ten o'clock the intense heat compelled us to halt at Cotar, a village on the banks of Choule river; where we found a number of travellers, and droves of oxen, refreshing themselves under a mango grove: we joined their party, and after a slight repast enjoyed a comfortable repose, until the declining sun permitted us to continue our route along the delightful banks of Choule river, winding through a populous and cultivated country, protected by two Mahratta fortresses on the hills.

Several of these small towns and villages were adorned with

Mahomedan tombs and mosques, in a good style of architecture; like the Hindoo temples, they were covered with a coat of fine chunam, in whiteness and brilliancy equalling the purest marble, or porcelaine, which it most resembles: these polished domes form a striking contrast to the mango and banian-trees, by which they are surrounded.

The Mahomedan mausoleums generally stand in a garden of pomegranates and custard apple trees, which take off from the gloom of a cemetery: the Hindoo temples in the Concan are also frequently surrounded by a garden, sometimes of singular beauty. The brahmins evince as much taste and judgment in the situation of their seminaries and temples, as the monks in the disposition of abbeys and priories in England; where some of the most lovely spots are still graced by their ruins. In this respect the monkish and brahminical taste exactly corresponds: to the latter, shade and water are indispensably necessary; and, contrary to the general restrictions of the monastic life, the Concan shades are enlivened by the songs and dances of the female choristers appropriated to the temples; the number of Brahmins engaged in their religious rites; and the concourse of people assembled to morning worship Nor are these gardens deficient in flowers, fruit, and vegetables; the latter indeed compose the principal part of the brahmin's food; their best orchards contain guavas, plantains, jambos, and every variety of Indian fruit; with grapes, figs, and mulberries: superior grapes, oranges, peaches, and apples, are supplied from Poonah and Aurungabad, in the Deccan. The whole country produces mangos and tamarinds: the mango season in the Concan commences in April, and ends soon after the heavy rains fall in

June: the best grape season in the Deccan is from March till June.

The most productive gardens in the Concan are on the banks of rivers, and in the beds of nullahs, or rivulets, which run from the mountains. In these situations, at the beginning of February they sow the seeds of musk and water-melons, cucumbers, gourds, and pumkins in great variety: these continue to supply their tables until the flurries, which generally precede the rainy season; then, on the first swelling of the rivers, the villagers take a licence to rob and plunder the plantations, to the great detriment of the owner. They have two excellent sorts of pumkin, the red and white; and a profusion of beans and vegetables, indigenous to this part of India.

Many of the rivers in the rainy season abound with good fish: the bheinslah, in general appearance and flavour, resembles the carp, having a large mouth, without teeth, and strong scales; they weigh from fifteen to twenty pounds: the poatlah is of a similar kind, but smaller. The sewrah is an excellent fish, without scales; it has a large mouth, several rows of teeth, and weighs ten or twelve pounds. There are five or six other sorts of fish in those waters, whose Hindoo names are of no consequence, and I am not icthyologist sufficient to know where to class them: they also abound with cat-fish, and very good eels.

I did not observe any wheat or cotton fields in the Concan; in the upper country they cultivate both: our journey was not indeed in the season to see many crops on the ground: as the rice, juarree, and most other grains, are sown at the beginning of the rainy season, in ground already prepared for the purpose: and during the fair intervals of the wet months they plow for wheat, gram, pease, and other articles, which they sow in October and reap in February: the wheat thrives best in ground wherein nothing has been produced the preceding year: for gram and pease, which they sow broad cast, they prefer low rice-grounds, and other wet places: for all the rest they use the drill. The juarree generally springs out of the earth on the fifth or sixth day; about a fortnight afterwards they weed it by a machine called coalpah, and repeat the operation in ten or fifteen days.

At the earliest dawn of morning in all the Hindoo towns and villages, the hand-mills are at work; when the menials and widows grind meal sufficient for the daily consumption of the family. There is a windmill at Bombay for grinding corn, but I do not recollect seeing another in India; where the usual method of grinding is with mill-stones, and always performed by women, who resume their task every morning; especially the forlorn Hindoo widows, divested of every ornament, and with their heads shaved, degraded to almost a state of servitude. Very similar must have been the custom in Judea, from the pathetical lamentation of the prophet, alluding to this very circumstance: "Come down, and sit in the dust, O virgin daughter of Babylon; sit on the ground, O daughter of the Chaldeans; for thou shalt no more be called tender and delicate: take the mill-stones, and grind meal; sit thou silent, and get thee into darkness, O daughter of Chaldea, for thou shalt no more be called the lady of the kingdoms!" Thus when the Hindoo female, who had perhaps been the pride and ornament of the family, is humbled on the death of her husband, it is not surprising to see her prefer his funeral pile to such a state of degradation: and we must cast the mantle of charity over the young virgin-widow, who infringes the celibacy imposed on her by such cruel and impolitic laws.

Soon after the day closed, we forded Choule river, and arrived at Ustom, a considerable village at some distance from its banks; which we found a great inconvenience; all the wells and tanks being exhausted, except one belonging to a mosque still further: thither we repaired to pass the night, and the fakeer who had the care of it, allotted one of the largest tombs for our accommodation. These are often elegant structures of marble, or polished chunam; consisting either of a dome supported by columns, or a sepulchral chamber with only one entrance to the tomb, generally placed in the centre under the dome: it was one of the latter to which we were conducted; but the stagnated air, and disagreeable smell of the bats, soon compelled us to retreat to a clump of custard-apple trees, where we lighted fires, dressed a curry, and enjoyed a sound repose amid the graves of departed Mussulmans, until break of day.

We then continued our journey through a pleasant cultivated part of the Concan, which afforded nothing particularly interesting until we met a Brahmin of consequence coming from a celebrated temple in the Deccan; whether he was a secular chieftain, or one of the priesthood, I did not learn. The road we were now travelling was a great thoroughfare from the low country to Poonah, the residence of the Brahmin peshwa, and the resort of all castes of Brahmins; especially the Gurus, a very select body of priests, of the highest dignity and authority in the brahminical hierarchy; in some respects similar to the bishops and archbishops in the Christian church; as they travel through their respective dioceses, at stated seasons, to visit the inferior priests, and administer particular rites at the Hindoo temples. Those of the greatest sanctity make more extensive pilgrimages, to perform the upaseyda, and other solemn ceremonies in their seminaries and sacred groves. The Guru is reputed a being of so holy a nature, that he is not only venerated, but worshipped when he appears in public: on some occasions their splendid processions unite the insignia of oriental grandeur, with the fascinating charms of the Hindoo religion, bearing a great resemblance to the former magnificence of the sovereign pontiff on the great festivals in the church of Rome. These sacred shrines are frequently visited by female senassees, brahmacharrees, and other devotees, who have entered into religious vows, and are highly respected: many of these devout women, as also of the Gurus and exalted Brahmins, are supposed to have arrived at such perfection and purity, as to be actually an incarnation of the deity, and consequently an object of worship.

So much sanctity is annexed to the Gurus, that all of inferior caste to the Brahmins are expected to retire from the public road when he passes by in public procession, that the air may retain its purity, unpolluted by plebeian breath. Whatever might be the sacerdotal or civil station of the Brahmin we encountered, humility of spirit was not his prevailing characteristic, if we may judge from the pompous titles, and high-sounding praises ascribed to him by the chopdais and heralds: for, like other great men, he had these precursors, and a number of pioneers to clear the road, and "make his paths straight;" by removing obstacles, and filling up the ravines and the hollow-ways in his route. All eastern potentates affect these distinctions, nor do they ever travel without their heralds and pioneers: this pervades the magistracy, from the poorest Hindoo rajah and Mahomedan nabob of a province, to the emperor himself; who in the days of Mogul splendour, vied with Semiramis in her progress through Media and Persia: in which, according to Diodorus, when rocks or precipices impeded the royal traveller, they were ordered to be removed: hills and mountains were levelled, and valleys filled up, for the accommodation of this mighty potentate: finely illustrating the figurative language on the approach of the PRINCE OF PEACE, when " every valley was to be exalted, and every mountain and hill be made low, to make straight in the desert a high way for the LORD!"

There are many celebrated temples in the Concan, but still more above the Gauts, where in some the revenues and establishment of the priesthood are enormous: one temple in the Deccan formerly maintained forty thousand officiating Brahmins; who with the dancing-girls dedicated to the deities, and the other expensive ceremonies of the Hindoo religion, must have consumed an immense income. The Hindoo deities are literally innumerable: in a note to Dr. Tennant's valuable publication, they are said to be thirty crore; which, at a diminished calculation, in round numbers exceeds three hundred millions: allowing this to be fabulous, the number of gods and goddesses in the Hindoo mythology must be infinite: the Brahmins instruct the other castes to worship them, although they themselves do not believe in polytheism, and only worship the Supreme Being, as the great mysterious OM;

and the creating, preserving, and destroying attributes, in Brahma, Vishnoo, and Seeva. Allowing the Brahmins, and a comparative few of the higher orders, to be enlightened by a purer system of religion, the lower classes of society are condemned to a state of ignorance in religion, art, and science.

The Gurus have great power: but the ordinary Brahmins have taken care to reserve a sufficient portion for themselves, sanctioned and enforced by the code of Menu. At Poonah, the secular Brahmins occupy all the important stations; especially the lucrative office called Jeiram Bopput; a sort of censor, whose province it is to collect fines, which under the authority of the minister, he imposes arbitrarily on deviations from brahminical purity; drinking, domestic and family quarrels amongst the high and rich classes of society: this he manages with the greatest extortion and injustice. This officer is frequently summoned at the pleasure of the minister, and fined; which has eventually the effect of multiplying his abuses, by way of reparation for the mulct he has been obliged to bear; these are again connived at by his superiors, that he may enrich himself sufficiently to answer the call of the minister, as occasion may require.

As the hot-winds commenced their fury, we reached the village of Chouna; a spot endeared to travellers for a spreading banian-tree, and a well of excellent water; no less attractive in India, than the Maison-rouge at Frankfort, or the vineyards of Monte Fiascone, to the European tourist. Running streams had hitherto refreshed us when we happily stopped on their banks; but a good well had not yet fallen to our lot: on the contrary, at Ustam, and most other villages, the water was so muddy as to be scarcely drinkable; and even this unpleasant beverage was so scanty, that we often saw the women wait several hours at a small hole in the earth, to collect sufficient to fill a jar: it is only in the months of April and May, just before the first fall of rain, that this scarcity prevails: during that sultry season, of most brooks and rivers it may be said, " dumb are their fountains, and their channels dry."

The commendation of an ancient patriarch who dug a well, must not be thought too trivial a circumstance for the sacred records: he could not have bestowed a greater charity in a parched and thirsty soil: the frequent allusions to living streams, flowing rivers, verdant banks, and shady fountains, were delightful to the natives of Palestine: no prospect more enchanting, no promise more alluring, than to " feed in a green pasture, and repose beside the still waters." A good well and umbrageous banian-tree, are the most desirable objects to a traveller in Hindostan; since, on account of the peculiarities of caste, and the variety of religious professions, although an European carry his own provisions, very few of the natives will allow him to enter their house to eat them. This indeed is not to be expected among a superstitious people; who, like the Pharisees of old, make clean the outside of the cup and the platter, while they neglect the weightier matters of the law; who regard, with scrupulous exactness, eating or drinking with an inferior caste, the performance of stated ablutions, and bodily purifications: if by any accident, a Hindoo tastes food forbidden to his caste, or touches what is deemed impure, he is subjected to the severest penance, or perhaps degraded from his rank in society; while the same man may be guilty of falsehood, perjury, and the most immoral actions, with impunity. Dr. Tennant, who has well discriminated the Hindoo character, after a long residence among them, asserts a melancholy truth, which must be confirmed by every impartial observer of these singular people.

"That private charity is by no means the bright part of a Hindoo's character: religious persons, or those who assume that character, certainly are liberally supplied; but this must be the offspring of superstition, rather than the dictate of humanity. On some particular occasions, such as opening a new serai, most extensive charities are distributed to the multitude which is invited there: but this is mere ostentation; neither in its principles, nor in its effects, does it come up to the rational idea of charity. The necessitous poor are more happily directed for relief to the door of an European, than to their brethren in the faith. Temples indeed are raised, choultries built, and on great occasions thousands are fed by a wealthy native: but all this may be done in compliance with the interested advice of the Brahmins, or to gratify ostentation: and we ought not to confound what is extorted by the fears of superstition, or what is lavished by vanity, with the charitable benefactions dictated by a sound understanding, and a benevolent heart. Another circumstance in which the religious system of the Hindoos is prejudicial to industry and moral virtue, and consequently to the happiness of society, is the multitude of ceremonious rites, and trifling observances, by which it occupies the mind: thus withdrawing the attention from the necessity of practising rectitude, and preserving integrity of heart. In almost every action of his life, the Hindoo is under the immediate influence of his superstition; his prayers are offerings to his gods; his purifications, and ablutions in the river; his dressing and eating his victuals; the objects which he touches; the companions with whom he associates, are to him all intimately and equally connected with religion, and the everlasting welfare of his soul. If there is any part of his conduct with which his religious ideas have no concern, it is his moral character. In "doing justly, or loving mercy," he is apparently left to act as he pleases: but if in the most trivial action he violate the rules of his superstition, he is, in this life, deprived of all the comforts of society; and in the next, condemned to animate the body of some noisome reptile, or contemptible animal."

These sentiments correspond with the reflections I minuted while reposing under the banian-tree at Choura, when not permitted to enter a Hindoo habitation. Having refreshed our bearers and cattle, we pursued our journey through an arid plain towards the lower Gauts; a chain of mountains separating the broad valley we were travelling through, from the Concan plains reaching to the sea. This part of India during the rainy months, is doubtless a perfect garden; but at the end of the dry season its general aspect is very different: although in mentioning a parched country or barren plains in Hindostan, I by no means liken them to the burning deserts of Persia and Arabia; a scene of desolation, where Pitts, during a journey of thirty-seven days from Mecca to Cairo, met with scarcely any thing green, and where neither beast nor fowl was to be seen or heard; nothing but sand and stones, except in one place which the caravan passed by night; this they thought to be a village with trees and gardens.

The general aspect of Hindostan, excepting the sandy plains

on the borders of Cachemire, and the deserted country near the Indus, presents a scene of lofty mountains and woody hills, skirting a champaign, irrigated by rivers, or artificial streams, which, with the tanks and wells, were the noblest works of former princes: the emperor Firoze, in the fourteenth century, made a canal of a hundred miles in length; and cut channels from the Jumna and other rivers, to supply distant towns with water, and facilitate the inland commerce of his dominions.

With great difficulty and fatigue we ascended the lower Gauts; only called so in comparison with the stupendous barrier of the Deccan, on the eastern side of the Concan plains: our guides mistook the proper route, and bewildered us in a wild and savage scene: no sooner had we attained the summit of what we imagined the highest mountain, than one still higher reared its majestic head, and thus continued in long succession: fortunately during the extreme heat of noon, the woods and rocks afforded a friendly shade. We at length accomplished the arduous task, and hailed the western sea with delight. Descending by a narrow pass, we entered the lower part of the Concan, through rocks, woods, and glens; the haunt of tigers, hyenas, and serpents.

On entering Ram-Rajah, the first town in the low country, we were welcomed by a venerable Mahomedan, who, like Abraham, was sitting at his gate to receive strangers: his snowy beard reached to his girdle; his countenance inspired reverence and love: an urbanity and courtesy marked a distinguished character; and his whole behaviour evinced a superior knowledge of the world. He conducted us to the portico of his house, where we saw him surrounded by many branches of his children and grandchildren, dwelling under the same roof: the females did not appear; but, in all respects, as far as oriental manners and religious tenets permitted, he entertained us with the greatest hospitality, and exhibited a striking picture of the patriarchal age. We dined in a garden refreshed by fountains, surrounded with flowers, and shaded by caringe trees; whose purple blossoms, in rich festoons, diffused a sweet perfume: the fruit affords a delicate lamp-oil. The cassia-fistula, a tree of nearly equal beauty, abounds in this country; exclusive of the medicinal value of the fruit, the blossoms are fragrant and clustering; it is esteemed among the sacred trees of the Hindoos, who erect altars, and offer flowery sacrifices under its shade to Mariatalee and the sylvan deities.

Our venerable friend at Ram Rajah was one of the most respectable Mahomedans I ever knew; although greatly advanced in age, he retained all his faculties, and had not lost the cheerfulness of youth: this I mention, because the natives of India seldom live to old age; few of the men exceed threescore years, and still fewer of the other sex attain that period: many causes may be assigned for this brevity of life; especially early marriages. As longevity among the Indians is not common, neither is it, perhaps, very desirable: when declining years render the superior classes of Asiatics incapable of enjoying the ambitious, avaricious, and sensual pleasures, which in their estimation comprise the summum bonum of life; with minds untaught by learning and experience, unstored by science and literature, and uncheered by a warm and benevolent religion, they have no relish for those calm delights which soften the declining path of the pious Christian, and gild the rays of his setting sun. Possessing a mind at peace with God, the world, and himself; encircled by a loving and beloved offspring, to "rock the cradle of declining age;"

> "Though old, he still retains
> "His manly sense, and energy of mind:
> "Virtuous and wise he is, but not severe;
> "He still remembers that he once was young;
> "His easy presence checks no decent joy.
> "Him, ev'n the dissolute admire, for he
> "A graceful freeness, when he wills, puts on;
> "And laughing, can instruct." *Armstrong.*

The Mahomedans, in power, are generally intolerant and cruel; bigotted to the theism of their own system, they treat all other religions with a sort of contemptuous abhorrence, and we may safely pronounce them cold and uncharitable in their religious opinions: the Hindoo character, though very different, is in many essential points extremely defective, and led by deep-rooted prejudice and barbarous custom, to the commission of crimes, which ought not to be sanctioned by any moral or religious code. Unlike our patriarchal friend at Ram-Rajah, or the venerable Christian just mentioned, how often is the aged Hindoo parent deemed an encumbrance and unnecessary expense, by his family; and carried, a living victim, devoted to die, on the margin of the Ganges, or some holy stream; there his own children fill his mouth and nostrils with mud; and thus, cutting off every prospect of recovery, they leave the author of their being to be carried away by the stream, as food for alligators and vultures. Although sanctioned by the Brahmins, and perhaps sometimes voluntary on the part of the aged victim, no religion should tolerate such a sacrifice: that it is not always voluntary, we have many undeniable proofs: but the fatal consequence of not submitting to this extraordinary viaticum, or of eluding its effect, by returning to his family, in case of a rescue or recovery, is so provided for by the brahminical laws, that death is far more desirable than the continuance of life on such terms: many instances might be produced to confirm this assertion; I shall rather recite what Captain Williamson, from more experience than myself, has recorded on this subject.

" Many Hindoos, in their old age, or when seriously ill, are removed to the banks of the Ganges, whose waters are held sacred; and when about to resign their breath, are taken to the edge of the river on their beds; where a Brahmin attends to perform the religious ceremonies: no doubt that many, who might recover, are thus consigned to premature death. The damp borders of the stream, with a burning sun, rarely fail, however favourable the season may be, to put a speedy termination to the sick person's sufferings; but it has often happened, that the attendants become tired by the delay the poor wretch makes in ' shaking off his mortal coil,' and perhaps with the humane intention of finishing his pain, either place the bed at low-water mark, if the spot be within the flow of the tide; or smear the dying man with the slime of the holy waters, and fill his mouth with the precious mud. When a person has been taken to the side of the Ganges, or other substituted water, under the supposition that he is dying, he is, in the eye of the Hindoo law, dead: his property passes to his heir, or according to his bequest; and in the event of recovery, the poor fellow becomes an outcast: not a soul, not even his own children, will eat with him, or afford him the least accommodation: if by chance they come in contact, ablution must instantly follow. The wretched survivor from that time is holden in abhorrence, and has no other resort, but to associate himself in a village inhabited solely by persons under similar circumstances. There are but few such receptacles; the largest, and most conspicuous, is on the banks of the Mullah, which passes near Sooksongah, about forty miles north of Calcutta."

Cruel indeed are these mandates of ignorance and superstition! and yet, so contradictory and unaccountable is human nature, even in men of the very same nation and caste, that, notwithstanding the above treatment of their aged and infirm parents by the natives of Bengal, I can with pleasure and with truth record, that the generality of Indians, of whatever religious profession, whether Hindoos, Mahomedans, or Parsees, pay a great respect and deference to age; the hoary head is by them considered "a crown of glory." In the public courts of justice, as in scenes of domestic life, I have witnessed with delight, the pious brahmin and the experienced mullah, informing the members of the adawlet, or instructing their youthful pupils; who looked up with veneration to "days that should speak, and multitude of years that should teach wisdom; they waited for their words, and gave ear to their reasons."

The hospitality of our venerable host at Ram-Rajah, detained us longer than we intended; the day was closing when we left his friendly shade, and proceeded towards Alla-Bhaug, a Mahratta town at a considerable distance; as the country was marshy, and the roads bad, we had no prospect of reaching it before midnight, and therefore dispatched a horseman to purchase provisions, and provide accommodations, before the inhabitants should retire to rest.

On approaching the town at that unseasonable hour, we were met by an officer and a troop of Mahratta cavalry, preceded by *mussulchees*, or torch-bearers, who announced the approach of the *duan*, or minister of Ragojee Angria, the Mahratta chieftain, to whom that territory belonged: he soon made his appearance, with a splendid retinue, and attended us to the durbar; where we were treated with the most polite and kind attentions, seated on embroidered cushions, strewed with flowers, and refreshed by servants fanning us with punkas of *coos* grass, cooled with rose water. Our beds and equipage not being arrived, we were abundantly supplied by our host: while kids, poultry, rice, butter, milk, and vegetables were consigned to the kitchen for our supper; pine-apples, mangos, custard-apples, and pomegranates, were spread before us in the durbar, with wreaths of mogrees, and nosegays of roses and jessamine. When supper was served, the duan and his attendants retired, that we might eat it without restraint, and enjoy the repose we so much wanted. This hospitality extended to our servants and cattle; all were amply provided for, according to their respective castes, and professions.

On expressing our grateful acknowledgments for these friendly attentions, the minister informed us, that his chieftain, Ragojee Angria, was in the strictest friendship with the English, and had the greatest respect for our nation: having heard we were passing through his country, he ordered every thing necessary to be prepared against our arrival at Alla-Bhaug, and intended to pay us a visit on the following morning, if we could postpone our journey.

It may not be unnecessary to remark, that one of our party was a colonel in the army; myself and the other gentleman held respectable posts in the civil service; which made us travellers of some consequence among people who pay great deference to rank and station.

Bagojee Angria resided at *Colabie*, a fortified island half a mile from Alla-Bhaug; in which were the palace, treasury, and other public buildings; but the stables, gardens, and larger edifices, were at Alla-Bhaug: the former contained a noble stud of Persian and Arabian horses, elephants, and camels; and every thing about the Durbar was in a princely style.

At nine o'clock Ragojee came from Colabie, mounted on a large elephant, richly caparisoned: the duan followed on horseback; and the procession consisted of several state elephants, led horses, camels carrying the large drums, trumpeters, and other musicians, a select detachment of cavalry, and a body guard of infantry. On dismounting from the elephant, Ragojee's chopdars, or heralds, proclaimed his titles, and conducted him with great state to the durbar, where the duan presented us in form; he embraced each with a smiling countenance, and sat down on a cushion prepared for his reception: he then sprinkled rose-water, decked us with wreaths of mogrees, and concluded his visit by a present of muslin and keemcab; pieces of satin, with gold and silver flowers: these ceremonies, and some general political conversation occupied about an hour, when the prince reascended his moving castle, and returned in the same state to Colabie.

Ragojee was splendidly dressed in a muslin vest, and drawers of crimson and gold keemcab; his turban and sash were of purple muslin, the former adorned with sprigs of diamonds and rubies, and a very valuable emerald: from his neck depended two rows of beautiful pearls, sustaining a cluster of diamonds: his ear-rings, according to the Hindoo costume, were four large pearls, and as many transparent perforated rubies, on gold rings two or three inches in diameter: he wore a rich bracelet on his right arm; the handle of his catarra, or short dagger, was studded with jewels; the hilt of his broad sword plain gold. He appeared about forty years of age; of a comely person, pleasing countenance, and princely manners.

This Mahratta chieftain was of the same family with Conajee Angria, the celebrated pirate, so long the terror of the European and Indian vessels trading on the Malabar coast, until the conquest of Ghereah by Admiral Watson and Lord Clive. Ragojee, as one of the tributary Rajahs, paid the Mahratta government two lacs of rupees annually; he held his lands on a military tenure, and furnished a supply of troops, similar to the feudal system which formerly prevailed in Europe. Some Europeans, who had deserted into his service, informed us he was generally beloved by his people, and less oppressive than the other Mahratta princes: these men were married and settled in the country, and made themselves useful in the artillery department.

The duan's name was Govindsett, a pundit of the banian caste; a man of good character, and considerable abilities: to him Ragojee entrusted the whole management of his revenue and disbursements: they were of the same age, and having been brought up together, a confidential friendship, uncommon in India, had subsisted between them from the earliest period: in the course of education, Ragojee observing their different pursuits, promised when he attained the government, and followed the profession of arms, Govindsett should be his duan, or prime minister: the latter shrewdly replied, that, according to the usual custom of princes, Govindsett would be forgotten when Ragojee became surrounded by the insignia of royalty; but no sooner was the days of mourning for his father accomplished, than the young sovereign promoted his favourite to the highest honours, and gave him the management of his treasury.

After an early dinner, we pursued our journey towards that part of the coast from whence we were to embark for Bombay. In the course of conversation during Ragojee's visit, he politely observed, that as our servants and cattle might be fatigued by the distance and heat of the weather, he hoped we would accept of his own palanquins, horses, and camels, to the water-side; and an armed vessel to convey us to Bombay: we declined all except the latter; and accompanied only by Govindsett and his suite, we proceeded, at his particular desire, to a dewal, or temple, which he had lately erected, in a better style of architecture than any I had then seen in India. It consisted of two separate temples: the outer one a square, well proportioned, covered by a large dome, and adorned at each corner by an elegant turret: the roof of the further temple was embellished by a lofty spire, composed of cupolas, gradually diminishing to the summit, with appropriate ornaments to produce a general effect. The outer temple was dedicated to public worship, the inner exclusively to the brahmins, who washed and dressed the idols, richly adorned with jewels, and ornamented with flowers; amongst them the nymphea lotos was most conspicuous. In front of these temples a spacious area contained a tank lined with hewn stone for the ablutions of the worshippers, with a handsome obelisk at each corner, illuminated on the great festivals: for such illuminations are as common amongst the Hindoos, as with the ancient Egyptians, or modern Chinese: the surrounding groves were enlivened by dancing-girls and musicians; and, far from any appearance of austerity or mortification, the brahmins at Govindsett's temple seemed to partake of every terrestrial enjoyment: the dancing-girls and Hindoo women at the tank and fountains were of the most delicate order, and their own personal appearance indicated no self-denial in the article of food: on the contrary, they were all as fat and sleek as rice and ghee could make them; and reminded me of a curious remark in Orme's Oriental Fragments, that "the brahmins have made their gods require, besides the necessity of endowing their temples, the practice of all other kinds of charities, by which the necessities of human nature may be relieved. A third part of the wealth of every Hindoo is expended on such occasions. The brahmins themselves profess great hospitality, and by this address preserve that extreme veneration, which otherwise would be lost through the effects of envy, in a detestation of their impositions. A very strange custom prevails in some parts of India: a brahmin devotes himself to death, by eating until he expires with the surfeit: it is no wonder that superstition is convinced of the necessity of cramming the priest, when he professes to eat like a cormorant through a principle of religion."

"Far be from me the malignity of attributing to the weakness of human nature, the effects which might justly be given to its virtues: were not the Hindoos infamous for the want of generosity and gratitude in all the commerces of friendship; were they not a tricking, deceitful people, in all their dealings; their charity could not be deemed to arise from the influence of superstition."

Such are the sentiments of one of the best judges, and most humane investigators of the manners and customs of the Hindoos. The sleek and glossy appearance of Govindsett's brahmins reminded me of the singular suicides abovementioned. The dewal itself answered Dr. Fryer's description "of a fair pagod, or temple beleagured with a grove of trees which cast a lustre bright and splendid, the sun reverberating against its refulgent spire, crowned with a globe white as alabaster." Such was Govindsett's temple, encircled by groves and fountains, among flowers, fruits, and a variety of aromatic shrubs so much esteemed in India: the extensive lake was covered with the nymphea, waving its lovely blossoms of azure, white, and rose-colour, to every motion of the breeze. This oriental beauty is often mentioned by the ancients: it was as much a favourite with the Egyptians as with the Hindoos; the former considered it an object of religious veneration; the latter offer it in sacrifice, and as a decoration in their temples. Herodotus mentions a people called Lotophagi, who lived entirely upon the fruit of the lotos; of what species I cannot determine; as the fruit was the size of the mastic, and sweet like the date, from which they also made wine. He says the Egyptians eat the root of the plant, which was of a pleasant flavour; and from the flour of the seed they made bread. These properties of the nymphea, and the rhamnus lotus of Linnæus, are confirmed by Pliny, and may possibly be known in some countries at this day.

The temple, lake, and gardens, at Alla-Bhaug, presented an excellent specimen of modern oriental magnificence, and evinced the taste and liberality of the munificent founder: on alluding to the immense expense of such an undertaking, Govindsett made a reply which sensibly affected us: "By the blessing of Providence and the generosity of my sovereign, I have been promoted to honour, and accumulated wealth, sufficient for present enjoyment, and the future provision of my family. In dedicating this temple and sacred groves for public worship, with the gardens, tanks, and fountains, which I have made for general ablution and refreshment in a sultry climate, I trust I have not only offered an acceptable sacrifice to the benevolent deity, and bestowed a useful charity on my fellow creatures; but, from the changes incidental to mortality, the sun of prosperity may decline, and the clouds of adversity gather over my posterity; when my children's children may derive a benefit from what now so highly gratifies their father's heart."

In this scene of mutability such changes are no where uncommon; but the rapid revolutions of wealth and power in Asia, gave double energy to the speech of this benevolent Hindoo: distinction of caste and profession vanished; and we cordially united with a heart of sensibility, replete with piety to God, and love to man!

"In faith and hope, the world will disagree,
"But all mankind's concern is charity;
"All must be false that thwart this one great end,
"And all of God, that bless mankind or mend:
"Man, like the generous vine, supported lives,
"The strength he gains, is from th' embrace he gives."

As Pope's lines occurred to me on the spot, and were inserted in my manuscript of the evening, I have not suppressed them: a Christian enjoying the light of revelation, will confine them within proper limits; and notwithstanding my general remarks on the moral character of the Indians, will not forget that *love* which forms the grand test of his own religion, nor the charitable sentiment of an inspired apostle, that God is no respecter of persons: I willingly allow the Hindoos all the merit they can claim; but the veil is now as much withdrawn from the inner temples and mystical reveries of modern brahminism, as from the ancient Eleusinian mysteries: nor can an unprejudiced mind, conversant with both religions, admit that the followers have no need of the gospel: those who best know the Hindoos, know them to be immersed in ignorance, superstition, and idolatry! happy is the humblest Christian, beyond all the attainments of ancient philosophy or brahminical absorptions, who, under the cheering beams of revelation, finds his heart influenced to love God, and to evince that love by benevolence to his fellow creatures: who, lamenting the evil propensities incidental to his fallen nature, is enabled to look up to a Redeemer, who made an expiation for sin, which not all the penance of the Hindoo fanatics, nor even the typical sacrifices of the Jewish altars could ever have effected.

Our ride from Govindsett's temple, to the place of embarkation for Bombay, offered nothing interesting: he took leave at his garden gate, ordering a party of horse to escort us to the sea-port, and an officer to accompany us in the vessel, to inform him of our arrival at Bombay. They conducted us several miles over the salt-marshes, and passing through the Mahratta town of Tull, we arrived late in the evening at Mandava, a small place in sight of the island of Bombay, from whence we were to embark on the following morning.

Notwithstanding we were under the protection of Ragojee's escort, the Hindoos of Mandava, fearful of contamination, would afford us no better accommodation than a cow-house; where we dressed our supper, and passed the night. To this humble roof, by order of the officers, the villagers brought poultry, butter, fruit, and vegetables; with fuel and earthen pots in abundance; which we were not permitted to pay for: this diminished our enjoyment of a repast obtained by oppression, and consequently repugnant to the feelings of an Englishman. No murmur reached our ears, but we knew from our servants, that it was not accompanied by the blessing of those from whom menace and compulsion obtained it.

Lady Wortley Montague remarks, that when the Turkish bashas travel, themselves, and their numerous retinue, not content with eating all that is to be eaten belonging to the peasants, exact what they call teeth-money; a contribution for the use of their teeth, worn with doing them the honour of devouring their meat. This humane writer, in her entertaining Letters from Turkey, was compelled to be an innocent partaker of similar oppressions: and the story related by Baron de Tott, with a degree of humour which in some measure diminishes the cruelty of Ali Aga, his mikmindar, or conductor, I have seen frequently realized from the whip to the cinnamon, during my own travels in India. The Baron travelling in Moldavia, on an embassy to the cham of the Tartars, at the expense of the Turkish government, would willingly have paid the Greek peasants for his supply of provisions; but that was not permitted: and so liable were they to such pillage, that they generally denied having the articles. At one place where the usual supply was demanded, the head of the village pretending he did not understand the Turkish language, the mikmindar knocked him down, and kicked him until he began to complain in good Turkish of being thus beaten, when it was well known the villagers were poor people, often in want of necessaries, and whose princes scarcely left them the air they breathed: "Pshaw! thou art joking, friend," replied Ali Aga, "thou art in want of nothing, except of being well basted a little oftener; but all in good time: proceed we now to business. I must instantly have two sheep, a dozen of fowls, a dozen of pigeons, fifty pounds of bread, twelve pounds of butter, with salt, pepper, nutmegs, cinnamon, lemons, wine, salad, and good oil of olive; all in great plenty." The Moldavian replied with tears, "I have already told you that we are poor creatures, without so much as bread to eat; where then must we get cinnamon?" On this, the conductor took his whip, and flogged the poor Moldavian until he could bear it no longer: when, finding Ali Aga inexorable, and that the provisions must be produced, he ran off: and in less than a quarter of an hour, the primate of the village, assisted by three of his countrymen, brought all the provisions required, not forgetting even the cinnamon."

I wish not by the preceding relation to diminish the hospitality of Ragojee or Govindsett: the conduct of their people who escorted us was consistent with the usage of Hindostan: where princes, governors, and officers, travelling through a country, pitch their tents near a village, and levy a contribution of kids, poultry, fruit, and vegetables, and many of Ali Aga's accompaniments for themselves and attendants. Not always contented with what is produced with inconvenience and ill-will, these officers frequently extort money from the oppressed inhabitants, which, after the usual exactions of government, they are very little able to furnish. How few of them can make the appeal of the venerable prophet to a people among whom he had walked from his childhood: " Behold, here I am, old and gray headed! whose ox have I taken, or whose ass have I taken? whom have I oppressed, or of whom have I received a bribe, to blind mine eyes therewith?"

The transaction at Mandava, which gave rise to these observations, concluded our adventures: the next morning we embarked for Bombay, and arrived there in a few hours: on taking leave, we offered our conductors a present, which they respectfully refused; saying, their prince's favour was beyond any other consideration, and they should forfeit it by accepting our bounty.

This was my first journey on the continent of India; I found it replete with novelty and entertainment: I recorded characters and events as they occurred; wishing on all occasions to be divested of prejudice, especially in a country famed for its serenity of climate, luxuriance of soil, and the mildness of its inhabitants: a country, which, perhaps, precedes Egypt as the nurse of science; and by its arts, manufactures, and valuable productions, has contributed from time immemorial to the comfort and luxury of other civilized nations; various reasons, however, induce me to prefer

" My native isle belov'd; by sounding waves
" Bosom'd remote, and hallow'd from the world!"

Aromatic gales and spicy groves; trees adorned by Flora and Pomona; pellucid lakes and murmuring fountains; charm in poetical descriptions: we wish to dwell in such delightful scenes; a residence in the torrid zone convinces us of their fallacy: hot-winds, and arid plains, unrefreshed by a cooling breeze or living spring, annoy the Asiatic traveller: and admitting the existence of such pleasures in the temperate climate and fertile provinces of Hindostan, we know from experience, that a constant possession of the loveliest objects, often renders them insipid: the revolving seasons and variety of Europe, seem more congenial to an Englishman than the luxurious monotony of India, even in its most pleasing form..

The inhabitants of the torrid zone are generally indolent and effeminate; the climate is equally inimical to bodily and mental exertion: physical causes produce these effects, but they are strongly aided by a system of tyranny which prevents every manly effort. History shews the fatal effects of arbitrary power, and effeminate indulgence; Alexander himself could not withstand them; after the conquest of Persia, he thought the habit and manners of the Macedonian kings inadequate to his greatness; he chose to be treated like the Persian monarchs, and reverenced after the manner of the gods: he therefore suffered persons, in token of their respect, to prostrate themselves upon the ground before him. Happily Phocion, Niocles, Sidney, and similar characters, occasionally shew us wherein true greatness consists: the Hindoo chieftain, and Mahomedan nobleman, kiss the mandate of death with the servility which marked their character through life, and submit to the mute and bow-string with the same stoical indifference, as when formerly invested with a *sirpau*, or dress of honour, from a tyrannic master: but this indifference, founded on predestination, is very unlike the heroic firmness which characterized the truly noble soul of Phocion, who whilst holding the poison to his lips, being asked if he had any commands for his son, answered, tell him to "forget this injury of the Athenians!" of that ungrateful country, then rewarding his patriotic love with the cup of death! Niocles, his friend, under the same sentence, desired he might drink the potion before him; Phocion replied, because he had never denied him any thing, he would not even this, the most difficult request he had ever made!

In the court of an Asiatic sovereign we look in vain for true magnanimity: the nobles approach him with distrust and fear, conscious that his frown deprives them of life; nor can they, on so frail a tenure, enjoy wealth or honours: those in the middle walk of life, instead of being subject to one tyrant, are oppressed by numerous petty despots, who, dead to every feeling of humanity, rule them with a rod of iron. The lower classes of ryots, or husbandmen, are not in a more enviable situation; the despotic system pervades all ranks, and whole villages emigrate, in the vain hope of finding a more equitable government: they have not indeed much to leave; their cottages being generally built of mud, and their furniture only a few mats and earthen pots: they live scantily on vegetables, rice, or inferior grain.

In travelling, it is easy to distinguish the ancient inhabitants from those whom conquest or commerce have dispersed throughout Hindostan; not so much in complexion and outward appearance, as in the peculiarities of character: the Mahomedan is comparatively bold, enterprizing, and resolute; the Hindoo tender, humane, and timid: this distinction may in part be attributed to the mildness of the climate and difference of food, but still more to the doctrine of transmigration; since a religion, which teaches them that the dearest connexions they once enjoyed on earth, may, on the system of the metempsychosis, now animate the mortal form of a bird, beast, or insect, not only inspires them with horror at the idea of shedding blood, but, in a great measure, prevents every kind of cruelty.

"Where the human race is struggling through such mighty ills, as render its condition scarcely superior to that of the brutes of the field," Orme naturally asks, "shall we not expect to find throughout Hindostan dreary plains, lands uncultivated, miserable villages thinly interspersed, desolated towns, and the number of inhabitants as much diminished as their miseries appear multiplied? On the contrary, we find a people, equalling, if not exceeding in numbers the most populous states; such as enjoy the best of governments, and the best of laws."

"The effects of climate of Hindostan seem to counteract, in favour of the human race, the violences to which it is subject from the nature of the government. The sun forbids the use of fuel, and renders the want of raiment to be scarcely an inconvenience: the bare earth, with the slightest hut over it, affords a repose without the danger of diseases to a people vastly temperate: productions peculiar to the soil of India, exceedingly contribute to the ease of various labours; a convenient house may be built in three days, with no other materials than what are furnished by the bamboo and kajan; a boat, with all its appurtenances, may be made from the single cocoa-nut tree, which at the same time supplies oil, and a nourishment in much request; the ease of producing and manufacturing cotton, is evinced by the plenty and price of linen; health is best preserved in this climate, by the slightest and simplest diet; perhaps it is from this consideration that religion has forbid the use of flesh meats and spirituous liquors amongst the Hindoos.

"Thus the general wants of other climates become extremely lessened in this. Now if men multiply in proportion to the ease of gaining a subsistence, it will no longer be admired, that the country of Hindostan should, even under the iron sway of despotism, continue populous; especially if we add this better fundamental cause, which, resulting like the other from the effects of the climate, is still rendered more effectual by the most sacred of customs. Every Hindoo is by his religion obliged to marry, and is permitted to have more wives than one: it has been proved, that the number of females exceeds that of the males; so that a plurality of wives produces not the effect in India, which it is imagined to do in other countries, that of decreasing the numbers of a people."

In this part of my letters, youthful imagination, and enthusiastic patriotism, heightened by distance from the beloved object, led me to draw a long comparison between the inhabitants of Britain and India. Warmed by the amor patriæ, I pursued the delightful theme from Windsor's royal towers, to the palaces of the nobles, villas of the opulent, commercial sea-ports, manufacturing towns, cheerful villages, farms, and hamlets: I traced the munificent endowments for art and science: from her splendid universities to the parochial schools. It was a picture, which, in a distant clime and secluded situation, delighted the heart, and animated my endeavours to secure a competence, that I might the sooner enjoy these unspeakable blessings: blessings! which, after five-and-twenty years experience, are still enhanced, by contemplating the misery of Europe: but, as the subject is here so happily understood, I suppress a juvenile rhapsody, which acquired a peculiar interest in a foreign country.

View on BANCOOTE RIVER; in the CONCAN.
taken from Dazagon Hill.

Jam. Forbes 1771

Blue LIZARD and NEVA Tree?

W. Hooker, fecit   Jam. Forbes Delin.

Engraved by Chas. Heath

A Distant View of the Temple at ALLA BHAUG, *with different Natives*

IN THE CONCAN.

Jam. Forbes, 1772

CHAPTER X.

A DESCRIPTION OF THE CITY AND INHABITANTS OF SURAT;
ITS OPULENCE, MANUFACTURES, AND COMMERCE;
THE COURT, PALACES, AND GARDENS OF THE NABOB;
GENERAL CHARACTER OF THE MOGULS;
THE NATURAL HISTORY OF THE SURROUNDING COUNTRY;
AND AN ACCOUNT OF THE HINDOO TEMPLES AND RELIGIOUS
CEREMONIES AT PULPARAH.

1772.

Let India boast her plants, nor envy we
The weeping amber, nor the balmy tree;
While by our OAKS the precious loads are borne,
And realms commanded, which those trees adorn. — Pope.

CONTENTS.

CHAPTER X.

Soon after my return from the hot-wells at Dazagon, I visited Surat, one of the principal cities in India; where the manners and customs of the natives are more oriental, than in those places immediately under the English government.

Surat is about a hundred and twenty miles to the northward of Bombay; the voyage thither affords an opportunity of viewing Bassein, Damaun, and some other sea-ports: the hilly coast terminates half way at the lofty promontory of St. John's; from thence to the entrance of Surat river, the shore is flat and uninteresting: the southern mountains are woody, and abound with teak trees, often called the oak of Hindostan, from their great value in ship-building. Teak timber is more durable than oak, from its oleaginous quality, preserving the wood, and the iron necessarily used in naval architecture, for a considerable time longer than the British oak, which contains a corrosive quality, tending to consume the iron-work. I saw a ship at Surat which had been built near eighty years; and which, from veneration to its age and long services, was only employed in an annual voyage to the Red Sea, to convey the Mahomedan pilgrims to Juddah, on their way to Mecca; and then returning with them to Surat, after the hodge, or religious ceremonies were finished; the vessel was oiled, and covered up on shore until the following season.

During the fair months, the sea between Surat and Bombay is covered with ships of different nations: large fleets of merchant boats, richly laden, sail every fortnight under convoy of the English cruizers, to protect them against the Coolies, a horde of pirates near the gulph of Cambay, whose swift-sailing vessels constantly infest that navigation.

On anchoring at Surat bar I left the ship which brought me from Bombay, and sailed up the Tappee in her pinnace: this river takes its rise at Maltay, a small town to the northward of Nagpore, the capital of Moodajee Bounselah, in the latitude of 21° 8′ north, and 79° 44′ east longitude: and after an increase by many tributary streams, flows into the sea at Surat bar, a distance of nearly five hundred miles.

We followed the serpentine course of the Tappee, or Tapty, through a flat uninteresting country, until we suddenly opened on the city of Surat, pleasantly situated on the southern bank of the river: the old Indian castle, with the English and Mogul flags on the principal towers, had a venerable aspect: the English, Dutch, French, and Portugueze colours, waved on their respective factories, and garden-houses near the river; and from that distance, Surat had a better appearance than on a nearer approach; when we found the walls and towers out of repair, the public buildings in a ruinous state, and the streets dirty, narrow, and irregular.

The bar, or sand-bank, where the ships anchor, and discharge their cargoes, is generally crowded with merchant-vessels from the commercial nations in Europe and Asia: the city exhibits a busy multitude of Hindoos, Mahomedans, Parsees, Jews, Turks, Armenians, Persians, Arabians, Greeks, and other Asiatic strangers; besides the Europeans, whose factories have been already mentioned, it is also frequented by merchants from Malacca, China, Abyssinia, Mosambique, Madagascar, and the Comorro isles; and by numerous traders from the seaports, and inland provinces of Hindostan.

In a former chapter I have particularized the trade of Bombay; that of Surat is very similar; although now one of the greatest emporiums in India, I do not find it mentioned in the oriental commerce of the ancients by Strabo, Arrian, or other writers on that subject, who describe the Arabian and Egyptian trade with Pattala, the modern Tattah, on the Indus; Barygaza, or Baroche, on the Nerbudda, and Musiris, now Murjee, on the Malabar coast. These Arabian vessels imported, from Egypt and other places, woollen-cloth, brass, iron, lead, tin, glass-ware, coral, wrought-silver, gold and silver bullion, and several kinds of wine: and they exported spices, diamonds, sapphires, pearls, and other gems; with cottons, silks, pepper, and perfumes. Dr. Robertson observes, that "the justness of Arrian's account of the articles imported from India, is confirmed by a Roman law, in which the Indian commodities subject to the payment of duties are enumerated. By comparing these two accounts, we may form an idea, tolerably exact, of the nature and extent of the trade with India in ancient times."

The diamonds, sapphires, and rubies of India, have always been held in the highest estimation; in topazes, amethysts, and some other gems, perhaps America may be equal: the most celebrated diamond mines are at Golconda, in the territory of the nizam; and at Raolcondah, near Visiapoor, in the Mahratta empire: Ceylon produces the ruby, sapphire, topaz, and other precious stones; especially one of superior beauty, called the cat's-eye: the pearl fishery of this island is very lucrative, and the pearls vie in size and lustre with those of Ormuz: gold mines are unknown in India; but that valuable metal is found in the torrents which flow from the mountains of Thibet into the Indus and Ganges: there is no silver in Hindostan, but what is imported from foreign countries: several places in the southern peninsula and Ceylon, produce iron, but the natives are very deficient in their method of smelting and manufacturing it.

Orme mentions that the first English ship which arrived at Surat was the Hector, commanded by Captain William Hawkins, in August 1608: the Captain brought a letter from the East India Company, and another from King James the First, to the emperor Jehangire, requesting the intercourse of trade. At this time the Portugueze marine predominated on the Indian seas, in so much that they made prize of all vessels which had not taken their pass; and the fear of their resentment on the ships which traded from Surat to the gulphs of Arabia and Persia, deterred the Mogul's officers from giving the encouragement they might wish, to the English strangers.

The Portugueze dreading the future power of the English, and actuated by the most inveterate jealousy, did every thing in their power to prevent the establishment of an English factory at Surat: they often attacked our vessels at sea with a great superiority, but acquired neither riches nor glory: yet by bribery and intrigues with the Surat government, they had for several years sufficient influence to frustrate our trade, and prevent a settlement. At length, in October 1612, a treaty was concluded by Captain Best with the Mogul government, that an ambassador from the King of England should reside at the imperial court; that on the arrival of the Company's ships at Swally, the anchoring ground near Surat bar, proclamation should be made, three several days successively, in the city of Surat, that the people of the country might freely come and trade with the English at the water-side; and settled the duties on their commodities at three and a half per cent.: it also exempts the trade, and the factory then permitted to be established, from responsibility for the robberies of *English pirates:* and that in all questions of wrongs and injuries done to the English nation, justice should be rendered without delay, or exorbitant charge.

Such was the commencement of our trade with Surat, which is situated in 21° 11′ north latitude, and 72° 50′ east longitude: the outer walls of the city are seven miles in circumference, with twelve gates: between each gate are irregular towers, mounted with cannon, and the walls are perforated for musquetry: the inner town is surrounded by a similar wall, and an equal number of gates: the streets are narrow, the houses generally lofty, and crowded with inhabitants: between the outer and inner walls, are many streets and houses; but, like most other oriental cities, much of that space is occupied by villas, gardens, and cultivated land, producing grain, fruit, and vegetables.

The bazars, filled with costly merchandize, picturesque and interesting groups of natives on elephants, camels, horses, and mules; strangers from all parts of the globe, in their respective costume; vessels building on the stocks, others navigating the river; together with Turks, Persians, and Armenians, on Arabian chargers; the European ladies in splendid carriages, the Asiatic females in hackeries, drawn by oxen: and the motley appearance of the English and nabob's troops on the fortifications, remind us of the following description of Tyre, by the prophet Ezekiel:

" O thou that art situated at the entry of the sea, which art a " merchant of the people for many isles! O Tyrus! thy builders " have perfected thy beauty. Thy wise men were thy pilots, and " the inhabitants of Zidon and of Arvad were thy mariners: the " ancients of Gebal, and the wise men thereof, were thy caulkers, " and all the ships of the sea occupied thy merchandize. The men " of Persia and Arabia were in thine army, the men of Arvad upon " thy walls, and the Gammadims in thy towers. Tarshish was thy " merchant for all kinds of riches; with silver, iron, and lead, they " traded in thy fairs. Javan and Tubal dealt with thee in the " persons of men, and vessels of brass. Togarmah supplied thee " with horses, horsemen, and mules. Syria was thy merchant for " emeralds, purple, and broidered-work; for linen, and agate; and " many isles brought thee horns of ivory, and ebony. Judah and " Israel traded in thy markets with wheat of Mennith and Pan- " nag, and honey, and oil, and balm. Damascus was thy mer- " chant in the wares of thy making, for the multitude of all riches, " in the wine of Helbon, and white wool. Dan also, and Javan, " occupied thy fairs with iron, cassia, and calamus; and Dedan " brought thee precious cloths for thy chariots. Arabia, and all " the princes of Kedar, supplied thee with rams, and goats, and " lambs; and the merchants of Shebah and Raamah, enriched thy

" fairs with the chief of all spices, with precious stones and gold. " Haran and Canneh were thy merchants for blue cloths, and " broidered work, in chests of rich apparel, bound with cords, and " made of cedar. All that handle the oar, and all the pilots of " the sea, come down from their ships, they did sing of thee in thy " markets, and thou wast replenished, and made very glorious in " the midst of the seas!"

This is a true picture of oriental commerce in ancient times; and a very exact description of the port, and bazars of Surat, at the present day.

The public buildings at Surat are few and mean: the durbar, or nabob's palace, though extensive and convenient, makes but a shabby appearance. The mosques and minarets are small, without taste or elegance. The Hindoo temples are not more conspicuous, and the serais, or caravansaries, much out of repair.

I need not at present enter into a detail of the disputes and disturbances which existed in Surat until the year 1759; at which time a firmaun, or grant, was obtained from the Great Mogul, constituting the English East India Company governors of the castle, and investing them with the office of admiral of the fleet; which dignities they still possess. Some alterations in favour of the English have since taken place at Surat; when I was in India the English and Mogul flags were both displayed on different towers in the castle: the Mogul's broad-pendant was hoisted in the principal armed vessel employed on the Surat station; and a sort of double government, divided between the nabob and the East India Company, existed in the city.

The Dutch, French, and Portuguese nations, had no share in

the government or police of Surat; but they lived in an elegant style at their town and country houses, with handsome equipages, and suitable attendants. The Dutch factory is the most regular and the best built mansion in Surat; the Dutch Company import sugar, arrack, and spices, from their settlements in the eastern islands; and export a considerable quantity of cotton piece-goods manufactured here. The French trade is greatly diminished; and the Portugueze, who once commanded the Indian seas, are every where on the decline: but the commerce of the English Company and private merchants at Surat, is very extensive.

In the English and Dutch burying-grounds, situated without the walls, are some handsome tombs, with domes and pillars in the style of the Mahomedan mausoleums; which, interspersed among shady trees, give these cemeteries a grand and solemn appearance.

The serai, or principal caravansary, at Surat, was much neglected: most of the eastern cities contain one at least, for the reception of strangers; smaller places, called choultries, are erected by charitable persons, or munificent princes, in forests, plains, and deserts, for the accommodation of travellers. Near them is generally a well, and a cistern for the cattle; a brahmin or fakeer often resides there to furnish the pilgrim with food, and the few necessaries he may stand in need of.

In the deserts of Persia and Arabia, these buildings are invaluable: in those pathless plains, for many miles together, not a tree, a bush, nor even a blade of grass, is to be seen; all is one undulating mass of sand, like waves on the trackless ocean. In these ruthless wastes, where no rural village, or cheerful hamlet;

no inn, or house of refreshment is to be found, how noble is the charity, that rears the hospitable roof, that plants the shady grove, and conducts the refreshing moisture into reservoirs. Beautifully does Sir William Jones describe such an act of beneficence in an Arabian female:

> "See yon fair groves that o'er Amana rise,
> "And with their spicy breath embalm the skies;
> "Where every breeze sheds incense o'er the vales,
> "And every shrub the scent of musk exhales;
> "See, thro' yon opening glade, a glittering scene,
> "Lawns ever gay, and meadows ever green!
> "To cheer with sweet repast the fainting guest,
> "To lull the weary on the couch of rest;
> "To warm the traveller, numb'd with winter's cold,
> "The young to cherish, to support the old;
> "The sad to comfort, and the weak protect,
> "The poor to shelter, and the lost direct;
> "These are Selima's cares, her glorious task,
> "Can heaven a nobler give, or mortals ask?
> "When chill'd with fear, the trembling pilgrim roves
> "Thro' pathless deserts, and thro' tangled groves,
> "Where mantling darkness spreads her dragon wing,
> "And birds of death their fatal dirges sing;
> "While vapours pale, a dreadful glimmering cast
> "And thrilling horror howls in every blast;
> "She cheers his gloom with streams of bursting light—
> "By day a sun, a beaming moon by night!"

There are many gardens between the outer and inner walls of Surat, surrounding the villas of the nabob and principal inhabitants; the finest of them is called Mahmud-a-Bhaug, where the nabob had extensive pleasure grounds; with small reservoirs of water, and fountains playing near the open saloons, which produced a refreshing coolness, and had a pleasing effect; the gardens, according to the season, were filled with balsams, poppies, and various flowers, of an equal height, closely planted, and so disposed, as to resemble a rich Turkey carpet: this formality seems to be the acme of Mogul taste. The walks are shaded by cypresses, champacas, and cocoa-nut trees; adorned with oleanders, myrtles, pomegranates, roses, jessamine, and odoriferous plants peculiar to India.

The method of watering these extensive gardens, and of drawing water for the purposes of agriculture in this part of India, is simple, and more efficacious than the soft showers from a watering-pot, which would by no means satisfy the parched and thirsty soil. The wells at Surat are large, and deep, enclosed with strong masonry; a walk of an easy descent is formed from the surface, ten or twelve feet wide, its length corresponding with the depth of the well: on the circumference, opposite to each other, are stone pillars, supporting an horizontal beam, from which is suspended a large leathern bucket, running by a strong rope over a pulley; to the other end of the rope is fastened a yoke of oxen; which, as they descend the sloping walk, elevate the bucket containing the water; this is emptied into a reservoir, and from thence conducted by the gardeners in small streams, to every tree and shrub in the garden. Many of the wells and walks are sufficiently large to admit of two or three pair of oxen drawing water at a time; and some of them are erected for the public use by charitable individuals, at the expense of many thousand pounds.

The haram, or women's apartment, at Mahmud-a-Bhaug, is a

distinct building, separated from the palace by a large garden: this, from the jealousy of the Moguls, is forbidden ground, when the nabob resides there; but being uninhabited, I had an opportunity of seeing it: all the windows look into enclosed gardens, and have no prospect of any thing beyond them. It seems calculated to furnish every pleasure that can be expected by the unfortunate females immured under the Argus-eyes of duennas and eunuchs. Baths, fountains, fruits, and flowers, the European fair ones would think a poor compensation for liberty: the Asiatic ladies, accustomed to this confinement, are not discontented with their lot. The advice which Telemachus gives to Penelope, is still realized in every eastern haram—

> "Retire, O queen! thy household task resume;
> "Tend, with thy maids, the labours of the loom:
> "There, rule, from public cares remote and free;
> "That care to man belongs, and most to me. *Homer's Odyssey.*

An intelligent oriental traveller, describing a scene in the nizam's country similar to Mahmud-a-Bhaug, justly observes, "that although these gardens cannot be compared to those of Europe in taste and variety, they are peculiarly adapted to the retired pleasures of a Mahomedan life: the principal requisites of which are coolness, space, and secrecy; besides that, they hold it both grateful and healthy to live much among the fragrance of plants and flowers; and that pride, jealousy, and modesty, unite in demanding perfect security from all intrusion. Hence the high walls, so inelegant in the eyes of a European, are the necessary guardians of a Mahomedan's honour, and the safeguard of his pleasures. Within this protection, secluded from the world, the voluptuous Mussulman, laying aside the grandeurs of the day, with the irritation of mind which accompanies ambition, abandons himself to soft repose; and, in the stillness of a starry night, acquires that serenity of mind which lulls the soul into pleasing complacency; forming a delightful contrast to the stormy passions of an agitated day. Negligently stretched upon his couch, he listens to the melodious song; and contemplates the graceful forms of the surrounding dancers; amid the odoriferous smoke of incense.

These oriental gardens bear a great resemblance to those of the Pheacian monarch, both in situation and general effect.

> ' Close to the gates a spacious garden lies,
> From storms defended, and inclement skies;
> Tall thriving trees confess'd the fruitful mould,
> The swelling mango ripens here to gold;
> Here the blue fig with luscious juice o'erflows,
> With deeper red the full pomegranate glows;
> The branch here bends beneath the weighty pear,
> And verdant olives flourish round the year;
> The balmy spirit of the western gale
> Eternal breathes on fruits untaught to fail:
> The same mild season gives the blooms to blow,
> The buds to harden, and the fruits to grow:
> A plenteous fountain the whole prospect crown'd;
> Which through the garden leads its stream around,
> Visits each plant, and waters all the ground."
>
> *Homer's Odyssey.*

The palace and gardens of Mahmud-a-Bhaug were out of repair; as the Moguls of rank are seldom at any trouble or expense, on a place which was not built by themselves: they had rather be the reputed founder of an insignificant villa, than preserve the grandest palace erected by their ancestors. These gardens were made by a former nabob, and called after his name; they cost an immense sum, and required many years to complete them: yet his successor never resided there, nor prevented their decay; while, with the iron rod of despotism, he was converting a populous part of the city into a large garden, adorned with extensive walks, groves, and fountains, to surround a summer pavilion: the reigning nabob dignified this favourite retreat with the appellation of "The Gift of God;" the suffering manufacturers, driven from their quiet habitations, and shady verdant looms, called it "The Garden of Oppression."

The baths at Mahmud-a-Bhaug had been on a grand scale: in most of the principal houses at Surat are private hummums, or bagnios; which consist of one or two small rooms, paved with marble, illuminated by a sky-light of coloured glass, and furnished with cisterns of hot and cold water. There are many public hummums on a larger scale, but of the same construction; where oils, perfumes, and pastes, are provided for anointing the visitors. You first enter a vestibule, paved and lined with marble, surrounded by benches for the convenience of undressing: from thence you are conducted by two men into the marble bathing room; which contains two cisterns of hot and cold water; these are mingled in copper vessels, until of the required temperature, and then poured upon the visitor by the attendants. The operation of these men is at first disagreeable to Europeans, especially in the champoing; which is a method of working or kneading the flesh, and cracking the joints, after being rubbed over with perfumed pastes: champoing affords delightful sensations to the Asiatics; and many Europeans, after being accustomed to this singular treatment, consider it a luxury.

The Banian hospital at Surat is a most remarkable institution; it consists of a large plot of ground, enclosed with high walls; divided into several courts, or wards, for the accommodation of animals: in sickness they are attended with the tenderest care, and find a peaceful asylum for the infirmities of age. When an animal breaks a limb, or is otherwise disabled from serving his master, he carries him to the hospital; and, indifferent to what nation or caste the owner may belong, the patient is never refused admittance. If he recovers, he cannot be reclaimed, but must remain in the hospital for life, subject to the duty of drawing water for those pensioners debilitated by age or disease from procuring it for themselves. At my visit, the hospital contained horses, mules, oxen, sheep, goats, monkeys, poultry, pigeons, and a variety of birds; with an aged tortoise, who was known to have been there for seventy-five years. The most extraordinary ward was that appropriated to rats, mice, bugs, and other noxious vermin: the overseers of the hospital frequently hire beggars from the streets, for a stipulated sum, to pass a night among the fleas, lice, and bugs, on the express condition of suffering them to enjoy their feast without molestation.

The Banian hospital in Surat has several dependent endowments without the walls, for such invalids and convalescents to whom pasturage and country air may be recommended; and especially for the maintenance of the goats purchased from slaughter on the anniversary of the Mahomedan festival, when so many of those animals are devoted to destruction.

The doctrine of the metempsychosis is commonly supposed to be the cause of founding this singular hospital; I, however, conversed with several sensible brahmins on the subject, who rather ascribed it to a motive of benevolence for the animal creation: nor can we do otherwise than approve of that part of the institution appropriated for the comfort of those valuable creatures who have exhausted their strength in the service of man. At the same time it must be acknowledged, that the belief in transmigration which pervades every part of the Hindoo system, has probably no small degree of influence in this endowment: for the metempsychosis is founded nearly on the same principle with that of Pythagoras, and the ancient philosophers, as we find from Ovid.

> "That all things are but alter'd, nothing dies,
> "And here and there, th' unbodied spirit flies,
> "By time, or force, or sickness dispossess'd,
> "And lodges where it lights, in bird or beast;
> "Or hunts without, 'till ready limbs it find,
> "And actuates those according to their kind:
> "From tenement to tenement is toss'd,
> "The soul is still the same, the figure only lost!
> "Then let not piety be put to flight,
> "To please the taste of glutton-appetite;
> "But suffer inmate souls secure to dwell,
> "Lest from their seats your parents you expel!
> "With rabid hunger feed upon your kind,
> "Or from a beast dislodge a brother's mind." DRYDEN.

The inhabitants of Surat are generally merchants or manufacturers: after the Mahrattas conquered Guzerat, the weavers of keemcabs, and other rich stuffs, the embroiderers, jewellers, painters, and inlayers of ivory, ebony, and sandal-wood, meeting with no encouragement from the Mahratta government, emigrated from Ahmedabad to Surat, and other flourishing cities in the western districts of Hindostan, where they have resumed their employments with great success.

Surat is also a considerable market for shawls, one of the most delicate fabrics yet brought from the loom: they are not indeed manufactured at Surat, nor in any of the southern provinces, being chiefly the produce of Cachemire, that "paradise of nations," where Acber, and many of the imperial princes retired from the cares of government: encircled by their favourite courtiers, and in the bosom of their family, they enjoyed in that mild climate the picturesque scenery of the surrounding mountains, and the rural beauties of the delicious valley, watered by the celebrated Hydaspes, and refreshed by many other streams from its lofty boundaries. The shawls manufactured in Cachemire, from the delicate silky wool of a goat peculiar to Thibet, are an elegant article of luxury, too well known in Europe, to need a particular description: this manufacture is not confined to Cachemire, but all others are deemed of an inferior quality: their prime cost is from twenty to five hundred rupees a shawl, according to the size, texture, and pattern: some, perhaps, may be more valuable.

The staples of Europe are disposed of by agents at the respective factories in Surat; but the commodities exported to Europe from India and China far exceed in value those imported from thence: the natives of India, from the mildness of the climate, and fertility of the soil, want but few foreign supplies: gold and silver have been always carried thither by European traders. The English commerce in Asia, and especially in China, towards the conclusion of the eighteenth century, never could have been conducted on such an extensive scale, had it not been for the inexhaustible mines of South America: their precious metals have, by various channels, been conveyed to the east, from whence they never return: it is singular, that the discovery of the new world by Columbus, from whence proceeds this influx of gold and silver to Europe, was nearly at the same period when Vasco de Gama opened the trade to India by the Cape of Good Hope.

Having accompanied the English chief on a public visit to the nabob of Surat, I will endeavour to describe the court etiquette at an oriental durbar. The chief went in state, attended by the members of council, aids du camp, and other officers, preceded by a detachment of European infantry, the British colours, and other insignia appropriate to his station. The castle guns fired a royal salute; and on approaching the Durbar, the nabob's troops were ready to receive us. The naib, or vizier, with the nabob's brother, met the chief in the inner court, and conducted him to the hall of audience, where he was seated on the nabob's right-hand; the other gentlemen, in chairs, according to their respective stations. On his left were the naib, the nabob's sons, brother, and officers of state. After a complimentary discourse, and a few political questions, we were served with coffee, in small porcelain cups, placed in silver saucers, and soon after with glasses of perfumed sherbet: the nabob then presented the chief with an Arabian horse, a diamond ring, and several pieces of gold and silver keemcab: his attendants brought to each of the gentlemen a present of shawls, keemcab, or muslin, suited to their rank; the ceremony concluded by presenting pawn, or betel-nut, folded up in a leaf of betel, with chunam, and spices, fastened by a clove: this is the usual indication of the visit being terminated. The nabob attended his guests to the bottom of the steps leading from the durbar to the area, and at parting took each by the hand; his eldest son and brother accompanied us to the outward gate, and took leave in the same manner.

The custom of giving and receiving presents, prevails universally in Hindostan, and in most parts of Asia; from sacred and profane history, we find it was equally customary among the ancients. On Telemachus leaving the Spartan court, Menelaus says to his departing guest,

> " No prince will let Ulysses' heir remove
> " Without some pledge, some monument of love:
> " These will the cauldron, these the tripod give,
> " From those the well-pair'd mules we shall receive,
> " Or bowl emboss'd, whose golden figures live.

The termination of the monthly fast of Ramadān, one of the strictest ordinances in the Mahomedan religion, afforded me an opportunity of seeing the nabob go in state to the jumai-musjod, or principal mosque: a ceremony he always performs on the appearance of the new moon after the Ramadan; in which month the Mussulmans believe the Koran was sent from heaven, and observe the fast with great austerity.

The procession left the durbar at nine o'clock in the morning, led by the cajee, a venerable Mahomedan priest, followed by a train of artillery, with two flags on each gun-carriage; an officer bearing the sacred standard of green silk, embroidered with gold, and mounted on an elephant, surrounded by young men with small banners, formed the first division. Then came a detachment of Mogul infantry, with a band of martial music, preceding the scidees, or Mahomedan caffrees, favourite slaves and chief officers of the nabob, mounted on excellent horses, richly caparisoned: the scidees are generally natives of Abyssinia, adopted into the family of the rich Moguls, and often married to their daughters. After them came a company of English troops, followed by an elephant, and camels carrying kettle-drums and musicians, with others on horseback: these were succeeded by an English gentleman of the council at Surat, in a state palankeen, representing the East India Company, as governor of the castle, and admiral of the Mogul's fleet: the nabob's empty palankeen and carriages went before his two sons, mounted on Arabian chargers, immediately preceding the elephant on which his highness was enthroned in a splendid houdah, with his principal attendant in a separate apartment behind: the nabob was richly dressed, and his turban adorned with jewels: the covering of the houdah and caparison of the elephant, were scarlet and gold. The buxey, or general of the army, at the head of a select body, closed the procession.

This magnificent cavalcade only occurring once a year, was very gratifying to a stranger; but I was still more delighted with the company I accidentally met on the occasion. A friend procured me a projecting window in one of the principal streets to view the spectacle; where I was soon accosted by an old duenna, to desire I would either turn my back, or walk down stairs, while some Mogul ladies passed through the room in their way to an adjoining latticed chamber: knowing the necessity of obedience, I preferred looking out of the window, and kept my station: but at the sound of foot-steps I was tempted to peep behind me; when instead of the ladies, I beheld the careful matron holding up a thick veil, to screen her charge: a similar curiosity to see an English stranger brought them to the lattice; fortunately one of the party had known me before, which induced her to break through an established custom, and pay me a visit, accompanied by one of the greatest beauties I ever beheld: her age did not exceed fifteen; her form was perfect, her features regular, and her large antelope eyes of brilliant lustre: although fairer than the generality of Indian females, neither the rose nor the lily adorned her complexion, yet the brunette tint rather enriched than impaired the softness and delicacy of her skin; "grace was in all her steps," and her whole deportment elegant and courteous.

This young beauty excelled in personal charms, but was not so superbly attired as her friend, whom I hastily sketched, as a specimen of a well-dressed Mogul. Her drawers, of green satin flowered with gold, were seen under a chemise of transparent gauze, reaching to her slippers, richly embroidered: a vest of pale blue satin, edged with gold, sat close to her shape, which an upper robe of striped silver muslin, full and flowing, displayed to great advantage: a netted veil of crimson silk, flowered with silver, fell carelessly over her long braided hair, combed smooth, and divided from the forehead, where a cluster of jewels was fastened by strings of seed-pearl: her ear-rings were large and handsome, that in her nose, according to our idea of ornament, less becoming: the Asiatic ladies are extremely fond of the nose-jewel, and it is mentioned among the Jewish trinkets in the old testament; a necklace in intermingled rows of pearls and gold covered her bosom, and several strings of large pearls were suspended from an embroidered girdle set with diamonds: bracelets of gold and coral reached from her wrist to the elbow, golden chains encircled her ancles, and all her toes and fingers were adorned with valuable rings. Like most of the oriental females, of all religions, her eyes were tinged by a black circle, formed with the powder of antimony; which produces a refreshing coolness, gives the eye additional lustre, and is thought to be a general improvement to Asiatic beauty.

The slippers, girdle, and other parts of the Mogul dress, of both sexes, are embroidered with gold, silver, and coloured silks, upon velvet, satin, or scarlet cloth: the jama is often richly embroidered; this is the name of the muslin robe, worn by Hindoos and Mahomedans, which falls in full folds from the waist to the feet; the upper part is made to fit the body, and crossing over the bosom, is tied on the left side by the Hindoos, and by the Mahomedans on the right. The veil is an elegant part of the female dress; and has been so esteemed, from the time of Rebecca, to the present day: Homer frequently mentions it as an ornament of Grecian and Trojan beauty:

> " A veil translucent, o'er her brows display'd,
> " Her beauty seems, and only seems, to shade."

We were acquainted with a young Persian, a temporary resident at Baroche, who one day brought his wife to our garden-house on a visit to my sister, which seemed productive of much novelty and pleasure to both parties: on taking leave they mutually exchanged presents; the Persian lady presented my sister with a veil of purple silk-net, embroidered with silver, such as the Moguls wear either to cover the face, or to throw back as an ornament: similar to that which Helen gave to Telemachus—

> " The beauteous queen, advancing, then display'd
> " A shining veil, and thus endearing said,
> " Accept, dear youth, this monument of love,
> " Long since, in better days, by Helen wove;
> " Safe in thy mother's care the vesture lay,
> " To deck thy bride, and grace thy nuptial day."
>
> ODYSSEY.

The art of embroidery is of great antiquity, as we learn from sacred and profane history: the dress of the princes and nobles in Homer's time resembled the jama, girdle, and kincob drawers, flowered with gold and silver, now worn by the Moguls; thus Homer describes Ulysses, in his royal attire:

> " In ample mode,
> " A robe of military purple flow'd
> " O'er all his frame; illustrious on his breast,
> " The double clasping gold the king confest:
> " In the rich woof a hound mosaic drawn,
> " Bore on full stretch, and seiz'd a dappled fawn:
> " Fine as a filmy web beneath it shone
> " A vest, that dazzled like a cloudless sun:
> " A sabre, when the warrior press'd to part,
> " He gave, enamell'd with Vulcanian art:
> " A mantle purple-ting'd, and radiant vest,
> " Affection grateful to an honour'd guest."

The note on the above passage in Pope's Homer illustrates the art of ancient embroidery, by remarking, that it was of divers colours, as we may gather from the epithet applied to the fawn, ποικιλον; and it is evident that this art was known amongst the orientals in the age of Ulysses; we read also in the book of Judges, "Have they not sped, have they not divided the prey? to Sisera a prey of divers colours, of divers colours of needle-work, of divers colours of needle-work on both sides, meet for the necks of them that take the spoil?" Tamar, after her humiliation, laid aside her royal robe of many colours, which, as a princess of Israel, she was accustomed to wear.

Such is the analogy between ancient and modern usages in the oriental world; where things are much less liable to change than in Europe, especially among the females, whose manners and customs keep them in a secluded state: yet the higher classes enjoy various pleasures in the haram; and many of them confirm Lady Wortley Montague's account of the ladies in Turkey, "where no woman, of what rank soever, is permitted to go into the streets without two *murlins*, one that covers her face, all but her eyes; and another, that hides the whole dress of her head, and hangs half way down her back: their shapes are also wholly concealed by a thing called a *feugee*, which so effectually disguises them, that there is no distinguishing the lady from her slave: it is impossible for the most jealous husband to know his wife when he meets her; and no man dare touch or follow a woman in the street. The great ladies seldom let their gallants know who they are, and it is so difficult to find out, that they can very seldom guess at *her* name, whom they have corresponded with for half a year together."

Nor must we suppose, because neither the Hindoo nor Mahomedan women are allowed to eat with the men, either at public festivals or family meals, that they are abstemious in the Haram; on the contrary they have very expensive entertainments in their own apartments: thus it was among the Greeks and Persians; when Ahasuerus king of Persia made a royal banquet for his nobles, Vashti the queen gave a feast to the women in the royal house. Maillet, the French consul at Cairo, was invited to a magnificent entertainment given by the Basha on the circumcision of his son, at which all the great men in that part of Egypt were present; at the same time the expence in the ladies' apartments amounted to nearly as much as the public festival; "there being the same liberalities, the same pleasures, the same abundance, the same magnificence, that appeared out of the Haram.'

The despotism and avarice of the Indian sovereigns generally prevent their subjects from making that display of fortune, which wealth and situation authorize in other countries; consequently within decayed palaces, ruinous courts, and closed gates, in modern oriental cities, it is not uncommon to find a house and garden fitted up in good style: this contrast was frequent among the Nabob's subjects in Surat; those who had claimed the English protection better enjoyed the gifts of fortune.

During my visit at that city, a young gentleman conversant in the Persian language, had an opportunity of rendering an essential service to a Mogul widow of distinction; who, in consequence of some deeds falsely translated, and misrepresented by the Mahomedan lawyers, was involved in a long series of trouble and expence: from the humane impulse of rescuing a respectable family from such chicanery, he interested himself in the cause, revealed the truth, and reinstated the lady in her fortune. Not having seen her generous benefactor during the whole transaction, and desirous of acknowledging the obligation, she requested an interview.

The young Englishman was conducted to a ruined edifice in a solitary part of the outer city, which appeared to have been an appendage to some magnificent mansion: passing through the portal and dark narrow passages common in eastern houses, he entered a spacious court, adorned with fountains, shaded by tamarind trees, and double tube-roses, the pride of Surat gardens; this led to an open pavilion surrounded by a veranda, and over-looking a further garden in a similar taste, terminated by a hall elegantly furnished with mirrors, carpets and Persian paintings; above were the family apartments. Here my friend was served with sherbet, fruit, flowers, and a hooka. The attendants withdrew on the approach of their lady, richly dressed and closely veiled; she entered with a graceful dignity; from the over-flowing of a grateful heart commenced an interesting conversation, and presenting him with ottah of roses, and a valuable jewel, seemed hurt at his refusal. Young and thoughtless, he made a transition from the brilliant gem, to her antelope eyes, sparkling through the veil; and, from a momentary impulse, requested he might behold a countenance irradiated by her superior mind: unwilling to deny the only favour he seemed inclined to accept, she withdrew her veil, and displayed a face still decked with youthful bloom, delicate features, and fine expression: in this singular situation the enamoured Englishman began a subject not easy to mistake, in the warm strains of the Persian and Arabian poets; to which she at first vouchsafed a smile; but assuming a dignified air, and impressive language, she assured him that the deep sense of her obligation had alone induced her to deviate from established custom, in requesting this interview; but a sense of her own honour, veneration to her husband's memory, and maternal example to her children, would ever regulate her conduct; that he might not, however, think her ungrateful, she appointed another meeting the next evening.

Encouraged by so flattering an invitation, the enamoured youth repaired to the pavilion, found every thing in the same style of elegance and hospitality, and in the further saloon was received by a lady, whom he accosted as the mistress of the house; until, throwing off her veil, he discovered a beautiful Mogul, young, witty, and elegant, who entertained him at the pavilion, while the widow and her children were visiting at a distant villa. He never afterwards discovered his lovely incognita, nor could he, consistent with propriety, continue his visits in a Mogul family.

We must not too hastily condemn this grateful Mahomedan, nor judge her conduct by the decorum of female manners in England, or the purity of the Christian religion: her education had been different, and the oriental standard of propriety is more relaxed than our own; on the present occasion gratitude predominated over every other consideration: and, as a modern traveller well observes, "in consequence of the peculiar prejudices and opinions of one people, the same practice may be viewed by them in the darkest light, which in another country may not only be tolerated but recommended."

In the vicinity of so populous and opulent a city as Surat, the country is highly cultivated, and a fertile soil amply repays the farmer; the fields, generally enclosed, and the hedges planted with mango and tamarind trees, produce wheat, rice, juaree, bahjeree, and other Indian grains; luxuriantly diversified by crops of cotton, hemp, tobacco, plants for dying, and a variety of seeds for expressing lamp oil; particularly the erindah, or palma-christi, which is also much esteemed for medicinal virtues. The wheat-fields afforded me great delight; they were the first I had seen since my departure from England, and the harvest had begun: the corn is trod out by oxen, walking over the ears, as described by Homer

> "Where round and round, with never wearied pain,
> "The trampling steers beat out th' unnumbered grain."

The gardens produce cabbages, cauliflowers, pease, french-beans, artichokes, asparagus, potatoes, carrots, turnips, lettuce, and salads, in abundance and perfection; besides a variety of indigenous roots and vegetables. Among other useful productions is a vegetable soap, called omlah; the nuts grow in clusters on a wild tree, and the kernels, when made into a paste, are preferred to common soap for washing shawls, silk and embroidery; it lathers in salt water, and on that account is valuable at sea, where common soap is of little use; retah, another vegetable soap, in the vicinity of Surat, has the same property.

The wood-apple, a fruit unknown at Bombay, grows on a large tree, in perpetual verdure; and, like many in the torrid zone, is covered at the same time with blossoms and ripe fruit; the apple is circular, heavy, and the size of an orange, hanging perpendicularly at the extremity of long slender branches, bending with their weight; which gives the tree a beautiful appearance: the fruit smells like a mellow apple, but on breaking the wooden shell, we find an acid pulp, full of seeds, ate only by the poorer natives.

Under the shade of these trees, and of the banian and tamarind groves, the weavers every morning fix their looms, and remove them in the evening: they are constructed with the greatest simplicity; it is astonishing how few materials are required to fabricate the most delicate muslins.

The lanes near Surat afford delightful rides; the eye wanders over extensive scenes of cultivation, villages, farms, and lakes, embellished by the nymphea in every pleasing variety: the lakes abound with water-fowl; the fields are enlivened by partridges, quails, and green pigeons; and the mango groves filled with monkeys, squirrels, and peacocks. Parrots, larks, doves, amadavads, toohties, and bulbuls, enliven the walks; but gay plumage generally supersedes melody in the Asiatic birds; the amadavads are very small, beautifully arrayed in scarlet, yellow, brown and white; I have seen a hundred together in a cage, but never two of them marked alike, and one only sings at a time, in a low simple note. The toohtee, a pretty bird, is so called from a monotonous repetition of its own name, like the cuckoo in England.

The surrounding plains abound with deer, antelopes, hares, and feathered game: the eastern hills, wild and woody, are infested by tigers, leopards, hyenas, wolves, and other ferocious animals, whom hunger impels to commit depredations in cultivated tracts near the city. The principal Moguls at Surat keep them in menageries; particularly the leopard cheeta, and syah gush, which afford them much diversion in hunting antelopes.

The tiger, leopard, and hyena are well known in Europe, and therefore need no minute description; the largest hyæna I ever saw was in the nabob's menagerie; his head resembled that of a wolf, but more fierce and ugly: the body partook of the wolf and hog, covered by long bristly hair, of a dusky gray colour, confusedly striped with black. The hyæna is said to be the most savage and ferocious of quadrupeds; when enraged its aspect is hideous. Jackalls abound in the country round Surat, and hunt in large packs. The panther, leopard, and cheeta, are of the same genus as the royal tiger, but smaller; and differ in having the skin spotted instead of striped: these spots vary in each species; in the panther and leopard several small black spots encircle a mark of bright orange colour, on a field of paler hue; the cheeta, felis jubata, is distinguished by black spots only, on a yellowish brown; the peculiar marks of the panther I am not acquainted with.

In my original letter from Surat, in the year 1772, I had written an account of the cheeta-hunt; but the friend to whom I am indebted for many interesting occurrences in this publication, favoured me with the following extract from his journal at Cambay; which, from a keen sportsman, is more accurate and entertaining than any thing I can offer: the extract was accompanied with a beautiful drawing by his lady, from an original sketch taken on the spot, by a native of Hindostan.

"The diversion of hunting with the cheeta is much admired and pursued by the princes and chieftains of Hindostan, both Mahomedans and Hindoos, excepting Brahmins. The cheeta, though of the leopard species, differs from it materially, although confounded with that animal by Buffon, and other naturalists: as to its relation to the panther, or whether it be the panther, I must be silent, never having seen the creature so denominated. In height the cheeta considerably exceeds the leopard, and greatly excels it in form and beauty. Its head is smaller in proportion; its eyes are brown or hazle, without an appearance of vice; its spots are black and solid, not in circles; its body is long, loins slender, chest deep, legs straight and taper, and its paws not larger than those of a common sized dog; its tail is long and gracefully turned. The cheeta is as much superior to the leopard in the docility and generosity of its nature, as in the elegance of its shape; of this I can speak with the greatest confidence from long possession, and a close observation of both animals.

"The cheeta is a native of many parts of Hindostan, but those of Guzerat are most esteemed: two of them were caught for and sent to me as a present, by a chief of that province, one of which is the subject of the annexed drawing. They were brought to me soon after they were caught; which was effected by digging deep pits, and covering over with boughs, near the places they frequented; which are easily discovered by certain trees, against which they are very fond of rubbing themselves. If they are caught young, and brought up by hand, they prove good for nothing, and lose that degree of activity and fierceness, which characterize those procured after having provided prey for themselves in a wild state.

"The cheeta introduced into the drawing, is, in every respect but size, a perfect representation of the one in my possession; he was broke in after he came to me, and was in the space of twelve months as familiar as a dog, and would follow his keeper loose through the streets of Cambay; though, from the apprehension of his killing goats and other tame animals, he was generally led by a chain; his common allowance of food is five seir, or something more than four pounds of solid mutton every day, except that preceding the day on which he hunts, when he is kept from food.

" I shall now describe the method of hunting with this animal: a reynkla, or Indian carriage, called by the English a hackery, as introduced into the drawing, is attached to the cheeta; on this cart, which is drawn by oxen, he leaps from custom without hesitation: he is then hooded, and his keeper, sitting by him, secures him by a string through his collar on the neck; in this manner he is conveyed to the scene of action, having a belt round his loins, the use of which will be hereafter explained.

" Antelopes are very common in the northern parts of Guzerat, and there is seldom any doubt of sport: when the game is descried, the sportsmen generally leave their horses and attendants, and get on hackeries, or country carts, like that of the cheeta, as being less likely to alarm the antelopes; all the followers on foot likewise keep close behind the hackeries; for, exclusive of the circumstance of frightening the game, the cheeta himself is apt to be alarmed, when carried out to a hunt, by a crowd, which he might disregard in the town; and so strongly has instinct implanted in him the fear of man, and the consciousness of his being obnoxious to him, that should a person appear at a distance in a line with the game, he will scarce ever run: but it should be remarked, that the introduction of the horses and attendants is only a favour allowable after the game is killed.

" Every sportsman being thus mounted on his vehicle, they proceed in pursuit of the antelopes; and the subsequent manœuvres depend upon the nature of the country; if it is woody, or a forest scenery, the cheeta may be unhooded at any distance; for the astonishing sagacity of the animal curbing his impulse to run, on first getting sight, he leaps carefully off the cart, and creeps on with the greatest cunning from bush to bush, narrowly observing the game, and most artfully avoiding discovery. If by these means he can get within the distance of about seventy yards, he rushes forth at full speed, and seldom misses. This method is by far the most entertaining, as it discovers the animal in every point of view, and shews the extent and turn of his force and genius.

" If the cheeta finds that he cannot proceed undiscovered, or if he perceives the game to be alarmed, he crouches, and lies close to the ground; thus posted, the hackeries take a circuit, leaving the cheeta, and getting on the other side of the antelopes; and then, edging down, urge them towards the ambuscade, which if they pass within the distance of seventy or eighty yards, there is every reason to expect success.

" A third method is in a bare and open country, where we are frequently obliged to follow the game sometime before we can get within distance; in which case the huntsman studiously avoids getting to windward; and endeavours by traversing to force the antelopes to run across him, at which time the cheeta is most likely to follow them; for, although he may be previously within distance, he generally hesitates, even when unhooded, to quit his cart, if the game is standing still, or looking towards him when he has no cover to conceal himself. But sometimes, with every advantage of distance, the cheeta will not run, and in this respect, so trying to an eager sportsman, he is very inferior to the dog, who never fails to do his utmost. When the cheeta resolves to exert himself, his velocity is astonishing; for although the antelope is esteemed the swiftest species of the deer, and the course generally begins at the distance of seventy or eighty yards, yet the game is usually caught, or else makes his escape, within the space of three or four hundred yards; the cheeta seldom running a greater distance, and in that I have measured repeated strokes of seven paces. On coming up with the game, especially if a doe or a fawn, which have less strength than the buck, and no horns, it is difficult to describe the celerity with which it overthrows its prey. But the attack of an old buck is a more arduous task; his great strength sometimes enables him to make a hard struggle, though seldom with success; for, although I have known a buck to get loose two or three times, yet I never saw one escape after having been fairly seized.

"The cheeta, on overtaking the deer, by a most powerful and dexterous use of its paw, overthrows it, and in the same instant seizes it by the throat; when, if it is young, or a doe, as already observed, it does not quit its hold until he finds the respiration ceased: but if it is a buck, whose neck is very thick and powerful, he is obliged to be more cautious, and to avoid in the struggle not only a blow from the horns, which from the mere convulsive motion of terror and agony, might be very dangerous; but from the hoofs, whose sharpness renders them equally so: the artful care with which he avoids these weapons is well and truly described in the drawing: the deer thus seized by the throat, loses all capacity of struggling, and in the interim the cheeta-keeper comes up, and instantly cuts the throat of the antelope; as it is an abomination among the Mahomedans, as with the Jews, to eat an animal killed in any way but with the knife. The cheeta finding the animal dead, would commence the work of laceration, which he generally begins between the hinder legs, but is prevented by his keeper; who either catches the blood from his throat in a ladle kept for that purpose, and presents it to him to lap, or nimbly cuts off the last joint of the leg, which is the operation represented in the drawing; and putting it into his mouth, he leaves him employed with it, and quickly carries off the game, to secure it behind the hackery. The cheeta having amused himself with his ladle or bone, his keeper leads him to the cart, which he ascends without taking any further notice of the game, though tied close under his nose.

" This is the mode generally practised when we intend to pursue our sport; and I have killed four antelopes in one morning: but when it is the intention to proceed no further, the cheeta has a handsome share of the deer last killed. It sometimes happens that the cheeta is thrown out, and misses his prey; he then lies down, and the keeper drives the hackery to him: disappointment sometimes sours his temper, and he shews signs of anger, but I never saw them attended with any danger. The keeper, after soothing him a little, takes him by the collars round his neck and waist, and conducts him to the cart, on which he readily leaps. I have heard of accidents happening on these occasions, but I never saw one, or a likelihood of one, though I always made a point of being near the animal, both after seizing and missing.

" One of my cheetas having frequently disappointed me by refusing to run, I resolved to keep him without food until he killed for himself; but although I had him out every day in sight of game, he forced me to keep my resolution until the eighth day; when he ran with surprizing velocity, and killed a black buck; though he had not ate any thing during the whole time."

I once joined some keen sportsmen on a cheeta hunt in the forests of Guzerat, but the animal was in a sullen mood, and afforded very little diversion. The Moguls train another beast for antelope-hunting, called the syah-gush, or black-ears; which appears to be the same as the caracal, or Persian lynx, felis caracal. The syah-gush resembles the lynx, but is smaller, and less fierce; with a more pointed head, and remarkably long ears, tufted with black, its general colour is a reddish brown; in the chace it affords much amusement, and is employed in the pursuit of herons, cullums, cranes, and large birds.

Porcupines are met with in most parts of Hindostan; they are generally about two feet long, and one in height, in appearance resembling the hedgehog; except that the prickles of the latter are on the porcupine hard pointed quills, which cover the whole body in different lengths, from one to fifteen inches; these quills are strongly fixed in the skin, and very sharp at the point: they are mostly white, variegated with a purplish brown, and harder than a goose-quill; some are thick, strong, and sharp, others long and flexible: every part of the body is closely covered with them, except the ears and feet: the porcupines are very destructive in gardens; they select the nicest fruit within their reach, and will pass over beds of common vegetables, to devour the lettuce, cucumber, french-beans, and other delicacies: when roasted, their flesh has the appearance and flavour of pork: I have frequently dined on this animal, as also on the small land-tortoise; both very common in Guzerat.

My walks from Surat were often directed to the village of Pulparra, pleasantly situated on the banks of the Tappee, and famous for its seminaries of brahmins: the drooping branches of the banian trees, planted on the steep banks, overshadow the steps leading to the sacred stream, for the convenience of ablutions, and spread a solemn gloom around the Hindoo temples and altars, which abound in this spot. Pulparra is esteemed peculiarly holy; it is the general resort of recluse brahmins, and gymnosophists of various descriptions: there also, at stated seasons, the other tribes of Hindoos repair to bathe, and offer their flowery sacrifices: the sacred edifices and groves are strewed with the champa, mogree, and nymphea; and the cottages and arbours of the Yogees and Senasses are crowded with visitors to behold the austerities of these devotees; who, forgetting they were created for active and useful life, endued with a capacity to improve their talents, and enjoy rational pleasures, consume their days in stupid indolence; or inflict on themselves severe penance and cruel torture, in hopes of rendering themselves acceptable to their deities, in a state of ignorance or forgetfulness of that Being whose tender mercies are over all his works.

> " What blessings Thy free bounty gives
> " Let me not cast away;
> " For God is paid, when man receives;
> " T' enjoy, is to obey!" Pope.

The bodies of the deceased Hindoos are burnt at Pulparra, and their ashes scattered over this sacred part of the river: here also their widows frequently immolate themselves on the funeral pile of their husbands. Herodotus mentions a similar practice among the Crestonians: where " each person had several wives;

and on the decease of the husband, a great contest ensued to determine which of them had been best beloved: she, to whom that honour was ascribed, was gaudily dressed, and then sacrificed, by her nearest relation, on the tomb of her husband, with whom she was afterwards buried: not to be elected was deemed an affliction by the surviving wives, and was imputed to them as a disgrace." This idea certainly prevails among the Hindoos; the memory of the wife who burns herself is venerated; the widow who survives her husband is condemned to a sort of domestic slavery. No immolation of a Hindoo widow took place during my residence at Surat; nor was I ever an eye-witness of this extraordinary sacrifice. I have heard many relations, and read several authentic manuscripts of the interesting scene; but none more satisfactory than the following letter from one of my medical friends, who saw a young brahmin go through the dreadful ordeal, and thus feelingly describes it.

"I have often thought, during my absence from Bombay, that it behoved me to write to you; but I have ever been at a loss for a subject of sufficient importance to license a trespass on your numerous avocations: one has at length occurred, which, if it cannot boast much weight, may not be unacceptable on the score of singularity; I shall therefore proceed to describe it to you without further exordium: it is an instance of the self-devotion practised among the brahmin females of distinction, on the death of their husbands.

"I was hastily summoned by a brahmin friend yesterday, about five in the evening, to be a spectator of this dreadful ceremony. Soon after my conductor and myself had quitted the house, we were informed that the *suttee* (the name given to these female victims), had passed by: and we soon traced her route by the *gulol*, or rose-coloured powder, she had thrown around her, and the betel-leaf, which, as is usual on these occasions, she had scattered.

"She had reached that part of the river set apart for religious ablutions, before we arrived, and, having performed her last ceremony of this kind, was sitting on the margin of the stream: over her was held an aftabgheer, or state umbrella; an attendant fanned her with a waving veil, and she was surrounded by her relations, friends, and select brahmins, the populace being kept aloof by a guard from the government. In this situation she distributed two thousand rupees among the brahmins, and the jewels with which she was decorated to her friends, reserving only the nose-ring, called bulawk, and the bracelets on her wrists.

"My position prevented my seeing more of her than her hands, the palms of which being joined, they were uplifted in an attitude of invocation: quitting therefore this place, I removed to an eminence, which gave me an opportunity of observing the construction of the funeral pile, and commanded the path-way by which I understood she would approach it: the spot chosen for its erection was about forty yards from the river, directly in front of her as she sat: when I came up, the frame alone was raised; it consisted of four uprights, each about ten feet high. Its length was about nine, and the breadth of it under six; from near the top of the uprights was suspended, by ropes, a roof of slender rafters laid lengthwise, parallel with each other; on this were soon placed as many billets as it seemed capable of bearing, while beneath, a pile was raised of more substantial timbers to the height of four feet; this again was covered over with bundles of the straw called curwee, and bushes of dried tulsee, one of the sacred plants of the Hindoos; the sides, and one end being then closed up with the same materials, the other end was left open, and formed an entrance.

"The dismal tenement being thus completed, soon after the widow rose and came forward, walking amidst her friends without support: she approached the door, and there having paid some further devotions for the occasion, retired a few paces, and sat encircled as before.

"The dead body was now brought from the water-side, where it had hitherto lain, and deposited within the hollow of the pile; several sweet-meats were put in after it, and a large paper bag, containing either flower or the dust of sandal-wood. The widow rising, walked three times slowly round the pile; when, seating herself on a small square stone, placed opposite the entrance, she accepted and returned the endearments of her friends with great serenity: this done, she again stood up, and having stroked her right hand in an affectionate manner over the heads of her dearest relations and intimate friends, with a gentle inclination of her person towards them, she let her arm fall round their necks in a faint embrace, and turned from them. Now, with her hands indeed raised to heaven, but her eyes cast, in a glare of abstraction, deep into that cave of anguish which waited her, she stood awhile a piteous statue!—good God, have mercy on her! At length, without altering a feature, or the least agitation of her frame, she ascended the threshold unassisted, and entering the cave, lay down on the right side of her husband's corpse; yielding her tender body, in the full meridian of its youth and beauty, a victim to a barbarous and cruelly consecrated error of deluded faith!

"As soon as the victim entered, she was shut from our view by several bundles of straw, with which the aperture was closed; and all the actors in this tragic scene seemed to vie with each other who should be most forward in hurrying it to a conclusion. In the same instant the air was darkened by a cloud of *gulol;* the cords being cut which sustained the roof, it immediately fell to crush the limbs of the yet living sacrifice; the dreadful flame was communicated to the pile in a variety of parts; and the loud clamour of the trumpets assailed the ear from every quarter! when the conflagration became general, and not till then, the pyre was fed for a time with a large quantity of *ghee*, or clarified butter, thrown by the nearest of kin; but no combustible whatever was used in preparing the wood, of which the pile was composed.

"It is said to be a custom, that as the victim ascends the pile, she is furnished with a lighted taper: I heard some brahmins assert that it was the case in this instance; but I traced the whole progress of the ceremonial with so close and eager an attention, that I think I may safely contradict them. Before I left the place, a guard was posted over the pyre, to remain until the fire went out, that no accident might befal the bones of the sacrifice, some of which are always collected by the relations, and sent to Benares; where they are either preserved as sacred relics, or made an offering to the holy stream of *Gunga*.

"The subject of this shocking, though by no means uncommon immolation, was *Toolsebhai*, the wife of Ragobah Tantea, a young man of thirty years of age, nephew to Junabhy Daddah, a person of distinction, and Amul of Poonah. Toolsebhai was about twenty years of age; her stature above the middle standard, her form elegant, her features interesting and expressive, and her eyes particularly large, full, and commanding: at the solemn moment in which I saw her, these beauties were eminently conspicuous; notwithstanding her skin was then discoloured with turmeric, her hair dishevelled, and wildly ornamented with flowers, and her looks like those of one whose senses wandered; or, to come nearer the impression, whose soul was already fleeting, and in a state of half-separation from the body.

" A beautiful little girl, not more than four years old, the fruit of their union, survives her parents, thus early removed into another state of existence."

Such is the simple account of this ceremony by a man of feeling; many relations are published, more highly coloured: the most extraordinary and affecting spectacle of this kind is related by Bernier, a celebrated French traveller in the seventeenth century, who resided many years, as physician, at the court of Aurungzebe. During a journey from Ahmedabad to Agra, he witnessed a shocking tragedy which roused all the feelings of his benevolent heart, nor has he suppressed a manly indignation in the recital. A young Hindoo widow, attended by five females, surrounded by brahmins, was advancing towards the funeral pile of her husband: when the usual ceremonies were over, he beheld the young and beautiful victim kindle the combustible altar on which she had placed herself near her husband's corpse: the flames were increased by the oil of sandal, poured in by the ministering priests:

and when the pyre burnt most furiously the five infatuated attendants rushed into the midst of the fire, and shared the fate of their mistress. The amiable Bernier, indignant at this horrid spectacle, passionately exclaims against a religion which could permit such a sacrifice, and still more so against "*les demons de brahmens,*" who not only encouraged these deluded females, but were the most active persons throughout the infernal tragedy.

Religious prejudices are very powerful, but how they can thus destroy the feelings of humanity, is rather paradoxical: the cruelties of the inquisition and other mis-named Christian tribunals proceed from a different cause: they were originally actuated by the spirit of Christianity; but bigotry has strangely perverted its benevolent influence. In the sacrifice of a Hindoo widow, (and some thousands are annually sacrificed,) religion herself inculcates the horrid deed; the laws of Menu approve it; and the priests of Brahma, who affect to shudder at the death of an insect, assist at the destruction of this most lovely part of the creation.

Well may these brahmins be called the priests of Siva, the destroying power in the Hindoo triad: who, with her sister-furies, the satkis, have so many votaries in Hindostan: whether they all agree in sanctioning this most abominable sacrifice, I cannot determine; because the brahmins themselves are divided into various sects, who differ in many religious points which they deem essential, and do not eat or intermarry with each other. Although I have, in conformity to the generally-received opinion among Europeans, divided the Hindoos into four grand castes, or tribes, subdivided into eighty-four inferior distinctions, we shall find, on a more minute investigation, that in the various districts of India, there is a much greater multiplicity of castes, or sects, who neither intermarry nor eat with each other; neither do they perform the same religious rites to their respective deities.

We learn from Diodorus Siculus, that the ancient Egyptians were divided into three distinct classes: the first were those of rank, who, with the priests, filled the most honourable situations in the state; then the military, who were also husbandmen; lastly the artizans, who occupied the meanest employments. Herodotus says the Calasirians must not follow mechanic employments, but the son regularly succeeds the father in a military life: and also among the Lacedæmonians, some classes of the people were obliged to follow the profession of their fathers; particularly the heralds, musicians, and cooks: he further remarks, that if a man, in any manner belonging to another tribe, had a louder voice than one of these heralds by descent, he could not be taken from one tribe into another. This is exactly conformable to the unchangeable custom of the Hindoos.

Although mingled with other sensations, it is pleasing to see the inhabitants of Pulparra, and most other towns and villages on the banks of the Tappee, Narbudda, and principal rivers of Hindostan, repair to the water to perform their devotions; no morning dawns, no evening closes without this pious ceremony. That the Hindoos worship the Ganges there is I believe no doubt, because a peculiar sanctity is annexed to its stream: in an inferior degree they seem to venerate other rivers; and generally enter them twice a day, not only to perform their devotions, but to purify their bodies, and wash their garments: both sexes assemble or the same purpose, and shift their clothes in the water, without he least idea of infringing the laws of decency.

After performing their religious ablutions, the Hindoos receive on their forehead the mark either of Visnoo or Siva; this mark, affixed by a brahmin, varies in form and colour, according to the ect they profess; the one being horizontal, the other perpendicuar: it is made from a composition of sandal-wood, turmeric, and cow-dung; the latter is deemed peculiarly sacred. The mark on he forehead is frequently alluded to in the sacred scriptures, as characteristic of the righteous and the wicked: we read "of those who had the mark of the beast; and of those blessed and happy beings, who were admitted to the pure river of the water of life, proceeding out of the throne of God and of the Lamb, whose name was written on their foreheads; and who had not received the mark of the beast upon their foreheads, nor on their hands."

The sacred groves of Pulparra, are the general resort for all the Yogees, Senassees, and Hindoo pilgrims who visit Surat, from the most remote regions of Hindostan; the whole district is holy, and the Tappee in that part has a more than common sanctity: all ablutions in a river are thought to be more efficacious than an immersion in stagnant water; the Levitical law enjoined the leper to bathe in the running stream; the Hindoos annex to it a greater degree of purity than in any tank at their temples. These devotees are great travellers; they wander, either collectively or individually, from the confines of Russia to Cape Comorin; and from the borders of China to Malabar-hill on the island of Bombay, where there is a fane of much celebrity.

SURAT *on the Banks of the* TAPPEE.

Jam. Forbes, 1772.

Engraved by Chas. Heath

The Conclusion of a CHEETA HUNT *at* CAMBAY,

from an original Drawing by Lady Malet.

Plutarch mentions one of them, named Calanus, who followed Alexander from India: being seized with a dysentery at Pasagardus, he prepared his own funeral pile; and, after performing some religious ceremonies, laid himself on it with great composure, until burnt to death. Diodorus describes the immolation of an Indian widow two thousand years ago, in the army of Eumenes, who burnt herself on the funeral pile of her husband, in the manner I have just related.

CHAPTER XI.

A VOYAGE FROM BOMBAY TO ANJENGO;

CONTAINING A DESCRIPTION OF THE PRINCIPAL SETTLEMENTS ON THE COAST OF MALABAR.

1772.

As Egypt does not on the clouds rely,
But to the Nile owes more than to the sky;
So what the earth, and what the heaven, denies
To Albion's favour'd isle, the sea supplies.

The taste of hot Arabia's spice we know,
Free from the scorching sun that makes it grow;
Without the worm, in Persian silks we shine;
And, without planting, drink of every vine.

To dig for wealth we weary not our limbs;
Gold, though the heaviest metal, hither swims:
Ours is the harvest where the Indians mow;
We plough the deep, and reap what others sow.

WALLER.

CONTENTS.

Voyage from Bombay to Anjengo—Rutna—Ghereah and Mahratta fortresses in the Concan—Ghereah harbour—Raree, Fort Augustus and Vingorla—Geographical division of the Malabar coast—Concan, Deccan, Visiapoor, and Malabar—Goa harbour—Alguarda fort—city of Goa, churches, palaces, and convents—tomb of St. Francis Xavier—inquisition—cruelties of that tribunal at Goa—inhabitants of Goa—commerce—arrack—mangos—decline of the Portugueze in Asia—causes assigned—account of Goa in the sixteenth century—Benezegur—Kankanco—political history of India—rise of the Mahratta empire—Carwar—manufacture of the terra-japonica—Mirzee and Barcelore, the ancient Musiris and Barace—navigation of Hippalus and commerce of the Greeks, Egyptians, and Arabians, with those ports—fortified island—Onore—beauty of the country—productions—sandal-wood, its cultivation and use—land and sea winds—water-spouts—Malabar frontier—Mangulore—gigantic statue at Kurkul—customs of the Buntar—Tulava—landed property in India—its tenure—Mount Dilla—Cannanore—Tellicherry—fortifications, houses, trade, and cultivation—cardamom, growth of that valuable spice—Dumapatam island, coffee plantations—ordeal trials in Malabar—Mucuars at Tellicherry—Mahie—Sacrifice Rock—edible birds-nests—Calicut—European factories—former trade—overwhelming the ancient city—Dr. Fryer's curious account of Calicut—provisions—Vapura—teak timber—sapan-wood—grand appearance of the Gaut mountains—Cochin-town, fort, inhabitants, and commerce—hospitality of the Dutch—Cochin-leg—Mattancherry—Jews-town—history of the

Jewish colony there—epitome of the Jewish history—Porca, Calliquilone—Quilone—Eddova—arrival at Anjengo, difficulty of landing—description of Anjengo—poverty and melancholy situation of that settlement—Portugueze and native inhabitants—trade and manufactures—birth-place of Sterne's Eliza, and Orme, the historian—his superior character—south-west monsoon at Anjengo—catamaran—abundance of fish—hippocampus—contest between the river fish and those of the ocean during the monsoon.

CHAPTER XI.

SOON after leaving Surat, I was appointed a member of the council at Anjengo, the most southern of the English settlements on the Malabar coast, about six hundred miles from Bombay, in the latitude of 8° 39′ north. We sailed from that island the beginning of February, 1772, and in a fortnight arrived at Anjengo, after a delightful voyage, during which we stopped at most of the principal places on the coast.

A favourable breeze soon carried us past Fort Victoria; the next day sailing along the mountainous shores of the Concan, we had a distinct view of Rutnah-Gheriah, and several other Mahratta fortresses; we then looked into the harbour of Gheriah, the chief sea-port on the Malabar coast, defended by a strong fortification, and surrounded by a rich territory. Gheriah is in the latitude of 16° 37′ north, twenty-three leagues from Goa; in which distance are the forts of Raree and Augustus, conquered by the English, from the Malwans, in 1765, then lately ransomed: still nearer to Goa is Vingorla, a small town in a hilly country, where the India Company had at that time a factory, and collected a small revenue.

The mountainous shore of the Concan is improperly called a

part of the Malabar coast; but as the western side of the Indian peninsula, almost from Surat to Cape Comorin, is generally included under that denomination, I will briefly describe the existing boundaries of the kingdoms and provinces in that part of the globe called by geographers the Hither-India.

The most northern district was the Deccan; bounded on the north by Guzerat, east by Golconda and Berar, south by Visiapoor, and west by the Indian ocean: Aurungabad, Satamah, and Poonah, were the principal inland cities: Poonah, from an obscure village, became after the brahmin usurpation, the capital of the Mahratta empire. The sea-ports were Tull, Dundee, Dabul, and Choule, once belonging to the Portuguese, but then to the Mahrattas, who possessed the whole coast: Bombay, Salsette, and all the contiguous islands were included in this division.

The next was the kingdom of Visiapoor, extending north and south, from Gheriah to the spot called the Malabar frontier, near Mangulore: this division was bounded on the east by the Gaut mountains, on the west by the Indian ocean; Visiapoor was the chief inland city; Ghereah, Goa, Carwar, Barcelore, and Onore, the principal sea-ports: the Mahrattas, and a few dependent Hindoo princes, possessed the northern districts, except Goa; the conquests of Hyder Ally added the country of Visiapoor to his dominions.

The third and last division was that of Malabar; which extended from the Malabar frontier north, to Cape Comorin, south: the Gauts were its eastern boundary, the ocean its western. That part of the coast was divided among many independent sovereigns: the principal towns were Mangulore, Cananore, Tellicherry,

Mahie, Calicut, Panana, Cranganore, Cochin, Porca, Quilone, Anjengo, and Coletchee: in this division, properly termed the Malabar coast, the persons, language, religion, and manners of the natives, differ very much from those in the northern districts.

We anchored in the spacious and beautiful harbour of Goa, defended by the Alguarda, and other fortresses, surrounded by gentle hills and fruitful vales, and embellished by churches, convents, and villas; whose white fronts were contrasted with the dark mango groves and cocoa-nut woods peculiar to that part of India. The vessel anchoring off the Alguarda, we sailed up the river, navigable for large vessels, and covered with barges and gondolas: the villas, domes, and spires, on its shady banks produce a fine effect. About mid-way the city of Goa suddenly opens on the view, founded, like imperial Rome, on many hills; the churches, palaces, and public buildings, at that distance, give it a grand appearance, but it disappoints on a nearer approach: on landing I beheld magnificent structures mouldering into ruin; the streets were faintly traced by the remains of their forsaken mansions, and squares and markets, once populous, were now the haunt of serpents and noxious reptiles: the few human inhabitants were priests, monks, half-starved soldiers, and low mechanics. Notwithstanding the general decline of Goa, the churches and convents retained their grandeur, and were in good repair: the Augustin monastery is very handsome, and the church of San Caitan exhibits a beautiful specimen of Italian architecture.

The Jesuits' college, one of the largest and most conspicuous edifices in Goa, contained apartments for several hundred of that society; after their expulsion, it was inhabited by monks of a different order: the church dedicated to St. Francis Xavier, is a fine structure, the high altar richly ornamented, and the chapel containing the monument of St. Xavier uncommonly splendid; the tomb, enclosed by glass to prevent damage, is only opened on particular occasions: we were admitted within the sacred enclosure, to examine the bassi-relievi, which in different compartments contain the life and miracles of the saint: the whole is composed of the choicest marble, sculptured by European artists: the superb shrine and silver ornaments were presented by a queen of Portugal.

I shall not detail the extraordinary legends which the priests gave us of their favourite saint, nor describe the more substantial entertainment they produced in the refectory. On leaving their convivial circle we visited several monkish convents, and the only nunnery then existing in the city; where, as usual, we saw many objects to pity, few to envy: on this subject I shall not enlarge, nor on that of the inquisition, the next public structure that we viewed: the cruelties inflicted on the native converts at Goa, especially among the wealthy Hindoos, made me shudder on entering the exterior courts of this iniquitous tribunal, which were all we were permitted to see: its history in Spain and Portugal is well known: the inquisitors at Goa have not been more merciful: how has misguided zeal tarnished a religion founded in loving-kindness and tender mercy! how have the judges of the inquisition departed from the benevolent spirit of its founder! what must the surrounding Hindoos, educated in the mild tenets of Bramah, think of the fires, the racks, and instruments of torture, used in that merciless prison? its cruel tyrants, clothed in the vestments of sanctity, but destitute of pity, have spared neither age, nor sex, nor condition, in human sacrifices to the God of mercy, and the compassionate Redeemer of man! Mistaken zealots! truly do ye fulfil the awful words, that he came not to send peace upon earth, but a sword! a sword too often wielded by those who are strangers to the merciful spirit of his gospel.

> "Mercy is as the gentle dew from heaven
> "Shed on the earth beneath—it is twice bless'd;
> "It blesseth him that gives, and him that takes:
> "It is the attribute of God himself." SHAKESPEAR.

Goa, situated in 15° 28′ north latitude, and 72° 45′ east longitude, was one of the finest European settlements in India; where the Portugueze generally kept a strong force of Europeans, and Topasses, who are the offspring of the Europeans and natives; their pay was small, but procured them a sufficiency of rice and fish (the usual food of the lower classes in that country): the ocean supplies great variety of the latter, and the rice grounds are very productive. The oil expressed from the cocoa-nut is exported from Goa, and forms a considerable article of commerce; it was also famous for the arrack, to which it gave its name; but that made at Batavia is now generally preferred: this spirit is distilled either from rice, sugar-cane, or the juice of the cocoa-nut tree: the fruit and flowers of several other trees in Hindostan produce by distillation, a spirit, to which the Europeans give the general name of arrack. Goa is famous for the Alphonso mango, a delicious fruit, which is sent in presents to other parts of India: mangos are abundant in the adjoining districts, but the Alphonso is as superior to the others, as the nonpareil to the crab-apple.

The commerce of Goa, and the northern parts of Diu and Damaun, is now unimportant; the rice, arrack, and oil, are exported to different parts of India; one or two ships annually arrive from Europe with military stores, and other articles; and return thither with printed cottons from Surat, and a few eastern necessaries for Portugal and her American colonies: this, with two or three vessels trading in Chinese articles from Macao to the Malabar coast, now comprise the whole of the Portugueze commerce in India.

Yet this is the nation, that in the fifteenth and sixteenth centuries called the Asiatic seas her own, and astonished the eastern world by her martial exploits: the discoveries of Gama, and the conquests of Albuquerque, were truly glorious: the latter subdued Goa in 1510, and secured many valuable possessions to the crown of Portugal. The emancipation of the Netherlands from the tyranny of Philip, was the principal cause of the decline of the Portugueze in India: they were then subject to Spain; and the Hollanders no longer groaning under the yoke of Alva, sent a large armament from Europe, who conquered Cochin, Ceylon, the spice-islands, and many other Portugueze settlements; their ruin in Asia was also accelerated by the vices of their governors and principal officers: the sudden influx of wealth wrought a dreadful change in their moral character: the noble conduct and patriotic virtues of the first conquerors were annihilated by the venality and corruption of their successors. De Gama, Albuquerque, and de Castro, appear a different race from D'Acughna, Coree, and the other monsters, whose atrocities have fixed an indelible stain on the annals of Portugal: their rapacity and cruelty, united to superstitious tyranny, occasioned a rapid downfall, from which they never recovered.

Cæsar Fredericke, two hundred years before my arrival, gave a very entertaining account of Goa, and the adjacent country. "Goa, the principal city that the Portugals have in the Indies, wherein the viceroy, with his royal court, is resident, is on an island which may be in circuit five-and-twenty or thirty miles: and the city, with the boroughs, is reasonably big, and reasonably fair; but the island is far more fair: for it is, as it were, full of goodly gardens, replenished with divers trees. This city is of great traffic for all sorts of merchandize, which they trade with in all those parts: the merchandize which went every year from Goa to Bezenegur, the capital of the kingdom of Naisinga, eight days journey from thence, were Arabian horses, velvets, damasks, satins, armesins of Portugal, and pieces of chian, saffron, and scarlets: and from Bezenegur they had in Turkey for their commodities, jewels, and pagodas, which be ducats of gold. In 1567, I went thither from Goa, in company of two other merchants, which carried with them three hundred Arabian horses to the king, because the horses of that country are of a small stature; and they pay well for the Arabian horses: and it is requisite that the merchants sell them well, for that they stand them in great charges to bring them out of Persia to Ormuz, and from Ormuz to Goa, where the ship that brings twenty horses and upwards, payeth no custom, neither ship nor goods whatsoever. So that the Arabian horses are of great value in those countries, from three hundred ducats, to one thousand ducats a horse.

"I rested in *Bezenegur* seven months, until the ways were clear of thieves, which at that time ranged up and down: and in the time I rested there, I saw many strange and beastly deeds done by the gentiles." Those particularly described are the cremation of Hindoo widows, voluntary penances, and rigid austerities already mentioned in these volumes.

Bezenegur is now generally written *Vijeyanuggur*, or more properly, *Vijaya-nagara;* in ancient days it was one of the most splendid cities in the east: and the capital of an empire, which nominally comprised under its jurisdiction the greater part of the southern peninsula: the dominions of Travancore, and some of the countries near Cape Comorin, are the only districts which preserved their independence, and by their distance were protected from the powerful sovereigns of Vijaya-nagara.

Many countries in the vicinity of Goa have at different times been almost depopulated by the mistaken policy, bigotry, and oppressions of the Portuguese government; especially the district of Kankana; from whence, Dr. Buchanan says, the inhabitants fled to Tulava, near Mangulore, to avoid a persecution in their native country, and are still called *Kankanies.* An order arrived from the King of Portugal to convert all the natives: the vice-roy being a lenient man, on the receipt of the order, permitted those who chose to retire to carry away their effects, and allowed them fifteen days to arrange their affairs: accordingly all the rich brahmins and Sudras retired to Tulava, with such of their property as they could in that time realize; they now chiefly subsist by trade, and many are in flourishing circumstances. The poor Kankanies who remained in the Portuguese dominions were all converted to Christianity; if the religion professed and practised by the Malabar converts can deserve that appellation.

In the second geographical division of the Malabar coast, I mentioned Goa among the cities in Visiapoor: this part of India, including the Concan and Deccan (which latter word means the south country, relatively to the northern provinces of Hindostan), has been from time immemorial inhabited by the nations of Canara and Malabar; people from Merhat and Telinga, mingled among them in the northern districts: until the middle of the sixteenth century, it formed a considerable part of the vast empire of Bezenegur, just mentioned. At that period, five of the Mahomedan princes who had usurped the dominion of their respective governments, north of the Kistnah, ambitious of new conquests, and of making converts to the mussulman religion, confederated in a war against Ram Raje, the Hindoo monarch of Bezenegur, who was killed in battle, A. D. 1565. In consequence of his death, and a disputed succession, many of the naiks, or governors of provinces, became independent; and formed the modern Hindoo governments of Mysore, Trinchinopoly, Madura, Tanjore, and some others: at the same time the zamorine of Calicut, the king of Travancore, and different Malabar princes, shook off all dependence upon the Hindoo empire; whose seat of government was removed from Bezenegur to Penekonda.

About this period, the Mahomedan prince of Bejapour, or Visiapoor, under his general Mustapha Khan, assisted by Sahoo

Bhosla, reduced the Carnatic Bala-gaut, afterwards called Bejapoury; and descending into the Payen-gaut, conquered the new principalities of Tanjore, Trichinopoly, and Ginjee. Meer Jumlah, another Mahomedan chief, was at the same time performing similar exploits in other quarters: they enjoyed their conquests only a very short time; for in 1687, the emperor Aurungzebe subverted their dominions, and reduced them to saubahs, or provinces, of the Mogul empire, placing them under the command of vice-roys, or nabobs; who for some time paid a tribute, and did homage to the imperial government at Delhi; but at length, on the imbecility and decline of the empire, they also threw off their allegiance, and became independent sovereigns.

Sahoo Bhoosla, or Shajee, was the father of Sevajee, the founder of the Mahratta empire: his ancestors were leaders in the tribe of Mahrattas, so named from their having immemorially inhabited the country called Merhat, which comprehends a great part of the Peshwa's dominions in the Deccan. The rise of the Mahrattas is fully detailed on a future occasion; nor would it be interesting to enter more into the politics or history of this part of India: Goa is now of very little consequence, and the influence of the Portugueze government very circumscribed.

Were I master of the subject, I should seldom introduce any oriental history previous to the Mahomedan invasion of India; having already proved that the pretended antiquity of the Hindoos is trifling and absurd: I will only insert one instance out of the number which might be quoted in corroboration of this assertion: I transcribe it from Dr. Buchanan's Travels in Malabar, where he procured a ring, in which was set a gold fanam, said to have been struck by Parasu Rama, when he created Kerala. These fanams are not easily obtained; being considered as relics of the greatest antiquity: according to the fables of the brahmins, Parasu Rama created Kerala above eight hundred thousand years ago; and Dr. Buchanan received an account from the Tulava brahmins, taken from an historical work in the Sanscrit language, by which it appears that Tulava was given to the brahmins 1,955,883,365 years, preceding A. D. 1801: in pursuing the history of Tulava, this intelligent writer observes, "the candid reader will not expect, that in a work comprehending the accounts of such a long duration of time, a few thousand years, earlier or later, in the chronology of these degenerate times, can be considered as of any consequence."

We sailed from Goa with the land-wind, and the next morning were off Carwar, a town of importance during the flourishing state of the Portugueze: the English had formerly a factory for the purchase of pepper, which has been for many years deserted: there are still a number of Portugueze inhabitants, with a bishop and inferior clergy; the Roman catholic churches at Bombay are in the diocese of Carwar.

In the neighbouring country, the peasants manufacture catechu, or terra-Japonica, from the keiri tree (mimosa catechu) which grows wild on the hills of Kankana, but in no other part of the Indian peninsula. Dr. Buchanan says, "the keira tree is felled at any season; and, the white wood being removed, the heart is cut into small pieces, and put, with one half of the quantity by measure, into a round earthen pot: it is then boiled for three hours; and when the decoction has become ropy, it is decanted. The same quantity of water is again added, and boiled, until it becomes ropy; when it is decanted, and a third water also is given. This extracts all the substance from the wood: the three decoctions are then mixed, and next morning boiled in small pots, until the extract becomes thick, like tar: it is afterwards allowed to remain in the pots for two days, and then has become so hard that it will not run. Some husks of rice being spread on the ground, the inspissated juice is formed into balls about the size of an orange, and placed on the husks, to be dried seven days in the sun: for two months afterwards they are spread out in the shade to dry; or in the rainy season for twice that length of time, and are then fit for sale. Merchants who live above the Gattes advance the whole price four months before the time of delivery; and give two rupees for a maund of forty *Chutcha seers* of twenty-four rupees weight; about nine rupees, or one pound sterling per hundred weight. The merchants who purchase reside chiefly at Darwara, Shanore, and other places in that neighbourhood; and are those who supply the greater part of the peninsula with this article; which, among the natives, is in universal use.

Not far from Onore we passed Mirzee, and Barcelore, two places famous for pepper, which grows spontaneously in those dis-stricts; as also the laurus cassia, and wild nutmeg.

These towns are supposed to be the Musiris and Barace of the ancients; whither Hippalus made the first voyage from the Arabian gulf: a voyage from Arabia to the coast of Malabar was then deemed of so much importance, that the monsoon wind, which wafted him over a tract of ocean, hitherto unattempted, was called Hippalus, after this celebrated navigator. Previous to this bold undertaking, the merchant vessels belonging to the Egyptians and Arabians had sailed from Berenice in the Red-Sea, along the Arabian shore to the promontory of Syagrus, now Cape Rasalgate; and held their course along the coast of Persia, to the different ports in India where they traded.

Dr. Robertson, describing the trade of the ancients with India, and particularly the voyage of Hippalus to Musiris, observes, that " as this was one of the greatest efforts of navigation in those days, and opened the best communication by sea between the East and West that was known for fourteen hundred years, it merits a particular description. Fortunately Pliny has enabled us to give it with a degree of accuracy, which can seldom be attained in tracing the naval or commercial operations of the ancients. Pliny observes, from Alexandria to Juliopolis is two miles: there the cargo destined for India is embarked on the Nile, and is carried to Coptos, which is distant three hundred and three miles, and the voyage is usually accomplished in twelve days. From Coptos goods are conveyed to Berenice, on the Arabian gulf, halting at different stations, regulated according to the conveniency of watering. The distance between these cities is two hundred and fifty-eight miles. On account of the heat, the caravan travels only during the night, and the journey is finished on the twelfth day. From Berenice, ships take their departure about midsummer, and in thirty days reach Ocelis (Gella), at the mouth of the Arabian gulf, or Cane (Cape Fartaque), on the coast of Arabia Felix. Thence they sail in forty days to Musiris, the first emporium in India. They begin their voyage homewards early in the Egyptian month Thibi, which answers to our December; they sail with a north-east wind, and when they enter the Arabian gulf meet with a south or south-west wind, and thus complete the voyage in less than a year."

The sight of Mirzee recalled to mind its former importance in the oriental commerce: nothing can be more clear or satisfactory, than Pliny's account of the trade to Musiris; and Arrian, describing the imports from the Arabian gulf, at that port, says they were much the same as those I have already mentioned at Surat; but as it lay nearer to the eastern parts of India, and seems to have had much communication with them, the commodities exported from it were more numerous and more valuable. He specifies particularly, pearls in great abundance, and of extraordinary beauty; a variety of silk stuffs, rich perfumes, tortoise-shell, different kinds of transparent gems, especially diamonds; and pepper in large quantities, and of the best quality.

After leaving Mirzee and Barcelore, there was nothing worthy of observation, until we passed Fortified Island, a little to the northward of Onore; it is about a mile in circumference, rocky, barren, and so strong both by nature and art, as to be deemed impregnable: it then belonged to the nabob Hyder Ally Caun, as did Onore, and all the adjoining territory.

Passing Fortified Island, we anchored off Onore, or *Honawera*, as it is called by the natives: the fort was situated on a rising ground, near a small town of indifferent houses; the best was the English factory, where two of the Company's servants resided, to purchase pepper and sandal-wood, for the English and Chinese markets: a considerable private trade was carried on with Bombay and the northern ports, in betel-nuts, and other articles.

Onore river, or rather a salt lake, is navigable at spring-tides for small vessels; it is indeed connected with a small river which flows from the inland mountains, through a hilly country, whose romantic rocks are softened by a wild assemblage of trees: among them the silk-cotton (bombax ceiba, Lin.), and the decannee-bean (butea superba), are very conspicuous; the former covered with buds and flowers of crimson, and the scarlet papilionaceous blossoms of the latter, contrasted by their black stalks, give a brilliant effect to the western woods, and appear at sun-set, like immense forests in a glow of fire. These sylvan regions are the haunt of tigers, and other wild beasts already described.

The low lands contiguous to Onore are well cultivated; and planted with cocoa-nut trees, areca, pepper, rice, and inferior grains: but the most valuable production in this part of India is the sandal, or saunders tree (santalum album, Linn.)

The sandal tree is indigenous on the rocky hills in the Onore districts, and if permitted, would grow to a tolerable size; but the wood is so valuable, that the tree is cut down at an early stage, and we seldom meet with any more than a foot broad: the wood is either red, yellow, or a whitish brown; and from its colour and size, is called the first, second, and third sort of sandal-wood; each varying in price: the best varied in price from one hundred and fifty to two hundred rupees the caury, of five hundred and sixty pounds weight. The wood of the brightest colour, and strongest scent, is most esteemed; having a fine grain, and an aromatic smell, which it communicates to every thing near it: it is therefore much used in small cabinets, escritoires, and similar articles, as no insect can exist, nor iron rust, within its influence: from the dust and shavings is extracted an aromatic oil; the oil and wood are used by the Hindoos and Parsees in their religious ceremonies; but the greatest part of the latter is reserved for the China markets, where it sells to great advantage.

The sandal is a beautiful tree; the branches regular and tapering; the leaf like the narrow willow, shorter, and delicately soft; the blossoms hang in bunches of small flowers, either red or white, according to the colour of the wood: the fruit is small, and valuable only for its seed: the tree thrives in a hilly rocky situation, and there produces wood of the finest grain, and strongest scent: on low land, and a richer soil, it degenerates, and is in all respects less esteemed.

It is often extremely difficult, as well as dangerous, to transport merchandize over Onore bar, on account of a tremendous surf: I never thought myself in such imminent danger as in attempting a passage through these surges: a little before my arrival, a young gentleman in the Company's civil service was overset in a ship's boat, and all perished! We took the advantage of the land wind at midnight to return to the vessel, when the surf was moderate.

I am not sufficiently conversant with the cause and effect of the land and sea breezes which so generally prevail during the fair season on the Malabar-coast. The Oriental Voyager assigns the most probable reason for the regularity of these periodical winds; although, in my opinion, not entirely satisfactory; as they seem to prevail equally along the whole extent of the Malabar coast, whether mountainous or flat.

"It is well known that from the time the sun begins to emerge above the eastern horizon, until he gains his meridian altitude, the earth is gradually acquiring a temperature above that of the sea.

This causing a rarefaction or expansion of the air over the surface of the land, it ascends into the higher regions; and a column of dense and cool air rushes in from the sea about mid-day, to preserve the equilibrium, thus producing the sea-breeze. The above cause continuing to operate while the sun is above the horizon, we of course have the sea-breeze during the remainder of the day: but at night, when the earth loses its acquired heat, and even sinks in temperature below that of the sea, the air which had ascended in a rarefied state during the day, begins to condense in the upper regions; and pressing upon that below, a column of air is sent off towards the sea; and thus the land-breeze is produced. The sole cause then of these semidiurnal breezes, being the capacity which the earth has for acquiring a higher temperature than that of the sea, the cause becomes evident why they do not take place on a mountainous coast, where the hills are covered with trees and verdure, which retaining the dews that fall in the night, the earth is as cool during the day as the sea: the mountains therefore do not obstruct the course of these periodical breezes, but prevent their existence."

The regularity of the land and sea-breezes on the Malabar-coast is sometimes interrupted by tempests: there were two during my residence in India, of fatal consequence, each about a month before the usual setting in of the south-west monsoon. Water-spouts are occasionally seen on this coast, but seldom attended with danger: those I observed from a distance, had an awful appearance; if, on a near approach, they realize Falconer's sublime description, they must be terrible indeed;

"Now from the left approaching, we descry
"A liquid column towering shoot on high;
"Its foaming base an angry whirlwind sweeps,
"Where curling billows rouse the fearful deeps!
"Still round and round the fluid vortex flies,
"Scattering dun night and horror through the skies!
"The swift volution, and th' enormous train,
"Let sages vers'd in nature's lore explain.
"The horrid apparition still draws nigh,
"And white with foam the whirling surges fly.
"The guns were prim'd, the vessel northward nears
"'Till her black battery on the column bears;
"The nitre fir'd, and while the dreadful sound
"Convulsive shook the slumbering air around;
"The watery volume, towering to the sky,
"Burst down, a dreadful deluge from on high!
"Th' affrighted surge, recoiling as it fell,
"Rolling in hills, disclos'd the abyss of hell!"

A pleasant land-breeze wafted us from Onore, to the fortress called the Malabar Frontier; where we properly entered on the Malabar coast: we anchored the same evening at Mangulore, in 12° 50′ north latitude, and 74°·44′ east longitude. It was then the principal sea-port of Hyder Ally, nabob of the Mysore; well situated for commerce, and frequented by foreign merchants for pepper, sandal-wood, rice, and betel-nuts.

The entrance into the river, or rather a salt-water lake, near which the town was built, is difficult and dangerous, occasioned by a rapid current running into the sea, through a narrow channel in the sandy beach, which extends along the coast: this entrance was defended by batteries; the principal fortress stood on the opposite side of the river, near a populous town; the houses were generally mean, and there were no public buildings of importance. During the succeeding wars with Hyder Ally, and his son Tippoo Sultaun, Mangulore, Onore, and the other sea-ports in their dominions underwent a total change.

At Kurkul, near Mangulore, is a celebrated Hindoo temple of great antiquity, and a gigantic image of *Gómatéswar;* inferior in size, but of a similar kind, to the famous idol, named *Gómatéswar Swami,* at Belligola, or *Sravana-Belligola,* the principal residence of the *Guroos,* or high priests belonging to the sect of *Jains,* a singular and separate tribe among the Hindoos, particularly described in the Asiatic Researches. The image at Belligola is said to be eighteen times the height of a man, but this I imagine to be exaggerated upon examining the engravings accompanying the account, where a man of the usual height stands upon the terrace near the gigantic figure, to shew the comparative height of art and nature: when these drawings were taken in 1801, the foot of the statue was measured, and found to be nine feet in length; hence the height of the statue is estimated at fifty-four feet. The records of the *Jains* also mention a golden image, of five hundred times the height of a man; which was inundated by the sea: but they believe it can still be sometimes seen at low water.

We staid a very short time at Mangulore, most of which was sacrificed to a formal visit at the governor's durbar; a Mahomedan oppressor, in great favour with his sovereign Hyder Ally; I should otherwise have gone to Kurkul, and some interesting places in its vicinity.

Travellers who sojourn only a few hours, or even a few days, in a place, and write decidedly upon the manners and customs of the inhabitants, can, in general, have acquired a very superficial knowledge, by whatever channel derived: I confess I have found myself involved in many errors, by believing the accounts both of Europeans and natives, whom I occasionally consulted, on the Malabar coast. Subsequent visits, and better information, have enabled me to correct those mistakes; many authentic sources of intelligence yet remain, and of these, few are equal to Dr. Francis Buchanan's journey through the Malabar districts: he mentions many singular usages in the country contiguous to Mangulore, particularly in the tribe of *Buntar*, who are the highest rank of *sudras* in *Talava*, and resemble the Nairs of *Malayala*, or Malabar. "Among them a man's own children are not his heirs: during his life-time he may give them money; but all of which he dies possessed, goes to his sisters, and to their children. If a man has a mother's brother's daughter, he must marry her; but he may take two or three wives besides: the ceremony is performed by the girl's father, or other near kinsman. When a man marries several wives, none of them can leave him without his consent; but when discord runs high, he generally sends one of the disputants back to her brother's house; and then she is at liberty to marry again. A man at any time, if he dislikes his wife, may send her back to her brother's house; and he can do no more if she has committed adultery. In all these cases, or when a widow returns to her brother's house on her husband's death, she is accompanied by her children; and may marry again, unless she has committed adultery with a person of low caste: but if that crime has been committed with a *brahmin*, *kshatri*, *vaisya*, or *bunt*, she is well received; her children become her brother's heirs, and no man will have any objection to marry her. The Buntar are permitted to eat animal food, and to drink spirituous liquors; they burn the dead, but seem to be entirely ignorant of a state of future existence.

"All the south part of Tulava formerly belonged to the Cumly Rajah, who pretends to be a *Kshatri* from the north of India. The manners of his family resemble those of the rajahs of Malayala. All the males keep Nair girls; but their children, who are called tambans, have no right to the succession. The eldest daughter in the female line cohabits with a Tulava brahmin; her sons become rajahs, and her eldest daughter continues the line of the family. Whenever she pleases, she changes her brahmin; the younger daughters also cohabit with brahmins, and produce a race of people called Bayllal, who have no right to the succession. The dominions of this family extended from the Chandra-giri river, to that on the north side of Cumley, and produced an annual revenue of fifteen thousand ikeri pagodas, about six thousand pounds. The rajah lives now in the country; but he has neither lands nor authority. Before the last war he lived at Tellicherry, on a pension from the Company; which has been doubled since we got possession of the country of his ancestors.

"In Tulava the state has no lands; the whole is private property: all the land-tax is now paid in money; but before the conquest, part of it was demanded in rice, and other articles of consumption for the troops, at a low rate, which was fixed by the officers of government: the accounts contain solely the tax which each proprietor ought to pay. When a man alienates part of his lands, he agrees with the purchaser to take a part of the tax, and then the revenue of the new proprietor is entered in the public accounts under his name. The sum which he is to pay is always mentioned in the title-deeds; and the government has a right to prevent any division that is not in proportion to the value of the lands alienated; otherwise the revenue might suffer greatly. The proprietors allege, that the tax amounts to more than the rent; and that they are obliged to borrow money, or to give part of the profit from the lands cultivated with their own stock, to enable them to satisfy the claims of government. Those whom Dr. Buchanan assembled to give him information, and most of whom were as fat as pigs, gravely told him that they were reduced to live upon *kanjee*, or rice gruel. From what they say, therefore, no estimate can be formed of the share of the rent which they pay to government. Every one thinks himself bound to conceal the truth, and none more so than the native officers of revenue. Every step, indeed, seems to have been taken, by a chaos of weights and measures, and by plausible but false accounts, to keep the state of the country a profound mystery."

This last quotation may not, perhaps, be generally interesting; but I have introduced it, because the subject of landed property in the British dominions in India, has lately occupied the attention of the different governments and boards of revenue; and is more largely discussed when treating of the agriculture and revenue of the districts under my charge in the province of Guzerat. Dr. Buchanan concludes his observations in the country near Mangulore, with a remark which is generally applicable throughout India: "That the universal cry of poverty, and the care, owing to long oppression, with which every thing is concealed, render it very difficult to know the real circumstances of the cultivator:

we may, however, safely conclude, from the violent contest for landed property of every kind in *Canara*, that each occupant has still a considerable interest in the soil, besides the reward due to him for cultivating whatever his stock enables him to do. It is indeed sincerely to be wished that this property may long continue unmolested, as no country can thrive where the absolute property of the soil is vested in the state."

The etiquette of the Mangulore Durbar detained us until a late hour; when we returned on board, and sailed with the land breeze for Tellicherry, along a hilly coast, particularly near mount Dilla, a high woody cape, twenty miles from Tellicherry. We next passed Cannanore, a large sea-port town belonging to a Mahomedan prince called Ally Rajah, who was also sovereign of the Maldivæ islands. Cannanore carried on a considerable trade in pepper and cocoa-nuts, and was situated in a beautiful country, the sea-coast being enriched by extensive groves of cocoa-nuts, with cultivated plains between them and the Gatte mountains.

Tellicherry was at that time a principal settlement of the English, in the latitude of 11° 48′ north, and 75° 23′ east longitude: the town, enclosed by a slight wall, contained several good houses, belonging to the English, and native Portugueze: situated on a rising ground near the sea, it was constantly refreshed by the western breeze; and, from the salubrity of the air, was called the Montpellier of India. The fort was large and well garrisoned; it contained an excellent house for the chief, with barracks and other public buildings: about a mile to the southward was another English fort, called Moylan, and batteries on the adjacent hills; but after the wars with the Mysore sultauns, the whole system on the Malabar coast was altered, and the present civil and military appointments in that quarter are foreign to the subject. A member of the Bombay council was then chief of Tellicherry; several junior servants formed his council, and filled the different departments: provisions were cheap and plentiful, especially fish, in great variety; it was famous for fine sardinias and excellent oysters. The trade consisted in pepper, sandal-wood, cocoa-nuts, cardamoms, and ureca, the produce of the country; with shark's-fins, dried fish, and similar articles.

The cocoa-nut groves on the sea-coast in this part of Malabar are very extensive: I have fully described this valuable tree at Bombay: in Malabar, from the time the nut is planted, until the tree begins to bear fruit, is about twelve years; it continues in perfection for fifty or sixty years; and in a decaying state, produces fruit twenty years longer: it then dies altogether, and is succeeded by a new plantation.

The low lands produce abundance of rice; those that can be irrigated give a second crop; the first harvest commences the middle of September, at the breaking up of the monsoon; the latter about the middle of January: after which, with additional manure and watering, they sometimes have a third crop of pulse.

The plantations of pepper in this part of Malabar are extensive and valuable; the jacs, mangos, and other high trees, on which the vines are trained, add much to the general beauty of the country.

The cardamom, amomum repens, Lin. which grows in this part of Malabar, is a spice much esteemed by the Asiatics; they chew it separately, or with betel; it is a principal ingredient in their cookery, and used medicinally as a stomachic. The plant in appearance resembles the ginger: it attains the height of two or three feet, and sometimes more, before it bears fruit; the blossoms are small, white, and variegated with purple; some have a brownish appearance: they are succeeded by small green pods, containing the seeds, which become of a light brown when the seed ripens, grows black, and acquires the aromatic flavour for which it is so estimable.

This valuable spice is indigenous to many parts of Malabar, but flourishes most on the acclivity of moist cool hills, among low trees, bushes, and little springs of water: although the cardamom delights in such a situation, it will grow in other places; and is sometimes planted in gardens and orchards of plantain trees; the roots are taken up and divided. The cardamom hills are generally private property; when the plants are discovered, they are preserved with great care, by cutting down the bushes, and attending to the shoots for three years, at which time they begin to bear; they have attained their full growth, and produce the best crops in the fourth year, after which they generally decay. The plants spring up in the rainy season; those under cultivation are not permitted to grow too close to each other; when it so happens the roots are divided, and planted at a greater distance: the seed begins to ripen about the middle of September, and continues more or less for the space of two months. The capsules, or seed-pods, sometimes grow on a high stalk, often in short clusters near the root: such as are ripe are daily gathered, and carefully dried for sale; otherwise the birds and squirrels would carry off a large share. It is supposed these animals scatter the seed in the unfrequented spots, where the cardamom is often unexpectedly found: diligent search is always made for the springing plants at the commencement of the rainy season. I was informed that in some places they burn the bushes, which are always cut down at that time; as the ashes produce an excellent manure without injuring the growing plant; by what means I know not. The cardamom is not general on the Malabar hills, but confined to particular districts, and especially to moist situations.

There were some thriving coffee plantations on the island of Durmapatam near Tellicherry; the seed was originally brought from Mocha, but the Malabar coffee is inferior in flavour and refreshment to the Arabian berry: it is a beautiful plant in its foliage, blossoms and fruit, but too well known to need a description.

The ordeal trials, mentioned in other parts of these volumes, were frequently practised at Tellicherry, even under the sanction of the British government: this custom, so contrary to the general opinion in Europe, is universally admitted under the sovereigns of Malabar. Under their administration, when a man, accused of a capital crime, chooses to undergo the ordeal trial, he is closely confined for several days, his right hand and arm are covered with thick wax-cloth, tied up and sealed, in the presence of proper officers, to prevent deceit: in the English districts the covering was always sealed with the Company's arms, and the prisoner placed under an European guard. At the time fixed for the ordeal, a cauldron of oil is placed over a fire; when it boils, a piece of money is dropped into the vessel; the prisoner's arm is unsealed, and washed in the presence of his judges and accusers: during this part of the ceremony, the attendant brahmins supplicate the deity; on receiving their benediction the accused plunges his hand into the boiling fluid, and takes out the coin: this I believe is sometimes repeated. The arm is then again sealed up, until the time appointed for a re-examination: the seal is then broken; if no blemish appears the prisoner is declared innocent; if the contrary, he suffers the punishment due to his crime.

In the account of ordeals, by Mr. Hastings, in the Dherma Sastra, or the chapter of oaths, he says "the word divya, in Sanscrit, is generally understood to mean an oath, or the trial by ordeal; being the form of appealing to the immediate interposition of the divine power." Nine kinds of ordeal are enumerated; but I shall here confine myself to what is said on that by oil.—"The ordeal by the vessel of oil, according to the comment on the Dherma Sastra, is thus performed; the ground appointed for the trial is cleared, and rubbed with cow-dung; and the next day, at sun-rise, the pundit worships Ganesa, presents his oblations, and pays adoration to other deities, conformable to the Sastra: then, having read the incantation prescribed, he places a round pan of gold, silver, copper, iron or clay, with a diameter of sixteen fingers, and four fingers deep; and throws into it one seer, or eighty sicca weight of clarified butter, or oil of sesamum. After this a ring of gold, or silver, or iron, is cleaned and washed with water, and cast into the oil, which they proceed to heat; when it is very hot they put into it a fresh leaf of pippala, or bilwa; when the leaf is burned, the oil is known to be sufficiently hot. Then, having pronounced a mentra over the oil, they order the party accused to take the ring out of the pan; and if he take it out without being burned, or without a blister on his hand, his innocence is considered as proved; if not, his guilt."

"On the trial by fire, the accused thus addresses the element; 'Thou, O Fire! pervadest all beings: O cause of purity! who givest evidence of virtue and of sin, declare the truth in this my hand.' In the ordeal by poison, the accused pronounces, 'Thou, O Poison! art the child of Brahma, stedfast in justice and in truth! clear me from this heavy charge; and, if I have spoken truly, become nectar to me!"

The Muckwas, or Mucuars, at Tellicherry are an industrious useful set of people; some are Mahomedans, some Hindoos: they are considered a very low tribe among the Malabars, but are more valuable in society than many of higher pretensions: they make excellent palankeen-bearers, boatmen, fishermen, and porters of goods from the landing place to the storehouses. Some of the young women are pleasing in their countenance, and person, which is generally very much exposed; their clothing consisting only of a white cotton cloth round the middle. The Hindoo Mucuars are kept in a most degraded state by the brahmins, who allow them to eat all animal food, except beef: they may also drink strong liquors; and are not very nice in their matrimonial connexions. Dr. F. Buchanan says the deity of this cast is the goddess *Bhadra-Kali,* who is represented by a log of wood, placed in a hut that is called a temple: they assemble four times a year to sacrifice a cock, and make offerings of fruit to the log: one of the caste acts as priest, but his office is not hereditary. The Mucuars are not admitted to enter within the precincts of any of the temples dedicated to the great gods of the brahmins, but they sometimes stand at a distance, and send their offerings by more pure hands: they seem to know nothing of a state of future existence; but believe in evil spirits, who inflict diseases, and occasion other misfortunes."

During our stay at Tellicherry, I spent an agreeable day at Mahie, a French settlement, a few miles to the southward, pleasantly situated on the banks of a river; trading chiefly in pepper, cocoa-nuts, and cardamoms. On sailing from Tellicherry to Calicut, we had a fine view of Mahie from the sea, from whence it appeared to greater advantage than on shore.

Sailing southward, we passed near Sacrifice-rock, a small island, so called, from the crew of an English ship having been massacred there by pirates, the beginning of the seventeenth century. It is famous for the edible birds-nests, found in the clefts of the rocks, which are esteemed so luxurious a dainty in China, as to have become a considerable article of commerce: the greatest quantity are produced on the coasts of Malacca; they are also procured from Sacrifice-rock, and other unfrequented islands. These nests are three or four inches in circumference, and one in depth: formed by a bird of the swallow tribe, (hirundo, nidis edulibus), either with the spawn of fish, or a glutinous frothy scum, which the sea leaves on the rock; with this they construct those little habitations, so highly prized by the Chinese epicure, and voluptuous Mahomedan, when stewed to a jelly, and seasoned with spices. Sharks' fins are dressed in the same manner; they are dried in large quantities at the fishing-towns on the Malabar coast, and constitute a valuable article of trade to China. The drying of these fins, sardinias, and other fish, all along the Malabar coast, renders the atmosphere extremely offensive, if not unwholesome; their putrid effluviæ generally overpower the aromatic odours, which would otherwise be wafted by the morning breeze from groves of cassia, sandal, and champach. The sharks' fins are sold at a reasonable price; but the newest and most transparent nests of the hirundo, are purchased by the Chinese at five or six dollars the pound. Those of an older fabric, dry, and less pellucid, are not so valuable.

A favourable wind carried us quickly from Sacrifice-rock to Calicut, in the latitude of 11° 18′ north: it is memorable, as being the place where Vasco de Gama, and his hardy followers, first landed from Europe in 1498; and where the English established a factory in 1616: at present it offers very little to interest a traveller, being chiefly composed of low huts, shaded by cocoa-nut trees, on a sandy shore; amidst an offensive effluvia from sharks' fins, and a variety of fish drying on the beach. In this unpleasant situation, the English, French, Danes, and Portugueze, had their respective factories, where they hoisted their national flags; and purchased pepper, cocoa-nuts, coir-cables and ropes, betel-nuts, timber, oil, and other articles. Beyond this sandy tract is a fertile plain, extending to the Gaut mountains; which in that part of the peninsula are of a stupendous height, and visible at sea seventy miles distance.

Calicut road, where the ships anchor, is deemed unsafe for those not well acquainted with the navigation; several vessels have been wrecked upon the ruins of the old city, now under water: as the mean town just described, formed no part of that emporium where de Gama landed: Calicut is said to have been then a large city, where the Zamorine, the sovereign of the country, held a splendid court, and merchants resorted from Persia, Arabia, Africa, and different parts of India, to purchase pearls, diamonds, spices, ivory, and other costly articles. From thence the persevering Vasco freighted the first ship to Europe, and introduced those oriental luxuries in much greater abundance, and at a cheaper rate, than they had been imported formerly by the Greeks of Constantinople, or the Venetians, who succeeded them in that valuable commerce.

Every vestige of that magnificent city is now whelmed beneath the sea, which flowed beyond its bounds, and no more receded: at very low water I have occasionally seen the waves breaking over the tops of the highest temples and minarets, but in general nothing is to be distinguished of this ancient emporium.

"The face of places, and their forms decay,
"And that is solid earth which once was sea;
"Seas in their turn, retreating from the shore,
"Make solid land what ocean was before:
"So Zancle to the Italian earth was ty'd,
"And men once walk'd where ships at anchor ride;
"And cities that adorn'd the Achaian ground
"Now whelm'd beneath the sea are sunk and drown'd:
"And boatmen there, through crystal surface show
"To wondering passengers the walls below." DRYDEN'S OVID.

Dr. Fryer's visit to Calicut, a century before I saw it, is pleasantly described, and his account of the interior part of this country is very interesting.

"In November 1673, we anchored against that anciently

traded port of Calicut: ashore, the first house facing us was the English; near it were placed six small pieces, resounding our salutes at our entry: on the back side lay two great guns, dismounted, of brass; all that is extant of the Portugal town and castle, which ran out into the sea, where our ships now ride, near four miles, overflowed by water; nothing remaining of it, but what is taken upon chronicle.

"What is left of Calicut, is not equivalent to what might be expected from the gleaning of so many ages of traffic: for the city that stood upon stilts is tripped up; for down it is gone; and the temple, whose marble pillars durst compare with those of Agrippa's in the Roman Pantheon, is topsy-turvy: and if any one that comes after me, make you believe it to be not above four miles in length, and in that not an house befitting a Christian; here and there a mosque, and burying-places with tanks; a good long bazar with trash, and ripe fruit; another with opium, and spices of this coast; changers and jewellers; unfenced and rude in building; he tells you but the truth. Indeed it is pleasantly situated under trees; and is the holy see of the zamorine, or pope."

"The country is enticing and beautiful, woody in the plain, up the country mountainous, where grows the pepper: it is a berry that is brought forth by a bind-weed, wedded to a tree, which it hugs as affectionately as the ivy does the oak; it is first green, when dried it is black, and husked white. Between this and Tellicherry, hills of cardamoms do bound the sight: on the east a gravelly forest, with tall benty grass, offers, besides its taking look, diversity of game; as hares, wild boars, tigers, and elephants, which are dreaded by travellers; they striking all down before them, trees as well as animals: the like terror is conceived by the crashing noise made among the woods by the wild bulls: for all which it is the practice of the wood-men to dig deep pits, and cover them with sods, laid over with boughs, to entrap them in their headstrong and unwary course. Monkeys, with white ruffs, and black shagged bodies, looking very gravely, are brought from hence."

"The first blackamoor pullen I ever saw was here: the outward skin of the fowl was a perfect negro, the bones also being as black as jet: under the skin nothing could be whiter than the flesh, more tender, or more grateful. On the sea-coast are water-snakes, which, by the goodness of Providence, warn the seamen, when all is obscured, of their too near approach to land: these are as sure presages on the Indian coast, as the Cape-birds are there."

The water-snakes, black monkeys, and black-boned fowls, like the native inhabitants of Malabar, remain unchanged; but the European settlements on the coast have been all metamorphosed since the French revolution, and the wars with the sovereigns of Mysore. The poultry, with a black skin and black bones, though disagreeable at first to strangers, are found to be more delicate in flavour, and superior in whiteness to the other kind: the hogs, fowls, and ducks in the southern parts of the coast, feed so much upon fish, that their flesh is frequently unpleasant, and offensive.

A few miles from Calicut is a small sea-port, called Vapura, pleasantly situated on the banks of a river; from whence a great quantity of teak-wood is exported, and where vessels are built of that timber. These valuable trees are felled on the Gaut mountains, and transported from thence to the river-side by elephants; where it remains to be floated down to Vapura, when the stream fills in the rainy season.

This part of Malabar also produces the chapingum, or sapan-wood (gullandina sapan): the trees are planted in gardens and orchards, for the sake of the wood, which produces a valuable dye.

From Calicut, we proceeded to Cochin, and arrived there on the 14th, after sailing along a bold coast, of cocoa-nut trees and rice-fields, extending over a sandy plain to the Gaut mountains: whose majestic summits in the morning are generally enveloped in clouds; but towards sun-set, their western acclivities display an assemblage of rocks and woods, in broad masses of light and shadow, which rival the Alps and Appennines of Europe; although deficient in those pinnacles and glaciers, whose sublimity and beauty, seen through the clear atmosphere of an Italian winter, baffle the artist's skill, and defy the power of language.

Cochin, in the latitude of 9° 58′ north, and 76° east longitude, was among the early conquests of the Portugueze; from them it fell into the hands of the Dutch, and is now in possession of the English. The town is pleasantly situated at the entrance of a broad navigable river, or more properly a lake, which extends southerly for near twenty leagues to Quilone, another Dutch factory, affording an inland navigation through that part of the king of Cochin's dominions.

When I was at Cochin it belonged to the Dutch; and as such only can I speak of it. The town was surrounded by a fortification, built by the Portugueze; of no great strength except towards the sea: the garrison consisted of five hundred Europeans, and some Malay troops from their more eastern possessions; the commanding officer had only the rank of major, and the civil governor was styled commodore.

I have occasionally resided there several weeks, when transacting business for the India Company: it was a place of great trade, and presented a striking contrast to Goa; where an empty harbour, forsaken houses, and mouldering walls, indicated its fallen state, and proved the wretched condition of a settlement destined from its advantageous situation to be a grand emporium: at Cochin, a harbour filled with ships, streets crowded with merchants, and warehouses stored with goods from every part of Asia and Europe, marked the industry, the commerce, and the wealth of the inhabitants.

The phlegmatic and formal character of the native Hollander generally accompanies him to other climates; but at Cochin, a constant intercourse with strangers had effected a pleasing change. I constantly received the kindest attentions from the governor and principal inhabitants; their tables were furnished with hospitality, and graced with politeness; their houses and gardens displayed the national cleanliness and neatness. Provisions of all kinds abounded; in the rainy season, when no ships frequent the port, a turkey cost only half a rupee; fowls and ducks in proportion: the beef, though small, was well-flavoured, and very cheap; as were fruit, vegetables, and other refreshments for the numerous vessels which touch there in the fair season. Europeans and natives find the water unwholesome; drinking it frequently causes that disagreeable disorder called the *Cochin-leg*, or elephantiasis, which is deemed incurable: it is the same as the lepra arabum, and considered as a species of leprosy. I have seen many with a leg thicker than their body; on the naked limbs of the natives it has a disgusting appearance; to the leg of a European, with a silk-stocking, shoe and buckle, something ludicrous is annexed; the Asiatic garb would be more comely. The swelling generally commences at the knee, and continues of the same wonderful circumference to the foot; few persons are affected in both legs; and I believe they are insensible of any other inconvenience than that of dragging such a cumberous load.

During my residence at Anjengo, I was deputed to transact some money concerns between the English Company and the Jews of Cochin; they do not reside in the city, but at Jews-town, or Mottancheree, situated on the banks of the river, about a mile distant; where they have two large synagogues, and many excellent houses and gardens; and are allowed the free exercise of their religion, and carry on the principal trade of the settlement. Jews from Poland, Spain, and other parts of Europe, were intermingled with those established in Malabar, many ages before the discovery of India by the Cape of Good Hope.

Samuel Abraham, a native of Poland, a man of learning, years, and respectability, was the most eminent merchant at Mottancheree in 1772. He managed my business for the Company, and gave me every information in his power respecting the Jewish tribes settled in the king of Cochin's dominions. They are a people distinct and separate from the surrounding Malabars, in dress, manners, and religion, as well as in their complexion and general appearance. This Hebrew colony is said to have emigrated from Judea soon after the destruction of the second temple by Titus

Vespasian; when a number of these devoted people, escaping from the dreadful massacres and sale of captives at Jerusalem, consisting of men, women, and children, priests and Levites, with such effects as they could transport, emigrated from Palestine to India: a country probably not unknown to the Jews in more prosperous days, at least to those tribes situated near Tyre and Sidon. The Medes, Persians, and Abyssinians, had a communication with distant parts of India for articles of luxury; and that they carried on a considerable trade to its remote provinces before Alexander's conquest, is evident from Strabo, Pliny, and other writers; exclusive of the maritime commerce already mentioned, from the Periplus and Grecian historians. It is therefore not improbable that some Jewish families, on their dispersion at the first captivity, or at some subsequent period, may have wandered to the Malabar coast; which my venerable informer assured me was believed by his people to have been the case with part of the tribe of Manasseh.

The fate of the expatriated Jews who wandered to India after the destruction of the second temple, until their arrival in Malabar, at the conclusion of the fifth century of the Christian æra, is, I believe, no where authenticated. At that period the colony reached their place of destination; the sovereign of the country, a brahmin, treated them with kindness, and allowed them to settle at Cranganore with considerable privileges. There they were established many centuries, increasing in wealth and consequence, until, from dissensions among themselves, they called in the aid of surrounding princes, and after much cruelty and bloodshed, were driven from Cranganore, with the loss of their possessions and property.

These unhappy fugitives were thus separated and dispersed among the Malabar districts, until a remnant again collected, and were permitted by the king of Cochin to settle at Mottancheree, on the banks of Cochin river, where their descendants have continued ever since. Samuel Abraham assured me, that they had in their possession a royal grant of Cranganore, and the district allotted to their ancestors, on their first establishment in Malabar, engraved on metal, and signed by the brahmin sovereign of the country. This is since confirmed by Dr. Claudius Buchanan, who procured a fac-simile, engraven on copper, from the original brass tablet which he saw in the possession of the Cochin Jews in 1807; he has also published a translation from that made by the Jews into the Hebrew language: the original grant, as dated in the Malabar annals, corresponds with the year 490 of the Christian æra.

The history of the Jews is the most wonderful of any in the annals of time: they are indeed a standing miracle! and however modern philosophy may raise doubts of revelation in some particulars, a people scattered over the face of the earth, yet preserved distinct and separate from every nation among whom they dwell, afford incontrovertible evidence of its truth. We trace them from the call of Abraham in Chaldea, and rest with delight at the tents and wells of the patriarchal shepherds: from those pastoral scenes we accompany them to Egypt, sympathize in their captivity and oppressions under an ungrateful monarch, and rejoice in their deliverance from cruel bondage: we share in their adventures in the wilderness, and participate in their wars and conquests in Canaan. Established there, and dissatisfied with the theocracy, we view them under the regal government, in a progressive increase of wealth and population, until, at the conclusion of David's reign, the men of Israel who drew the sword, were a thousand thousand, and an hundred thousand, and Judah was four hundred threescore and ten thousand men; all descended in a direct line from Abraham, the pastoral patriarch. In the reign of Solomon the temporal prophecies were completed; the wealth, power, and greatness, of that extraordinary monarch, surpassed all the kings of the earth: they sought his presence to hear his wisdom, and brought every one a present; vessels of silver, and vessels of gold; raiment, armour, and spices; horses and mules; until he made silver in Jerusalem as stones, and cedar trees as the sycamore trees in the plains: all the drinking vessels of king Solomon were of gold, and all the vessels of the house of the forest of Lebanon of pure gold; none were of silver; it was not any thing accounted of in the days of Solomon. For the king's ships which went to Tarshish with the servants of Hiram, king of Tyre, returned every three years with gold and silver, ivory, apes, and peacocks. The queen of Sheba came from a far country to hear his wisdom, and to behold his glory, accompanied by a very great caravan of camels, that bare spices, and gold, and precious stones; and when she beheld his greatness, and the splendour of his court, there was no more spirit in her; on her return to her own land, she gave the king an hundred and twenty talents of gold, and of spices, and precious stones, great abundance: but far beyond all was the approbation of his Maker, and his manifestation of his divine presence in the temple; where, after he had finished his prayer at the dedication, the fire visibly descended from heaven, and consumed the sacrifice: and the glory of the Lord filled the house; so that the priests could not enter because of the glory!

We cannot easily imagine a more splendid monarch, nor a happier people: heaven and earth united to exalt them in the face of the nations: but alas! how soon did the gold become dim, and the fine gold changed! Solomon forgot the guide of his youth; and, in his old age, bowed down to Ashtaroth, the goddess of Zidon, and to the abomination of Ammon; and built altars, and sacrificed unto the gods of his strange wives. His example was followed by many of his successors, until their idolatry became so abominable in the sight of JEHOVAH, who had peculiarly styled himself the GOD of Israel, that, after a succession of heavy judgments, blended with signal mercies, he finally withdrew his protection from the ungrateful tribes of Israel and Judah; and "Nebuchadnezzar "king of Babylon came up against Jerusalem, and besieged it, "with a large army: and famine prevailed in the city, and there "was no bread for the people; the city was broken up, and all "the men of war fled by night, by the way of the gate which is "by the king's garden; and Zedekiah king of Judah, went by the "way towards the plains: and the army of the Chaldees overtook "him in the plains of Jericho, and brought him to Nebuchadnez-"zar, who gave judgment upon him; and they slew the sons of "Zedekiah king of Judah, before his eyes, and then put out the "eyes of Zedekiah, and bound him with fetters of brass, and car-"ried him to Babylon. And they slew the young men with the "sword, and had no compassion upon the young man or maiden; "nor upon the old man, nor him that stooped for age: and all the "vessels of the house of GOD, great and small, and the treasures

" of the house of the LORD, and the treasures of the king and of " his princes; all these were carried to Babylon! And they burnt " the house of GOD; and brake down the walls of Jerusalem, and " burnt all the palaces thereof with fire, and destroyed all the " goodly vessels thereof: and them that had escaped from the " sword caused he to be carried away to Babylon, where they " became servants and slaves for seventy years." There we behold them in a deplorable state of captivity, hanging their harps upon the willows of Euphrates, unable to sing the songs of Zion to their taunting oppressors, and suffering a cruel bondage until released by the decree of Cyrus: then with their millions reduced to forty-two thousand, they were numbered by hundreds, and by twenties, in their small encampment near the river Ahava: there Ezra, their pious leader, proclaimed a fast, and prostrated himself before the GOD of Israel, who had delivered their fathers, their kings, and their priests, to the sword, to captivity, and to spoil: but had now extended his mercy to them in the sight of the kings of Persia, and had left a remnant to escape, and to set up the house of GOD, and to repair the desolations of Jerusalem! Their history is still interesting, from the building of the second temple until the final destruction of Jerusalem by Titus; predicted by the SON of GOD, for their rejecting him as the Messiah. From that dreadful period, to the present day, what a spectacle do they exhibit! how fully accomplished are all the prophecies respecting them! they daily present a miracle which no sophistry can controvert, no scepticim elude. Scattered over the face of the earth, how awfully do their expatriated tribes fulfil the denunciation of their great law-giver! " If thou forgettest the Lord thy GOD, and servest other gods, the

" Lord shall scatter thee among all people, from the one end of " the earth even unto the other; and thou shalt become an asto- " nishment, a proverb, and a by-word, among all the nations, " whither the Lord shall lead thee; if thou wilt not observe to do " all the words of the law; that thou mayest fear this glorious and " fearful name, THE LORD THY GOD!"

These meditations occupied my mind in many a moonlight walk, on the spot where this Jewish colony are now settled: they formed a part of my original letters from Cochin, and although in some respects they may appear foreign to the general subject, I was unwilling to suppress them.

We sailed for Anjengo on the 17th, passing near a sandy coast, covered with cocoa-nut trees: we had a transient view of the Dutch factories at *Porca* and *Calliquilone*, where they procure pepper and cassia, abundant in that part of Malabar: the next morning we arrived at *Quilone*, or *Coulan*, another Dutch settlement; it was formerly a large town, belonging to the Portugueze, with extensive fortifications; these are now destroyed; the churches are converted into warehouses, and the European inhabitants reduced to a factor, surgeon, and a small garrison: the natives are chiefly Roman catholic Christians.

Quilone is six leagues from Anjengo; about half way we passed *Eddava*, formerly a Danish factory; but at that time a country villa belonging to the English chief of *Anjengo:* it stands on the high bank of a river, commanding a view of the sea, and a pleasant country, covered with groves of cassia, and plantations of pepper. From thence to *Anjengo* the coast is hilly and romantic; especially about the red cliffs at *Boccoli;* where the women of

Anjengo daily repair for water, from a very fine spring; which they sell at *Anjengo*, the water there being generally brackish and unwholesome.

Although the weather was moderate, we found a violent surf rolling on the shore at *Anjengo;* no English boat ever attempts to pass through it: on approaching these rolling surges, we quitted the pinnace, and got into a canoe, in which we were thrown on shore by their fury.

Thus terminated our voyage down the Malabar coast; which during the fair season is delightful: its shelving shores afford a safe navigation, present many beautiful scenes, and a number of opulent towns: the alternate land and sea breezes are equally favourable for vessels bound either north or southward. While the captains are engaged in commercial concerns, the passengers have the advantage of stopping daily at some new settlement, where they meet with hospitality and variety. Paolino has beautifully described it, in few words. " At three or four leagues from the southern coast of Malabar, the country appears like a theatre of verdure: here a grove of cocoa-trees, and there a beautiful river pouring its tribute into the ocean, through a valley irrigated and fertilized by its waters. In one place a group of fishing vessels, in another a white church peering through the verdure of the groves: while the gentle land-breeze of the morning wafts the fragrance extracted from the pepper, cardamoms, betel, and other aromatics, to a great distance from the shore, and perfumes the vessel on her voyage with their odours; towards noon succeeds the sea-breeze, which speeds them to their desired haven."

Anjengo, the place of my destination, was at that time the last

English factory on the Malabar coast, something more than six hundred miles from Bombay, in the latitude of 8° 39′ north, and 76° 40′ east longitude. On a narrow bank of sand, its western side bounded by the sea, and the eastern by a river, were two rows of houses, forming a street about five hundred yards in length; the north end terminated by the Portugueze church, and the English burying-ground; the south by the fort and lower batteries: this fortress, which reached nearly from the sea to the river, contained store houses, accommodations for the garrisons, and apartments for the chief, who was a member of council at Bombay. The civil servants and military officers resided in tolerable houses; the natives generally in thatched huts. The Portugueze church, white tombs, a respectable fortress, and other accompaniments, surrounded by cocoa-nut woods, gave Anjengo a pleasing appearance.

Before I left Europe, I had cherished delightful ideas of Palmyra groves, and umbrageous banian trees: I said with our sweet descriptive bard,

" Lay me reclin'd
" Beneath the spreading tamarind; or in the maze
" Embowering endless of the Indian fig;
" Or stretch'd amid the orchards of the sun,
" Where high palmetos lift their graceful shade;
" Give me to drain the cocoa's milky bowl;
" And from the palm to draw its freshening wine!
" Gather the rich anana, India's pride
" Of vegetable life; beyond whate'er
" The poets imag'd of the golden age:
" Quick, let me strip thee of thy tufted coat,
" Spread thy ambrosial stores, and feast with Jove! THOMSON.

Poets are allowed to soar beyond the boundaries of humble prose: the lovely isles in the Odyssey, and Virgil's rural scenes, captivate the youthful mind, and store it with pleasing recollections: the embellishments of Tasso, Ariosto, and many of our British bards, charm the imagination.

> "O'er golden sands does rich Pactolus flow,
> "And trees weep amber on the banks of Po. ADDISON.

These poetical fictions belong to Utopian scenery: Anjengo groves were not of that delightful kind; there no verdant turf, or mossy bank, invited to repose; no purling streams, warbling bulbuls, or aromatic shrubs, regaled the senses; our slumbers were lulled by the roar of a tremendous surf; the atmosphere was impregnated with the fetid odour of fish to manure the rice-fields; and the arid sands in which the cocoa-trees were planted, offered no temptation for a walk. Without crossing the river, I had but little inducement to leave my house; which indeed was a cottage thatched with palmyra leaves, so small, that a sofa I carried from Bombay could not enter the door, and I remained in a veranda the whole time of my banishment. Without a road, carriages and horses would have been useless; our only recreation was sailing on the river, landing on its verdant banks, and strolling among the wilds; where, I allow, the scenery was delightful.

Most of the inhabitants of Anjengo are Christians of the Romish church; either descended from the Portugueze, or converted from the lower tribes of Malabars; a poor ignorant people, with whom we could not associate: many were fishermen; others made cordage and cables, from the coir, or husk of the cocoa-nut, a principal article of trade at Anjengo; where they also manufactured some common cotton cloth; but in the kingdom of Travencore were various and extensive manufactures of that article, which in every respect rivalled the *long-cloth* of the Carnatic. The English gentlemen traded in cassia, but the Company had the exclusive purchase and exportation of pepper. Among the Anjengo manufactures may be reckoned the trunks, travelling-cases, and camp-baskets, composed of cane-work, covered by a composition of quick-lime and butter-milk, mingled with a black powder, prepared from the burnt shells of cocoa-nuts: this is afterwards repeatedly varnished with the juice of a tree, common in Travencore, until it acquires a polished solidity capable of resisting the weather: two or three families excelled in gold and silver fillagree work, which they executed with the simplest implements; and imitated silver utensils of the best English fashion, with great facility and neatness.

I do not immediately recollect the Abbé Raynal's rhapsody at Anjengo: it implies, that however insignificant the settlement may be in itself, it will be for ever celebrated as the birth-place of *his* and *Sterne's* Eliza; a lady with whom I had the pleasure of being acquainted at Bombay; whose refined taste and elegant accomplishments require no encomiums from my pen. But it is, perhaps, not so generally known, that Anjengo gave birth to Robert Orme; a writer who has frequently been denominated the British Thucydides, and the Father of Oriental History; a man, as his epitaph modestly records, endeared to his friends by the gentleness of his manners; and respected by the public as the elegant historian of the military transactions of the British nation in India: a man, whose criticisms, or strictures upon style, were requested by Dr. Robertson, that his history might profit by one who had attended so much to the purity and elegance of language; and to whom Sir William Jones thus writes: "Your History of the Military Transactions in India, is not one of those books which a man reads once in a cursory manner, and then throws aside for ever; there is no end of reading and approving it; nor shall I ever desist giving myself that pleasure to the last year of my life. You may rely on this testimony, as it comes from one, who not only was never guilty of flattery; but, like Cæsar's wife, would never suffer himself to be suspected of it."

This amiable man was born at Anjengo in 1728, and died in England in 1801. I have occasionally introduced his sentiments in these volumes; his account of the Hindoo and Mahomedan inhabitants of Hindostan, their laws and justice, their manners and customs, and peculiar traits of character, is admirably correct, and his conclusion remarkably striking.

" Having finished this essay on the government and people of Hindostan, I cannot refrain from making the reflections which so obviously arise from the subject. Christianity vindicates all its glories, all its honour, and all its reverence, when we behold the most horrid impieties avowed amongst the nations on whom its influence does not shine, as actions necessary in the common conduct of life: I mean poisonings, treachery, and assassinations, in the sons of ambition; rapines, cruelty, and extortions in the ministers of justice. I leave divines to vindicate by more sanctified reflections, the cause of their religion and their God. The sons of liberty may here behold the mighty ills to which the slaves of a despotic power must be subject: the spirit darkened, and depressed by ignorance and fear; the body tortured and tormented by punishments, inflicted without justice and without measure: such a contrast to the blessings of liberty, heightens at once the sense of our happiness, and our zeal for the preservation of it."

The south-west monsoon generally sets in very early at Anjengo; it commences with great severity, and presents an awful spectacle: the inclement weather continues, with more or less violence, from May to October: during that period, the tempestuous ocean rolls from a black horizon, literally of "darkness visible," a series of floating mountains heaving under hoary summits, until they approach the shore, when their stupendous accumulations flow in successive surges, and break upon the beach: every ninth wave is observed to be generally more tremendous than the rest, and threatens to overwhelm the settlement. The noise of these billows equals that of the loudest cannon, and with the thunder and lightning, so frequent in the rainy season, is truly awful. During the tedious monsoon I passed at Anjengo, I often stood upon the trembling sand-bank, to contemplate the solemn scene, and derive a comfort from that sublime and omnipotent decree, "Hitherto shalt thou come, but no further; and here shall thy proud waves be stayed!"

My cottage and garden were so near the beach, that during the monsoon, the gauze curtains of the bed, although in a retired chamber, were constantly wet with a salt moisture, the glasses and pictures ran down with a briny fluid, and the vegetables in the garden were incrusted with salt. In that gloomy season, no vessel approaches the inhospitable shore; in the fair months, their boats never attempt passing through the surf, but wait at a distance, for the coming off of the light canoes, called *toneys*, to bring on shore the goods and passengers; who are never landed without trouble, and are sometimes exposed to danger: even then the sea is often so rough, that neither a canoe, nor even a catamaran, can put off; although the latter is only a small raft, on which the fishermen venture in severe weather to vessels in the offing: they are frequently overset, and the men washed off; yet they are such dexterous swimmers, as soon to regain their situation, and paddle away until their purpose is accomplished.

I shall not enter on the icthyology of the Malabar coast, except to mention the *hippocampus*, or sea-horse, which, in its dried state, forms a part of most European collections: it is not among the edible fish, though caught in great numbers with them: the hippocampus is generally from four to six inches in length, and two in circumference in the thickest part: the head and curvature of the neck resemble a horse; from whence a short swelling body gradually tapers to the extremity of the tail: some parts of its form are quadrangular, others hexangular, and the body has seven or eight divisions; the whole separated by ridges, and furnished with fins, to shape its course in its own element.

A principal amusement, during the rainy season, was to assemble at the bar of Anjengo river, to behold a curious contest, not only between the deities of the sea and the river, but also between the finny race in their respective dominions. In those months when the south-west monsoon blows with the greatest violence, the floods pour down from the mountains, swell the rivers, inundate the plains, and with astonishing rapidity, carry trees, houses, men, and beasts, to the ocean: the finny tribes, disturbed in their calm retreats, are impelled to the embouchure of the river: where, led by instinct, or accidentally driven by the monsoon winds, they meet the monsters of the deep ready to devour them. The floods from the mountains impetuously rush to this outlet, and there meet a sandy bar, accumulated by the western surges, which presents a formidable barrier between the contending waters: Neptune's terrific billows dash furiously against the river streams, precipitating over the bar, and present a scene easier to conceive than describe. The floods contain immense shoals of fish, which, unused to such violent convulsions, attempt to escape the noise and fury by leaping over the bar, into the distended jaws of the tyrants waiting to devour their timid prey. An alligator is sometimes involuntarily impelled to act a part in this extraordinary gymnasium; and of course perishes in the ocean.

Engraved by J. Shury.

VIEW OF GOA HARBOUR.

Jam. Forbes, 1772.

Published by White, Cochrane & Co. Fleet Street, June 1st 1812.

Engraved by J. Greig

View of the CITY *of* GOA, *from the River.* Jam. Forbes, 1772.

Published by White, Cochrane & Co. Fleet Street, June 1st 1812.

The MAZAGON MANGO of Bombay,
with the PAPILIO BOLINA or Purple-eyed Butterfly.

W. Hooker. fecit. Jam. Forbes, 1768.

Engraved by J. Storer [illegible]

TELLICHERRY on the Coast of MALABAR.

Jam Forbes, 1772.

Published by White, Cochrane & Co. Fleet Street, June 1st 1812.

Engrav'd by J. Shury

CALICUT, on the Coast of MALABAR. Jam. Forbes, 1775

Published by White, Cochrane & Co. Fleet Street June 1st 1812.

Engraved by J. Alay.

COCHIN *on the Coast of* MALABAR.

Jam Forbes 1772.

Published by White, Cochrane & Co. Fleet Str. Febr 1st 1812

Engraved by J. Storey

ANJENGO, on the Coast of MALABAR. Jam Forbes, 1772

Published by White, Cochrane & Co. Fleet Street, June 1st 1812

CHAPTER XII.

CONTAINING

THE NATURAL HISTORY OF ANJENGO;

AND THE SOUTHERN PART OF THE COAST OF MALABAR.

1772.

Learn from the birds what food the thickets yield;
Learn from the beasts the physic of the field:
Thy arts of building from the bee receive;
Learn of the mole to plough, the worm to weave;
Learn of the little nautilus to sail,
Spread the thin oar, and catch the driving gale.
Here subterranean works and cities see;
There towns aëreal on the waving tree.
Learn each small people's genius, policies,
The ant's republic, and the realm of bees;
How those in common all their wealth bestow,
And anarchy without confusion know;
And these for ever, though a monarch reign,
Their separate cells and properties maintain.
Mark what unvaried laws preserve each state,
Laws, wise as Nature, and as fix'd as Fate. Pope.

CONTENTS.

Reasons for leaving Anjengo—natural history of Travencore—beauty of the lakes and rivers—mountain scenery and solitary wilds—cultivation of pepper, and value of the produce—cassia lignea, and cinnamon—oil plants—olive tree—silk cotton—wild animals—wild buffaloe particularly described—civet cat; mode of extracting the perfume—crocodile and alligator; that of India in its form and character; battle between the alligator and royal tiger—crocodile of scripture—ichneumon—seal of Travencore rivers—birds of Travencore—beauty of the paroquets—devastations by the Malabar parrots—bird of Attinga—crescent snake—black amphisbœna—number of noxious reptiles—termites, or white ants, their extraordinary depredations; anecdotes of these marauders—public roads shaded by trees—gold dust in Malabar rivers—iron mines, forges, and smelting-houses in Malabar—salt-pans—molungies or salt-boilers of Bengal, their wretched situation in the Sunderbunds.

CHAPTER XII.

The climate of Anjengo not agreeing with my constitution, and the situation I held affording no emolument equivalent to the sacrifice of my friends and a delightful society at Bombay, at the expiration of the year I obtained permission to return there, and wait for some other appointment.

During my residence at Anjengo, I endeavoured to acquire a topographical knowledge of that part of Malabar; and the manners and customs of the natives of Travencore: its natural history opens a very ample field for investigation, and the inhabitants differ in many respects from the northern Hindoos.

The sandy soil on the sea coast is planted with extensive woods of cocoa nuts; beyond the river are fruitful fields of rice, natchnee, and other grain; large plantations of pepper and groves of cassia; which add a delicious fragrance to the morning breeze.

Although not partial to Anjengo as a residence, I never made a distant excursion without being charmed with the beauty of the country, and the variety of its rivers: sometimes we glide through narrow devious channels, between steep craggy rocks, with woody summits, where the branches uniting over the stream, form a verdant canopy, impervious to the tropical sun: from these dark recesses we suddenly emerge into an extensive lake

"pure as the expanse of heaven;"

again we enter a romantic scene of rocks and woods, or pursue the serpentine course of a broad gentle river, fringed by odoriferous plants, and encircling many verdant islands, some inhabited, others woody and wild: these scenes are animated by beautiful birds; and the waters abound with excellent fish. Cultivation extends to some distance eastward of the rivers; from thence to the foot of the Gaut mountains the country is an entire forest, never frequented by travellers, and little known even by those who live in its vicinity: there, amid the solemn stillness of uncultivated nature, I have ranged for miles, rapt in solitary musings.

These excursions were my chief enjoyment at Anjengo: the fertile plains, the hills clothed by mango, cashers, and cassia trees, bounded by the stupendous Gauts, towering in rude magnificence, formed a landscape not often exceeded; its grandeur was augmented when seen from the heights of Eddova and Quilone; where I have often beheld the sun majestically rising above the summit of the eastern mountains, and throwing a broad expanse of light over the western sea. In such situations we experience the truth of Addison's remark, that "our imagination loves to be "filled with an object, or to grasp at any thing that is too big for "our capacity: we are flung into a pleasing astonishment at "such unbounded views, and feel a delightful stillness and amaze-"ment in the soul, at the apprehension of them."

Among the various productions of the southern districts in Malabar are the pepper-vine, and cassia, (piper nigrum, & laurus cassia, Lin.) The former is a staple commodity at Anjengo, and grows on a beautiful vine, which, incapable of supporting itself, entwines round poles prepared for it, or, as is more common in the Travencore plantations, the pepper-vines are planted near mango and other trees of straight high stems, which being stripped of the lower branches, the vine embraces the trunk, covering it with elegant festoons, and rich bunches of fruit, in the picturesque style of the vineyards in Campagna Felice. The mango and jac trees are generally used for this purpose; few pepper gardens contain more than eight or ten trees: the vines are planted near the trunk, and led to it while young; the stem is tough, knotty, and strong: some begin to bear in the fourth year, others not till the sixth; they are in perfection about the ninth or tenth year, and continue bearing as many years longer, if in a congenial soil; from that period the vine gradually decays; a new soil is then prepared for a considerable depth round the tree, for the reception of fresh shoots from flourishing vines.

The leaf of the pepper plant is large, and of a bright green; the blossoms appear in June, soon after the commencement of the rains; they are small, of a greenish white; succeeded by bunches of green berries, which turn brown and hard as they ripen: the pepper is gathered in February, and has the same appearance as in Europe. The flavour of pepper is more or less communicated to the fruit of the tree which supports it; a circumstance not at all relished by the proprietor, as many mangoes taste strong of turpentine, and are not improved by the additional pungency of pepper.

Assiduity and cleanliness are essentially necessary in a pepper garden; not a weed is permitted to grow; the produce, however, amply compensates the trouble: for although the Anjengo pepper is not so much esteemed as that produced at Onore and Carwar, it is sold, on an average, at eighty rupees a candy; five hundred and sixty English pounds weight. It is treason to destroy a pepper-vine in Travencore, where the king monopolizes that branch of commerce; but permits the merchants of Anjengo to have a free trade with his subjects in cassia, coir, cables and cordage, made from the outer husk of the cocoa-nut.

As warehousekeeper at Anjengo, I received all the pepper purchased by the Company from the king of Travencore; whose agents brought it to the warehouses, and delivered it by the maund, a weight of twenty-eight pounds: I kept a particular account of the quantity annually received from the Travencore country, together with the average price, per candy; but the changes in Malabar, since the death of Tippoo Sultan, render those documents less interesting than the observations at a later period by Dr. F. Buchanan, respecting the general produce of pepper in the Malabar province, which has now become a national concern.

" Before the invasion of Hyder Ally, in 1764, that country produced annually about fifteen thousand candies, of six hundred and forty pounds each: from that period the crop has gradually diminished to half the quantity: so that a good season will now produce only eight thousand candies; a bad one not more than four thousand. Europeans usually purchase about five-eighths of all the pepper that is produced in Malabar; and the price which they give absolutely regulates that of the whole. Since the French have been driven from Mahie, the whole of this has of course fallen into the hands of the Company."

"In 1797 the Company exported four thousand one hundred and fifty five candies of Malabar pepper, of six hundred pounds each; which was the largest exportation during seventeen years: since the capture of Mahie, in 1793, the Company has, according to Maccay, sent annually about four thousand candies to Europe direct, to Bombay, and to China. The remainder of the pepper is exported chiefly by native traders. The largest quantity goes to the Bay of Bengal; the next largest to Surat, Cutch, Scindy, and other ports in the north-west of India; and a considerable quantity goes to the Arabian merchants of Muscat, Mocha, Hodeida, Aden, and Judda. The demand from Seringapatam was the smallest, and used to amount to about five hundred candies a year. The pepper that went to Coimbetore came chiefly from the Cochin and Travencore dominions."

"The Company have always made their purchases by a contract entered into with a few native merchants. In December and January, when the crops are so far advanced that judgment can be formed of the quantity of pepper likely to be obtainable, the commercial resident assembles the contractors, and a written agreement is entered into with them, settling the price, and the quantity that each is to deliver: at this time, sometimes the whole, and in general at least one half of the money is advanced to the contractors. The contract for pepper in 1800, was five thousand candies, at one hundred and thirty rupees the candy, of six hundred pounds; the price varies from one hundred to one hundred and forty rupees; and a contract was made for four thousand candies, in 1794, at two hundred rupees the candy."

The same writer mentions that, in the year 1757, the king of Travencore having received some assistance from the English was willing to favour their commerce: on this occasion Mr. Spencer, the English chief of Anjengo, took an account of the pepper produced in the dominions of that prince, where there was no land-tax, but where the king monopolized all the pepper, and gave the cultivators a fixed price for whatever they could raise. The whole quantity of pepper raised in the dominions of Travencore amounted to eleven thousand seven hundred candies; for this the king gave to the cultivators thirty rupees a candy. The amount of the sales, even including two thousand candies that were given to the English Company at the low price of eighty-two rupees, came to 13,12,260 rupees, or on an average one hundred and eleven rupees a candy: the king did not, therefore, allow the cultivators more than twenty-seven per cent. of the produce; yet the cultivation was carried on with the greatest spirit.

The cassia resembles the bay-tree, of which it is a species: it is called cassia lignea, to distinguish it from the laurus-cinnamomum, or true cinnamon, to which it is very inferior: the finest cassia sometimes possesses the peculiar properties of that valuable spice, but is in general of a coarser texture and less delicate flavour. The real cinnamon seems indigenous to Ceylon; there are some trees in the Company's garden at Anjengo, as a curiosity. The leaves of the cassia are smaller than the laurel, and more pointed; those of the cinnamon still more delicate: the blossoms of both, like the flowers of the Arbutus, hang in bunches, white and fragrant; the fruit resembles a small acorn. The young leaves and tender shoots are of a bright red, changing to green as they approach maturity; they taste of cinnamon, but the only valuable part of the tree is the inner bark; which being separated from the exterior, is cut into pieces, and exposed to the sun, when it dries and curls up, and is packed in cases for foreign markets. The tree decaying on being deprived of its bark is cut down, and new shoots spring from the root; it is also raised from seed.

The Travencore country abounds with indigenous trees, whose blossoms and foliage have a pleasing and diversified appearance; most of the fruit and seeds produce oil; one by way of distinction is called the olive-tree, and bears a fruit in shape, size, and taste like the olive; and the oil is rather pleasant; but the leaf and character of the tree is altogether different, and far more beautiful in landscape than the grey tint of the Italian olive.

The silk-cotton tree (bombax cerba, Lin.) grows luxuriantly in those districts: it produces beautiful cotton, but of too delicate a texture for manufacture. This tree is extremely curious in its growth; the branches regularly project in horizontal stages, gradually diminishing as they approach the top, forming in the Malabar woods a crimson pyramid, of singular appearance; the flower resembles a single peony, or round tulip, of bright red, succeeded by a pod, in size and shape like a plantain, green at first, but ripening to a dark brown, when it bursts open, and covers the adjoining groves with snowy flakes, light as the floating gossamer.

The animals in the southern provinces and mountainous regions of Malabar are tigers, leopards, elephants, buffaloes, hogs, civet-cats, and a variety of monkeys and squirrels; some of the monkeys are large, and covered with black glossy hair, except a very full white beard and mustachios; which give them a venerable, and almost a human appearance.

The wild buffaloe is common in many parts of Travencore: I had never before been in a country where these animals were indigenous. The Malabars, and especially the Nairs, form large hunting parties to destroy them, as also the wild elephant, tiger, and leopard. They assemble by hundreds, armed with strong spears, and large bows and arrows: forming a circle round the thickets frequented by the wild beasts, they make a loud noise to rouse them from cover, and drive them towards the centre: then gradually contracting the circle, they unite in an armed phalanx, and fall upon their prey, of which very few escape: but they sometimes wound each other in their furious onset, and often sustain dreadful attacks from their enraged foe.

The buffaloe is one of the strongest and most formidable of the savage race; with short horns, powerful neck, and large tuft of hair on the head. It is justly remarked in the oriental field-sports, that his aspect is extremely fierce; he seems to look with disdain on every living object, and to rely on the great strength he possesses, to overthrow whatever may be opposed to his rage. The smallest provocation irritates him incredibly! and such is his courage, that he will sometimes attack even a group of elephants going for fodder. There cannot be a more menacing object than a single wild buffaloe, disturbed from wallowing in the mud. His looks are ferocious in the extreme; and the knowledge of his brutal disposition by no means allays the apprehensions to which his countenance and gestures give birth: the whole race, whether wild or tame, have an eye full of mischief, and are never, on any occasion, to be trusted."

It is commonly understood that Providence has allotted to every animal a climate suited to its nature; and a general review, throughout the universe, will add no small weight to this opinion. Whether it be from the original order of things, as arranged by the Great Founder of the world; or, that, supposing some chance to exist, such animals as were not in their habits or constitutions, suited to particular soils, or temperatures, necessarily perished, and became extinct in such situations, we find the most marked attention to that system. But to this general rule we have to plead one exception: namely, that the buffaloe of India is by no means suited to the climate of the country: that animal not only delights in the water, but will not thrive unless it have a swamp to wallow in: there rolling themselves, they speedily work deep hollows, wherein they lay immersed. No place seems to delight the buffaloe more than the deep verdure on the confines of pools and marshes, especially if surrounded by tall grass, so as to afford concealment and shade, while the body is covered by the water: in such situations they seem to enjoy a perfect extasy; having in general nothing above the surface, but their eyes and nostrils, the horns being kept low down, and consequently entirely hidden from view.

The civet-cat (viverra civetta, Lin.) so called, though not of the feline, but weasel genus, is a very ferocious animal, and unless taken young, extremely difficult to tame: it is larger than a common cat, the body and feet shaded with dark stripes over a brindled brown; the head, eyes, and ears resemble a large rat, their food consists of birds, mice and reptiles, for which they insidiously watch, and seize with wonderful eagerness: I kept one for some time in a wooden cage, but the smell at length became so insufferable, that I gave him liberty; for, however the perfume may be esteemed, the odour of the animal is always disagreeable. The civet, or musk, is formed in a glandular receptacle under the tail, from whence it is squeezed out by little at a time, twice or thrice a week; it is then an offensive unguent like thick greasy milk, but afterwards changes to a hard brown substance. A full grown cat always yields more of this perfume when first caught, than after it has been any time confined.

The eastern districts of Travencore, intersected by lakes and rivers, abound with amphibious animals, especially alligators and seals. There seems to be no essential difference between the alligator of India, and the Egyptian crocodile; lacerta alligator, and lacertus crocodilus. Naturalists seem to confine the alligator to South America, the crocodile to Asia and Africa; but in India the lacerta crocodilus, generally called the alligator, is from five to twenty feet long, shaped like the genus to which he belongs: the back is covered with impenetrable scales; the legs short, with five spreading toes on the fore-feet, and four in a straight line on the hinder, armed with claws: the alligator moves slowly, its whole formation being calculated for strength, the back-bone firmly jointed, and the tail a most formidable weapon: in the river he eagerly springs on the wretch unfortunately bathing within his reach, and either knocks him down with his tail, or opens a wide mouth for his destruction, armed with numerous sharp teeth of various length; by which, like the shark, he sometimes severs the human body at a single bite: the annals of the Nile and Ganges, although wonderful, are not fabulous. The upper jaw only of the alligator was thought to be moveable; that is now completely disproved: the eyes are of a dull green, with a brilliant pupil, covered by a transparent pellicle, moveable as in birds: from the heads of those of large size, musk is frequently extracted.

The alligator sometimes basks in the sun-beams on the banks of the river, but oftener floats on its surface; there, concealing his head and feet, he appears like the rough trunk of a tree, both in shape and colour: by this deception dogs and other animals fearlessly approach, and are suddenly plunged to the bottom by their insidious foe: even the royal tiger becomes his prey, quitting the cover to drink at the river; the wily alligator, concealed under water, steals along the bank, and suddenly emerging, furiously attacks the tiger, who never declines the combat: the alligator generally loses his eyes, and receives dreadful wounds on the head, but at length plunges his adversary into an unnatural element, and there devours him.

The astonishing size and strength of the alligator and crocodile render them very terrible: the small ones live chiefly on fish; and, far from attacking the human species, dive instantly on their approach: the female sometimes lays three or four hundred eggs, which she covers with sand to be vivified by the sun; in about a month the brood break the shell and instinctively take to the water. I kept a small one several months in a garden pool, but growing large and destructive to my poultry, I set him at liberty.

I shall conclude this desultory account of the alligator, with a few passages from the sublime description of the Egyptian crocodile in the book of Job. "Canst thou draw out leviathan with a hook, or his tongue with a cord? canst thou fill his skin with barbed irons, or his head with fish-spears? Lay thine hand upon him, remember the battle, do no more! none is so fierce that dare stir him up; shall not one be cast down even at the sight of him? who can open the doors of his face? his teeth are terrible round about: his scales are his pride, shut up together, as with a close seal; one is so near to another, that no air can come between them: they are joined one to another; they stick together, that they cannot be sundered. By his neesings a light doth shine; and his eyes are like the eye-lids of the morning; out of his mouth go burning lamps, and sparks of fire leap out; out of his nostrils goeth smoke, as out of a seething pot, or caldron. In his neck remaineth strength; his heart is firm as a stone; the sword of him that layeth at him cannot hold; the spear, the dart, nor the habergeon: for he esteemeth iron as straw, and brass as rotten wood: darts are counted as stubble, he laugheth at the shaking of a spear. Upon earth there is not his like, who is made without fear!"

The ichneumon, or mongouse (viverra ichneumon, Lin.) which is said to destroy the eggs of the crocodile on the banks of the Nile, are equally destructive to those of the alligator, deposited near the rivers of Travencore; where these useful animals abound; they also devour the young ones on shore, as their food is vermin, and reptiles of every description: they are enemies to serpents, with whom they wage perpetual war; and when wounded by their poisonous fangs, instinctively go to an herbaceous antidote, with which they are well acquainted. This animal was adored by the ancient Egyptians for his national services; and is domesticated by their descendants, to destroy rats, mice, and other vermin. The ichneumon is formed, like the weasel, with a slender head, long nose, bright eyes, very sharp teeth, and a long coat of hair beautifully brindled, often shining like silver. It sometimes springs suddenly on its prey with wonderful agility; at others, it steals insidiously among the high grass and bushes, and seizes it unawares: it is very courageous, and frequently attacks animals much larger than itself.

The salt waters of Travencore abound with a seal of that species, which is called phoca pusilla, an animal seemingly between the beaver and the otter, in some respects partaking of both, and differing from the phoca vitulina, and others of the genus, found on the rocky islands of the ocean. The Travencore seal has a round head, short ears, thick neck, tapering body, and flat tail, like a fish; it is web-footed, and the skin covered with a soft oily hair: this amphibious creature, uniting in so many respects the quadruped with the aquatic animal, seems to link the two species in the great chain of creation: they vary in size and appearance in different countries; at Anjengo they seldom exceed four feet in length: they are gregarious and sociable; form parties on the banks of the rivers, but always plunge in at the approach of a stranger.

The birds in the southern parts of Malabar, as in most tropical climates, are gaily clothed; but less melodious than the northern songsters. The parroquets are remarkably handsome; the head shaded with red, purple, and blue, finishes in a black circle round the neck, from whence to its long tapering tail the plumage is a lively green: the parrots are not so beautiful, but their number is astonishing: they are as much dreaded at the time of harvest as a Mahratta army, or a host of locusts: they darken the air by their numbers, and alighting on a rice-field, in a few hours carry off every ear of ripe corn to their hiding places in the mountains: I have often witnessed these depredations, and thought of Pope's significant queries:

> Is thine alone the seed that strews the plain?
> The birds of heaven *shall vindicate* their grain.
> Thine the full harvest of the golden year?
> Part pays, and justly, the deserving steer.

The bird of Attinga, or pied bird of Paradise (picus orientalis, Lin.) is common in the queen of Attinga's dominions; its elegant form, purple crest, snowy plumage, and long tail, constitute it one of the most beautiful in the Indian ornithology.

Like most other countries between the tropics, Anjengo is infested by a variety of noxious insects and reptiles: the most curious is a small black snake, called by the natives the crescent snake, though I should rather class it with the polypus: it is two or three inches long, with a head shaped like a crescent; from the outer line of the semicircle are small teeth, easily discerned through a microscope; I could not discover any eyes: on cutting off this head, the other end immediately supplied the loss; it moves in a retrograde manner, and lives after the amputation: it is entirely covered with a glossy slime, which, like the snail, it leaves wherever it goes: this is said to be poisonous, and the bite mortal; a characteristic often ascribed to the Indian serpents without foundation.

There was also at Anjengo a small black species of the amphisbœna, or double-headed snake. The tail is shaped and marked so like the head, as not to be easily distinguished from it. The idea of the amphisbœna having two heads, with perfect organs, is erroneous; but as it proceeds, at pleasure, with either head or tail foremost, this opinion has been adopted. The bite of this snake is also reputed mortal by the natives; but being, like the former, destitute of fangs, the usual conveyance of a serpent's poison, I am doubtful of its malignity.

The houses at Anjengo, being mostly thatched with the matted leaves of the cocoa-nut tree, afford shelter to snakes, scorpions, centipedes, lizards, and insects of all descriptions.

I mentioned the termites, or white ants of Bombay; these extraordinary insects are far more numerous and destructive at Anjengo, where it is difficult to guard against their depredations: in a few hours they will demolish a large chest of books, papers, silk, or clothes, perforating them with a thousand holes: we dare not leave a box on the floor without placing it on glass bottles, which, if kept free from dust, they cannot ascend: this is trifling, when compared with the serious mischief they sometimes occasion, by penetrating the beams of a house, or destroying the timbers in a ship;

> Where in some gallant ship, that long has bore
> Britain's victorious cross from shore to shore,
> By chance, beneath her close sequester'd cells
> Some low-born worm a lurking mischief dwells;

Eats his blind way, and saps with secret guile
The deep foundations of the floating pile.
In vain the forest lent its stateliest pride,
Rear'd her tall mast, and fram'd her knotty side;
The martial thunder's rage in vain she stood,
With every conflict of the stormy flood;
More sure the reptile's little arts devour
Than wars, or waves, or Eurus' wintry pow'r. WARTON.

These destructive animals advance by myriads to their work, under an arched incrustation of fine sand, tempered with a moisture from their body, which renders the covert-way as hard as burnt clay, and effectually conceals them at their insidious employment.

I could mention many curious instances of depredation by the termites; one happened to myself: I left Anjengo in the rainy season to pass a few weeks with the chief at his country house at Eddova, in a rural and sheltered situation. On my departure, I locked up a room, containing books, drawings, and a few valuables; as I took the key with me, the servant could not enter to clean the furniture: the walls of the room were white-washed, adorned with prints and drawings, in English frames and glasses: returning home in the evening, and taking a cursory view of my cottage by candle-light, I found every thing apparently in the same order as I left it; but on a nearer inspection the next morning, I observed a number of advanced works, in various directions, towards my pictures; the glasses appeared to be uncommonly dull, and the frames covered with dust: on attempting to wipe it off, I was astonished to find the glasses fixed to the wall, not suspended in frames as I left them, but completely surrounded by an incrustation cemented by the white ants; who had actually eat up the deal frames and back-boards, and the greater part of the paper, and left the glasses upheld by the incrustation, or covered-way, which they had formed during their depredation. From the flat Dutch bottles, on which the drawers and boxes were placed, not having been wiped during my absence, the ants had ascended the bottles by means of the dust, eat through the bottom of a chest, and made some progress in perforating the books and linen. The chief's lady with whom I had been staying at Eddova, on returning to her apartments in the fort, found, from the same cause, a large chest, in which she had deposited shawls, muslins, and other articles, collected preparatory to her leaving India, entirely destroyed by these voracious insects.

The story of the termites demolishing a chest of dollars at Bencoolen, is commonly told, if not commonly credited throughout India. Captain Williamson in a great degree clears up that singular anecdote, by introducing another of a gentleman who having charge of a chest of money, unfortunately placed it on the floor in a damp situation; the chest was speedily attacked by the white ants, who had their burrow just under the place where the treasure stood. They soon annihilated the bottom, and were not more ceremonious in respect to the bags containing the specie; which being thus let loose, fell gradually into the hollows in the ants' burrow. When the cash was called for, all were amazed at the wonderful powers, both of the teeth and stomachs, of the little marauders, which were supposed to have consumed the silver as well as the wood. After some years the house requiring repair, the whole sum was found several feet deep in the earth; and the termites were rescued from that obloquy which the supposed power of feasting on precious metals had cast on their whole race! The captain does not give this story on his own authority; but adds, "the cunning of the white ants is truly admirable. They ordinarily work within plastering, occasionally appearing externally, and forming a shelter, by means of earth; which though taken from situations apparently dry as powder, when worked up, is perfectly moist. Whence they derive the moisture is not yet known. In this manner they construct a kind of tunnel, or arched passage, sufficient to admit passing each other in their way up and down, with surprizing rapidity. Hence they not only arrive unseen, though their ways are obvious, at any part of a house; but, when from finding such articles as they might else attack, insulated by means of frames, of which the feet are placed in vessels full of water, they have been known to ascend to the upper flooring, and thence to work downwards in filaments, like the ramifications of the roots of a tree; and thus descend to their object. In fact it is scarcely possible to prevent them from injuring whatever they take a fancy to."

When a bear finds a nest of any kind of ants, but especially white ants, he demolishes the whole burrow: licking up all the clusters he can get at; and lying with his tongue out, to entice the prey into his mouth: by this means he often obtains an ample meal; for a bushel of them may frequently be found in the same nest. The white ant is about the size of a small grain of rice; has a white body, appearing like a maggot, and a very strong red head, armed with powerful forceps: it has four short legs. They are an article of food among some of the low castes in Mysore, and the Carnatic.

A nest of these extraordinary insects, in a very singular situation, is mentioned in the drama of Sacontala. "A little beyond "the grove you see a pious Yogee, motionless as a pollard, hold-"ing his thick bushy hair, and fixing his eyes on the solar orb! "Mark; his body is half covered with a white-ants' edifice made "of raised clay; the skin of a snake supplies the place of his "sacerdotal thread, and part of it girds his loins; a number of "knotty plants encircle and wound his neck; and surrounding "birds'-nests almost conceal his shoulders."

In the king of Travencore's dominions are some useful public works, but nothing comparable to those in the northern parts of Hindostan: among other beneficial undertakings of the former sovereigns are rows of chashew-apple trees on each side of the principal public roads, extending for many miles: these trees are shady, and beautiful in foliage, blossoms, and fruit. Formerly the road from Lahore to Agra, a distance of near five hundred miles, was in the same manner shaded by large trees; and where there was a deficiency of wells, persons were placed in small arbours at convenient distances, to supply water gratis, to the traveller.

Gold dust is said to be sometimes found in the Nelambur river and other mountainous torrents of Malabar; iron is certainly produced in many places, where they have erected forges for smelting it; these are capable of much improvement. Dr. F. Buchanan, who had excellent opportunities of ascertaining the fact, and whose knowledge of mineralogy gives him a decided advantage over most other travellers, observes, that in the hills of the southern district of Malabar the " iron ore is found, forming beds, veins, or detached masses, in the stratum of indurated clay, of which the greater part of those hills consists; the ore is composed of clay, quartz in form of sand, and of the common black iron sand: this mixture forms small angular nodules closely compacted together, and very friable: it is dug out with a pick-axe, and broken into powder with the same instrument; it is then washed in a wooden trough, about four feet in length, open at both ends, and placed in the current of a rivulet; so that a gentle stream of water runs constantly through it. The metallic sand remains in the upper end of the trough, the quartz is carried to the lower end, the clay is suspended in the water, and washed entirely away. In this ore the quantity of metallic sand is small, in comparison with that of the earthy matter."

At Velater in Malabar this judicious writer observed thirty-four forges for smelting iron; he gives a long description of the process, from which the forges appear very defective compared with similar works in Europe. Each smelting requires 2160 lb. of washed ore, which costs about three pence halfpenny the hundred weight: the process obtains only from eleven to seventeen per cent. of iron from the ore, and what is produced is very imperfect; the Malabar iron sells at seven and eight shillings the hundred weight, but is in all respects very inferior to that imported from Europe. This comparison seems to give force and beauty to a passage in the prophecy of Jeremiah, denouncing judgment on the Jews; "shall iron break the northern iron and the steel?"

Salt-pans, or rather salt-fields, are formed in Travencore, as in most other parts of the Malabar coast: they are large reservoirs enclosed by mounds of earth, into which the sea flows at high tides; from whence, by a simple process, the water is conveyed into a range of small enclosures, where in the course of the day the fluid is evaporated, and the salt gathered in the evening. These reservoirs are most productive in the hot months preceding the rainy season; and from every part of the coast salt forms the chief article of inland commerce.

These salt-pans being generally near populous towns and villages, the men employed there are not more exposed to tigers and beasts of prey, than those occupied in the usual pursuits of husbandry: not so the Molungies, or salt-boilers, in the Sunderbunds, or wild regions of Bengal; who, of all the castes and tribes throughout the whole extent of Hindostan, seem to have the hardest fate: I would rather be a Pariah or Chandala, subject to their most ignominious treatment, and cruel oppression, than one of these unfortunate Molungies living in constant terror from the fiercest tigers, without any means of safety or redress. Their situation had often been represented to me by gentlemen from Bengal, and as often excited my commiseration; but I had no idea of their complete misery until I read the account of the Sunderbunds by captain Williamson; where, he says, "the royal tigers are often seen swimming across the various rivers which form the innumerable islands inhabited only by wild beasts, and presenting an immense barrier all along the sea-coast, from *Saugur* island to the great mouth of the Megna. Of this propensity in tigers the *Molungies* are so thoroughly aware, that, while performing their duties on the long spits of sand which project into the sea, from the impenetrable jungles that skirt the soil, a look-out is always kept for tigers on the opposite banks of the rivers; and as soon as any appear, the whole take to flight, and conceal themselves in caves excavated for the purpose; from which, it however sometimes happens, the hungry animal removes every obstacle with his claws, and drags out one or more of the inhabitants, already half dead with terror."

"The reader will naturally inquire, why some means are not adopted for opposing devastations of this nature, and for securing the *Molungies* from such a dreadful misfortune? The fact is, that no one is a *Molungie* from choice; but, according to the principle prevailing throughout Hindostan, the occupation of the father and his ancestors is continued invariably by his posterity. The *Molungies* would, however, readily deviate from this principle if they had the power to do so; but, being kept to their posts by various guards of revenue peons, or officers, they are unable to quit their miserable situation. These revenue officers are, in addition to some provincial militia, posted at all the places whereby it is possible to escape in boats: as to making off by land, it would be utterly impossible; the surrounding country being an immense wilderness, full of tigers, abounding in snakes, and intersected by a labyrinth of rapid waters, replete with alligators and other reptiles. This unfortunate race of human beings sometimes obtains an addition to their number when trespassers attempt to escape from the pursuit of justice, and to wind through the mazes of the inland navigation. These are handed over to the salt-pans, whence not one in a million ever returns. To arm persons of such a description, would be to afford them an immediate emancipation; and would subvert that establishment which supplies Bengal with salt, and affords to the government a revenue not much under a million of money annually! No doubt but time will furnish the means of substituting some less objectionable means of providing so indispensable an article of consumption, and do away what must, till then, be classed among the many necessary evils with which humanity is burthened!

A HINDOO TEMPLE, *near* EDDOVA *in* TRAVENCORE.

Jam Forbes 1772

The CAJEW or CASHEW APPLE of Malabar.

W. Hooker fecit. Jam. Forbes, Anjengo 1772.

CHAPTER XIII.

AN ACCOUNT OF THE INHABITANTS IN THE KINGDOM OF TRAVENCORE; AND PARTICULARLY OF THE BRAHMINS, NAIRS, AND POOLEAHS, IN THE SOUTHERN PARTS OF THE MALABAR COAST.

1773.

> In links of steel, here superstition binds
> The unsuspecting native; to his caste
> Tethers him; cramps his powers, condemns to ply,
> With joyless hands, the trade his sires have plied
> For centuries; proscribes all hope of change!
>
> GISBORNE.

CONTENTS.

tribes mentioned by Herodotus—their manners and customs illustrated by those of the Malabars—Paramahansa—Hindoo anthropophagi—further particulars of the Pooleahs and Pariars—Moplahs, Mahomedan Malabars—their character, ferocity, manners, and customs—run-a-muck—massacre of the English at Attinga—queen of Attinga, a shadow of royalty—interesting particulars of the St. Thomé, or Syrian Christians in the interior of Malabar.

CHAPTER XIII.

In describing the Hindoos, the aborigines of Hindostan, I divided them into four principal tribes, the Brahmin, Chuttree, Byse, and Sooder; subdivided into a number of smaller castes: the Malabars in this distinguishing characteristic, and many other essentials, resemble the northern Hindoos: as a nation, their four grand divisions are the Brahmins, Nairs, Thivees, and Pooleahs.

The Malabar brahmins, like those in other parts of India, form two distinct classes, engaged in different pursuits: both are held sacred by the other castes: one has the absolute and entire management of every thing relating to religion: occupied by no secular concerns, they spend their days under the sacred groves of their temples in superstitious ceremonies, and listless indolence, or study the sacred volumes, treatises on astrology, medicine, and fabulous legends; they inculcate benevolence to man, and kindness to the animal creation, and are reverenced by the inferior tribes, who swear by their heads, and treat them with filial affection.

The brahmins who live in large towns, and hold situations under their respective princes, as officers of government, collectors of the revenue, and other political departments, do not merit this amiable character: they may, on the contrary, be classed with the despots so often mentioned, who unfeelingly exercise the rod of oppression over the lives and property of their fellow-creatures: although, by a strange inconsistency, these very people are taught to shudder at the death of an insect, and tremble at the idea of inhaling an animalcule. Superstition leads her votaries to the most extraordinary actions; during my residence among the Malabars, where the ignominious distinction of castes is carried to the utmost extent, I was fully convinced that it puts a stop to the noblest exertions of *real* charity, blunts the finest feelings of humanity, and estranges man from man.

The Malabar brahmins, like the rest of that priesthood, have such faith in the purifying waters of the Ganges, as to believe their sins are absolved by a pilgrimage thither, or even by their virtue when transported to a distant country. The Ganges, Kistna, and Indus, enjoy this preeminence among the numerous rivers of Hindostan; they fertilize the finest tracts in its extensive plains: the Nerbudda, and other northern streams, claim a share of veneration; but I did not hear of any peculiar sanctity annexed to the rivers of Malabar: all waters excite a sentiment of affection and gratitude in a people whose climate and religion require such frequent ablutions, and where shade is so desirable, that the banian tree, and many others, are deemed sacred. In their fertile imagination all nature is animated by an endless number and infinite variety of inferior deities and benevolent spirits; who occupy every grove, preside over every fountain, and fill the heavens and the earth with forms invisible to mortal eyes.

The Malabars regard the cow with as much superstitious veneration as the northern Hindoos; and, if possible, are more severe in their punishment of those who ill-treat them, or cause their death: a subject of Travencore who is detected in selling a bullock to an European is impaled alive. Religious prejudice operates powerfully in the preservation of this animal; but it is politic in a country where milk forms a great part of the food, and oxen are very useful in commerce and agriculture.

Irrigation being absolutely necessary in a climate where rain only falls during four months in the year, the preservation of water is a most important object; the brahmins, therefore, judiciously persuade their disciples to build reservoirs, and construct wells, as the most acceptable charity they can confer: in the Travencore dominions are many expensive works of this kind; some made by the generosity of individuals, others at the public expense. The high roads are planted on each side with cajew-apple, tamarind, and mango-trees; which adorn the country, and shade the traveller: caravansaries, or choultries, are erected at convenient distances for his accommodation. Charity of this kind is every where inculcated; and it is equally the ambition of a southern Malabar as of a northern Hindoo, to have a tank, a well, or a choultrie, called after his name. Under despotic princes, where property is never secure, and to be reputed rich is to be really unfortunate, such munificent acts are far from being uncommon: the fame of these benevolent works, and the tranquillity of domestic life, form the chief happiness of a people unaccustomed to public spectacles, or the refinements of polished society.

The Nairs of Malabar are equally brave, and more energetic than most of the warlike Hindoos; the national characteristics of both people are otherwise very similar. A mild climate, and the peculiar tenets of their religion, inspire meekness, temperance, and listlessness: they abstain from intoxicating liquors, are seldom guilty of debaucheries, and not subject to many of those passions which enslave the civilized Europeans.

Strangers to patriotism, and the blessings of liberty, the Malabars, as well as the northern Hindoos, are governed by fear; loyalty and affection form no part of their political system: amongst such a people, ambition has no scope: every man is confined to his own caste, follows the profession of his ancestors, is married in childhood to his equal, and never rises higher than the limited sphere in which he was born: there may be exceptions, but they are very uncommon. One indeed of an extraordinary nature, occurred during my residence in Travencore: the reigning sovereign, who was of an inferior caste of Brahmins, advanced himself into a higher, by purifications, gifts, and ceremonies; part of which consisted in his majesty passing through the body of a cow, of the size of life, and made of pure gold: this was the last stage of purification; and when performed, the cow was divided among the Brahmins.* It is said, that Ragonath Row, the Mahratta paishwa,

* Orme ascribes a different cause for the king of Travencore's regeneration to that given to me by his subjects, who, perhaps, were withheld by fear from assigning the true reason. "The king of Travencore has conquered, or carried war into all the countries which lay round his dominions, and lives in the continual exercise of his arms. To atone for the blood which he has spilt, the brahmins persuaded him that it was necessary he should be born anew: this ceremony consisted in putting the prince into the body of a golden cow of immense value; where, after he had laid the time prescribed, he came out regenerated, and freed from all the crimes of his former life. The cow was afterwards cut up, and divided amongst the Seers who had invented this extraordinary method for the remission of his sins."

when expelled from his capital, and defeated by his enemies, passed through a golden cow, in hopes of better fortune: and two brahmins, whom he sent as ambassadors to England, were, on their return to Hindostan, compelled to pass through the sacred yoni, or female lingam, made of the finest gold. After performing this ordeal, and making valuable presents to the brahmins, they were restored to the privileges of their caste; which they had lost, by the impurities contracted in travelling through so many polluted countries. The celebrated Sevajee, in the seventeenth century, on the day when he assumed the Mahratta sovereignty, was publicly weighed against gold; his weight was equal to that of sixteen thousand pagodas; which, with a hundred thousand more, were distributed among the brahmins.

Herodotus mentions, that Mycerinus, king of Egypt, having lost his daughter, an only child, it caused him the greatest affliction; and wishing to honour her funeral with more than ordinary splendour, he enclosed her body in an heifer made of wood, and richly ornamented with gold.

The Malabar brahmins, more ignorant and less tolerant than their northern brethren, assume greater consequence than I ever met with in other parts of India: when travelling, they have always precursors to clear the road; who make a loud noise, and compel all of inferior degree to retire: even when their provision is carried along the highway, the same cry is made; and the vulgar are under the necessity of hiding themselves, or falling down with their faces to the earth, that the atmosphere may not be polluted by plebeian breath, while the food of a brahmin passes by. Even the king himself is obliged to alight from his elephant, horse, or palanquin, when he approaches a temple; no person being allowed to ride near those structures.

These ignorant and bigotted priests seem to hold strangers in abhorrence, and detest every intrusion into their holy retreats: I nearly lost my life by indulging an innocent curiosity near Quilone, a Dutch settlement, twenty miles to the northward of Anjengo. Strolling one evening through a wild scenery of woods and forests, I accidentally saw a Hindoo temple, almost concealed by banian-trees. Pleased with the scenery, I ascended a rising ground within the grove, to take a sketch; and in an adjoining tank saw a Nair girl performing her ablutions: she instantly snatched up her garment, and ran to an inner court; aware of her high caste, I did not attempt to speak to her; but seating myself on the bank, finished my drawing. In the grove was a Nair at his devotions, who, on the female speaking to him with earnestness, looked stedfastly at me, and departed with her to the temple. Thinking no more of either, I returned leisurely towards Quilone; when hearing a noise, I looked round, and perceived the same man, joined by several others, armed with sticks and stones, hastily following, and alarming the forest with their cries. I had neither time for deliberation, nor any weapon to defend myself; but, with a little distance in my favour, ran to the nearest village, and claimed the protection of some Moplahs, having received a few stones in my flight.

Upon inquiring from these Mahomedans the nature of an offence so undesignedly committed, they told me I had, in the first instance, ventured on sacred ground, untrod by Europeans; and had seen a woman of high caste in a consecrated tank; crimes of great atrocity among that superstitious people; and had they overtaken me, my life might have been the forfeit of my temerity. The next day the brahmins sent orders to the English party at Quilone to keep at a distance from their districts, lest the atmosphere should be tainted by our breath; and some of the milder sort sent a basket of live poultry to an English lady of our party, that during our abode there, we might abstain from eating beef.

Civilization, as far as the Malabars are susceptible of it, has long attained its height: Egypt, Assyria, Persia, Greece, and Rome, from the pinnacle of grandeur, perfection in the fine arts, and the luxury of opulence, have dwindled to a name: the Malabars seem to have been for some thousand years in the same state of mediocrity; on such a system, no new designs in building, no alteration in manners or dress, no improvements in art or science, are to be expected.

This may be alleged of a great part of the world besides; but I do not compare the Negroes and Hottentots of Africa, nor the savages of America, with the natives of India, or the generality of Asiatics: these are certainly placed on a higher scale: as already mentioned in the northern cities of Hindostan, especially among the Moguls, we find eloquence, poetry, painting, and architecture, in a considerable degree of perfection: the Chinese shine with still brighter lustre in the scale of civilized society: as a nation they have never been conquered, although the Tartars usurped the sovereignty, and introduced some changes in their customs: during numerous revolving centuries they have cultivated the arts of peace, have been governed by wise laws, and have enjoyed many enviable blessings; considering their limited intercourse with the rest of the world, and how little they are beholden to strangers for improvement, we must regard them as an enlightened, polished, and independent people.

That the heat of the torrid zone debilitates the body, and enervates the mind, is very obvious: to this cause may be attributed the want of curiosity, enterprize, and vigour, among the Malabars: their inclinations are chiefly passive; indolence constitutes their happiness, and you cannot impose a severer task than mental employment: with the exception of the warlike Nairs, they pass days, months, and years, in swinging in their verandas, or under the shade of a tree, chewing betel, and singing dismal ditties, without a reflection on the past, or a plan for the future: from this habitual indolence they become incapable of exertion; and thus the laws, manners, and customs, are the same at this day as they were some thousand years ago.

There are, however, occasionally exceptions to this state of listless indolence among the Malabars: during my residence at Anjengo a circumstance occurred which would not have disgraced a Roman matron. The English were at war with the Marawars, a people inhabiting a mountainous country in the southern part of the peninsula: a considerable force from Madras was sent against them, who with great difficulty obtained a conquest: the obstacles chiefly arose from the wildness of the country, and the almost inaccessible fortresses to which the Morawars retreated, in the midst of thick forests and morasses; the rajah was killed in defending his last castle, whither he had retired with his family and treasure: he expired in the arms of his wife; who immediately ordered one of the guards, as he valued his master's honour, to stab her to the heart before the fortress surrendered: the soldier obeyed; and the English found the unfortunate pair clasped in a last embrace: the commanding officer caused them to be burnt on the same funeral pile, agreeable to the custom of their caste.

The king of Travencore, in whose dominions Anjengo is situated, governed a country extending from Cape Comorin south, to the kingdom of Cochin north: a district which has always remained free from Mahomedan invaders, and most probably was never subject to any of the great Hindoo rajahs. Travencore is mountainous and hilly, difficult of access, and defended at the passes: the most formidable, though badly fortified, was the pass of Tinevelli, leading into that country. The king usually resided in a town called Trevanduram, about eighteen miles from Anjengo, mean in appearance, and without defence, the palace excepted, which was surrounded by an indifferent fortification near three quarters of a mile in extent. His force consisted of four thousand sepoys, disciplined in the English style, many of them deserters from the Madras army; and about twelve thousand irregulars, armed with English muskets: his cavalry never exceeded one thousand. On an emergency he could assemble a formidable militia, consisting of a hundred thousand men, armed with spears, and bows of a large construction. The Malabars are very expert with these weapons, especially the Nairs; who always assemble under their respective leaders, on the festival of the full moon in September, at the breaking up of the moonson; and being drawn up in two divisions, commence a serious engagement with bows and arrows, spears and lances: this is sometimes protracted for a considerable time, and many fall on both sides; who confer a great honour on their family by this sacrifice to glory. The principal brahmin and Nair ladies are always present on these occasions, covered with ornaments, if not with drapery.

The throne of Travencore does not descend from father to son, but invariably devolves to the eldest son of the eldest sister, that the blood-royal may be clearly and indisputably preserved. The king on particular occasions is splendidly apparelled, and adorned with the royal jewels; but in general dresses, like the other brahmins, in a muslin turban, with a piece of white cotton cloth round the waist, reaching to the knees: this is the usual dress of the Malabars. The hereditary prince has no outward distinction from the other nobles; and the king's sons, whether by his wives or concubines, have no privileges annexed to their royal descent, neither are they by birth entitled to any importance in the government.

I always found more suspicion and jealousy in conversing with the Malabars, than among any other people in India: they were very cautious of giving information, and deemed the most common questions intrusive; it was therefore impossible from such a people to obtain much knowledge either of a religious or political nature. Whether the Malabars, like the northern Hindoos, adore the triad-deity, with the subordinate divinities in their endless mythology; or whether their idolatrous system comprizes a different set of gods and goddesses, especially of the dii lares, I could not determine; neither could I ascertain the jurisprudence of Travencore, or other Malabar rajah-ships: in those dominions, it is perhaps altogether a nominal science: for in Travencore, as in most despotic states, the subjects are seldom governed by written laws, but implicitly obey the will of an arbitrary despot. The king is considered as heir to all his subjects when he chooses to exert his full prerogative; consequently they require no laws respecting landed property, or titles of inheritance: as he monopolizes all the pepper, and such other articles as he thinks proper in his dominions, commercial laws are also needless: the women, except among the Nairs, being entirely dependent, and almost in a state of slavery, have no occasion for statutes to regulate dowers or marriage settlements: for as the sovereign is absolute in his kingdom, so is every master of a family in his own house: moral actions and relative duties are regulated solely by the will of a father and a husband. Thus, occasions of wrangling and law-suits are removed: despotic power is allsufficient; and the people, excluded from general information, contentedly submit to the oppressive system.

The Nairs, or nobles, form the second tribe in the kingdom of Travencore: they are a well-made handsome race, of a fairer complexion than the inferior castes, from whom they entirely separate themselves; and neither eat nor intermarry with any other. Their marriages are very extraordinary, and directly contrary to the usual system of polygamy adopted in Asia. Among the Nairs, one wife is common to many husbands, who cohabit with her by turns; during this temporary attachment, the arms of the inmate are placed over the door of the house, to prevent the intrusion of another husband. These marriages are attended with fewer disputes, and disagreeable consequences than might be imagined: the wife nominates the father of the child; and he is obliged to provide for it.

In consequence of these marriages, it is an established custom, both in the royal house of Travencore, and the whole tribe of Nairs, that the son does not inherit his father's estate; which, if permitted by a despotic prince, devolves at his death to his sister's children; where there can be no doubt of the consanguinity. The same law exists among the Hurons in America; on the demise of a chief in that tribe, he is not succeeded by his own child, but by the son of his sister; and in default of such an heir, by the nearest relation in the female line. A similar custom prevailed among the princes of Ethiopia. Montesquieu assigns the following reason for the polyandrian system of the Nair ladies. "In this tribe the men can have only one wife; while a woman, on the contrary, is allowed many husbands: the origin of this custom is not difficult to discover. The Nairs are the tribe of nobles, who are the soldiers of the nation: in Europe soldiers are not encouraged to marry; in Malabar, where the climate requires greater indulgence, they are satisfied with rendering marriage as little burthensome as possible: they give one wife amongst many men; which consequently diminishes the attachment to a family, and the cares of housekeeping; and leaves them in the free possession of a military spirit."

The Nairs, and other high castes of Malabars, burn their dead, intermingling the fuel with sandal-wood, cinnamon, and cassia: the lower classes are contented with a pyre of common wood; and sometimes bury the deceased in their own plantations.

As a further illustration of these extraordinary people, I subjoin the following particulars from Dr. Francis Buchanan's observations in Malabar; travelling by authority in the provinces then subject to the British government, he was able to obtain more accurate information than it was in my power to do among a people so bigotted, and so jealous of the intrusion of strangers.

" The Nairs marry before they are ten years of age; but the husband never afterwards cohabits with his wife: such a circumstance would be considered as very indecent: he allows her oil, clothes, ornaments, and food; but she lives in her mother's house; or, after her parents' death, with her brothers; and cohabits with any person that she chooses, of an equal or higher rank than her own; but never more with her husband. If detected in bestowing her favours on any low man, she becomes an outcast. It is no reflection on a woman's character to say, that she has formed the closest intimacy with different persons; on the contrary, the Nair women are proud of reckoning among their favoured lovers many brahmins, rajahs, or other persons of high birth. When a lover receives admission into a house, he commonly gives his mistress some ornaments, and her mother a piece of cloth; but these presents are never of such value as to give room for supposing that the women bestow their favours from mercenary motives. A Nair man, who is detected in fornication with a Shanar woman, is put to death; and the woman is sold to the Moplahs: if he have connection with a slave girl, both are put to death; which is a most shocking injustice to the female, who, in case of refusal to her lord, would be subject to all the violence of an enraged and despised master.

" In consequence of this strange manner of propagating the species, no Nair knows his father; and every man looks upon his sister's children as his heirs. He, indeed, looks upon them with

are called Chagos; and as this tribe includes the bulk of the people, what may be said of them is applicable to the Malabars in general. They are well shaped, of a middle stature, and dark complexion: their dress is a cotton cloth, tied loosely round the waist, reaching below the knee; some wear a turban, others tie the hair on the back of the head, and throw a loose piece of muslin over it: but the brahmins are always distinguished by the sacred cord on the left shoulder. The dress of the Malabar women is similar to that of the other sex; their black glossy hair, tied in a knot on the middle of the head, is copiously anointed with cocoa-nut oil, and perfumed with the essence of sandal, mogrees, and champahs; their ears, loaded with rings and heavy jewels, reach almost to their shoulders; this is esteemed a beauty; instead of a small gold wire in the orifice, as is practised in other countries, the incision is filled with a filament from the cocoa-nut leaf, rolled around; the circles are increased, until the orifice sometimes exceeds two inches in diameter, the ear is then healed, and being stretched to the perfection of beauty, is filled with rings and massy ornaments. Round the waist they wear a loose piece of muslin, while the bosom is entirely exposed: this is the only drapery of the Malabar women; but they are adorned with a profusion of gold and silver chains for necklaces, mixed with strings of Venetian and other gold coins; they have also heavy bangles, or bracelets: a silver box, suspended by a chain on one side, forms a principal ornament, and contains the areca, or betel-nut, with its appendages of chunam, spice, and betel-leaf. Their skin is softened by aromatic oils, especially among the Nairs and Tetees, who are peculiarly attentive to cleanliness in their persons. The Tetees are of the tribe of cultivators, and the Muckwas of the fishers; both are well made women, sometimes tall, and always graceful.

The Moplahs, or wives of the Mahomedans, who have been for many centuries settled among the Malabars, are in all respects a contrast to the natives; far from exposing any of their personal charms, they muffle themselves up in a covering of thick cotton cloth, and always retire on the approach of a stranger: they are extremely dirty, and pride themselves on their chastity; the young Tetees, on the contrary, never consider it among the cardinal virtues; but after marriage, they make good wives, and affectionate mothers.

I inquired into the truth of Mr. Grose's anecdote of a Malabar woman, who living with an English lady at Anjengo, to please her mistress, dressed in the European manner; but appearing afterwards in the queen of Attinga's presence with her breasts covered, the cruel despot ordered them to be cut off, for such a mark of disrespect: it was confirmed at Attinga. It is not only the vulgar who are thus sparingly clothed; for the first princesses wear only a finer muslin, with costly jewels.

Most of the Malabar men have a knife stuck in their girdle; and the steel pen with which they write their letters, accounts, and records, on the leaf of the Palmyra tree, there called olas: they write in a straight line, in a neat manner, and with great expedition: their books consist of several leaves, fastened together by a thong. The northern Hindoos write with the calamus, or reed, on a smooth glossy paper, made of hemp, rice, and different ingredients.

The Malabar Christians dress like their pagan neighbours,

except that the women cover the bosom. The Christians I usually met with were of the lowest class; the Roman catholic missionaries made but few converts of superior rank, although many of them were settled in the Travencore dominions, and permitted to build churches for public worship.

The poorer Malabars live on rice, salt-fish, and jagree; which is a coarse sugar produced from the cocoa-nut tree, wholesome and nourishing; those who cannot afford rice, content themselves with natchnee, a grain of inferior quality. The despotism of the government frequently occasions an artificial famine, and the inhabitants fly the country: a real famine is sometimes attended with dreadful consequences. Rice is sown at the commencement of the rains; which do not always fall as expected, and in some instances they have been entirely withheld for a whole season. Should the ground be only partially inundated, the ear droops, and yields but half a crop. On such occasions the poor wretches are driven by hunger to Anjengo, and other sea-ports, where you see a youth selling himself for sustenance, a mother offering her infant son for a bag of rice, and a desponding father parting with his wife and children for forty or fifty rupees.

Malabar children are generally a cheap commodity at Anjengo; at the end of the rainy season, when there was no particular scarcity in the interior country, I purchased a boy and girl about eight or nine years of age, as a present to a lady at Bombay, for less money than a couple of pigs in England: I bought the young couple, laid in two months provision of rice and salt-fish for their voyage, and gave each of them four changes of cotton garments, all for the sum of twenty rupees, or fifty shillings. English humanity must not pass a censure on this transaction: it was a happy purchase for the children; they were relieved from hunger and nakedness, and sent to an amiable mistress, who brought them up tenderly, and, on leaving India, provided for their future comfort; whereas, had I refused to buy them, they would assuredly have been sold to another, and probably have experienced a miserable bondage with some native Portugueze Christian, whom we do not reckon among the most merciful task-masters.

A circumstance of this kind happened to myself: sitting one morning in my veranda, a young fish-woman brought a basket of mullets for sale; while the servant was disposing of them, she asked me to purchase a fine boy, two years of age, then in her arms: on my upbraiding her want of maternal affection, she replied with a smile, that she expected another in a few weeks, and as she could not manage two, she made me the first offer of her boy, whom she would part with for a rupee. She came a few days afterwards, with a basket of fish, but had just sold her child to Signor Manoel Rodriguez, the Portugueze linguist; who, though a man of property and a Christian, had thought it necessary to lower the price to half a rupee. Thus did this young woman, without remorse, dispose of an only child for fifteen pence!

The houses of the Nairs, and better sort of Malabars, are neat and clean; generally situated in a garden, with a few cocoa-nut and jac trees, betel plants, indigenous roots and vegetables: a small grove of areca, or a shady tamarind, and a well within the inclosure, furnish a Malabar habitation: the furniture seldom consists of more than a few mats, earthen pots, grind-stones, and utensils for cleaning the rice, with the swing already mentioned; where the thoughtless proprietor passes most of his time in apathy and indolence.

The tools and implements of agriculture and mechanism, are extremely simple: a light sandy soil requires only one yoke of oxen to a wooden plough, which slightly turns the surface: the rice, natchnee, and early grains, are sown at the commencement of the rainy seasons, and reaped soon after they cease; the latter crops are then sown, as already mentioned in the Concan.

The method of inflicting punishment on criminals and debtors in Travencore, is in some respects singular: for capital crimes the culprits generally suffer death; although, as in most oriental governments, money and interest may purchase a pardon; except for the dreadful sin of killing a cow, or selling one for slaughter: this subjects them to the most cruel death. For debts, and non-payment of fines, inflicted as a punishment, they are confined by the caricar, or chief of the district; who draws a circle round the prisoner, from which he dare not move; then, gently laying a sharp stone on the crown of his head, demands payment of the sum required: on a refusal, he places a large flat stone over the other, and ties it firmly on; additional weights are gradually accumulated, with a repetition of the demand, until the sharp stone penetrating the head, either insures payment, or causes a painful death.

Having described the higher castes, and drawn a few sketches of the inferior tribes of Malabar, I now descend to the degraded Pooleahs; an abject and unfortunate race, who, by cruel laws and tyrannical customs, are reduced to a wretched state; while the monkeys are adored as sylvan deities, and in some parts of Malabar have temples and daily sacrifices. I have often lamented the treatment of the poor Pooleahs, and the cruel difference made by human laws between them and the pampered brahmins: banished from society, they have neither houses nor lands, but retire to solitary places, hide themselves in ditches, and climb into umbrageous trees for shelter: they are not permitted to breathe the same air with the other castes, nor to travel on a public road; if by accident they should be there, and perceive a brahmin or Nair at a distance, they must instantly make a loud howling, to warn him from approaching until they have retired, or climbed up the nearest tree. If a Nair accidentally meets a Pooleah on the highway, he cuts him down with as little ceremony as others destroy a noxious animal: even the lowest of other castes will have no communication with a Pooleah. Hunger sometimes compels them to approach the villages, to exchange baskets, fruit, or such commodities as they may have, for a little grain: having called aloud to the peasants, they tell their want, leave the barter on the ground, and retiring to a distance, trust to the honesty of the villagers to place a measure of corn equal in value to the barter; which the Pooleahs afterwards take away. Constant poverty and accumulated misery, have entirely debased the human form, and given a squalid and savage appearance to these unhappy beings.

Yet, debased and oppressed as the Pooleahs are, there exists throughout India, a caste called Pariars, still more abject and wretched. If a Pooleah, by any accident, touches a Pariar, he must perform a variety of ceremonies, and go through many ablutions, before he can be cleansed from the impurity. With such ideas of defilement, no marriages are contracted between the Pooleahs and Pariars; nor do they eat together; although the only difference in their epicurean banquet is, that the Pooleahs eat of all animal food, except beef, and sometimes of that which dies of itself: the Pariars not only feast upon dead carcases, but eat beef, and carrion of every kind. The brahmins of Malabar have thought proper to place christians in the same rank with the Pariars.

Dr. Robinson truly says, "the condition of the Pariar is undoubtedly the lowest degradation of human nature: if a Pariar approach a Nair he may put him to death with impunity: water or milk are considered as defiled, even by their shadow passing over them, and cannot be used until they are purified. It is impossible for words to express the sensation of vileness that the name of *Pariar* or *Chandala* conveys to the mind of a Hindoo: every Hindoo who violates the rules or institutions of his caste sinks into this degraded situation. This it is which renders Hindoos so resolute in adhering to the institutions of their tribe; because the loss of caste is, to them, the loss of all human comfort and respectability; and is a punishment beyond comparison more severe than excommunication, in the most triumphant period of Papal power."

Rejection of caste must to a Hindoo appear much worse than death: hurled from the high privileges of a brahmin or a Nair, the delinquent of either sex is obliged to enter the tribe of Pariars, the outcasts of all ranks of society; in which both them and their offspring are compelled to remain for ever! No virtue, no talent, no merit of a child can ever atone for the venial sin of the parent, whose whole posterity must feel the full effect of the dreadful sentence: none are to pray, to sacrifice, to read, or to speak to the hapless culprit; none are to be allied by friendship or by marriage, none to eat or to drink with him: he is to become abject, and excluded from all social duties; to wander over the earth, deserted by all, trusted by none; never to be received with affection, nor treated with kindness; but to be branded with infamy and shame; the curse of heaven, and the hatred of all good men!

"Stand off, for I am holier than thou," seems to be the predominant sentiment of the brahmin, whether dwelling under the banian shades in northern Hindostan, or secluded among the cassia groves of Malabar. How different is the pride and intolerance of the Hindoo priest from the charity and benevolence of the Jewish monarch, who assembled a mixed multitude of all descriptions, from Dan to Beersheba, to celebrate the passover at Jerusalem; how different the supplication of the pious king to the anathema of the brahmin! "The good LORD pardon every one that prepareth his heart to seek GOD; though he be not cleansed according to the purification of the sanctuary! and the prayer ascended to HIS holy place, even unto heaven!"

The brahmins of Travencore, as in most other parts of India, have taken care to be exempted as much as possible from punishment; at least their sentence is far more lenient than that passed on the other castes for the same crimes; and their power and influence in Malabar are more unbounded than in the north of India.

Consulting Herodotus on the purifications and ceremonies of the priests in ancient Egypt, we find a striking resemblance between them and the brahmins in India, whose time ought to be divided between study and devotion. The Egyptian priests possessed many and great advantages; the brahmins enjoy still greater privileges, by the laws of Menu, and the invariable respect and affection of their followers.

Beloe, the elegant translator of Herodotus, says " he is dignified by courtesy with the title of the Father of History; that his matter is no less curious than diversified; and his history, as far as his own knowledge and diligent researches could make it, is entitled to attention and belief." This is readily admitted, as far as his own knowledge extends; and it is not impossible to throw light upon many passages in his history, which appear to have no more foundation in truth than the fables in the Odyssey, or the voyages of Sinbad the sailor.

Herodotus says that Darius, king of Persia, on a certain occasion sent for some of the Greeks who were subject to his power, and asked them what recompence would induce them to eat the bodies of their deceased parents; they replied that no sum could prevail on them to commit such a deed. In the presence of the same Greeks, who by an interpreter were informed of what passed, he sent for the Callatiæ, a people of India known to eat the bodies of their parents; he asked them for what sum they would consent to burn the bodies of their parents; the Indians were disgusted at the question, and entreated him to forbear such language. This has staggered the belief of those who have only taken a general view of Hindoo manners and customs, and have always observed them burn the bodies of their dead: but this strange assertion is wonderfully illustrated by the following passage in Moor's Hindu Pantheon; " Not only do the Hindoos, even the brahmins, eat flesh; but they eat, one sect at least, human flesh. They do not, I conclude, kill human subjects to eat; but they eat such as they find in or about the Ganges, and perhaps other rivers. The name of the sect is *Paramahansa;* and I have received authentic information of individuals of this sect being not very unusually seen about Benares, floating down the river on, and *feeding on a corpse.* Nor is this a low despicable tribe; but, on the contrary, esteemed, by themselves at least, as a very high one; and my information stated that the human brain is judged by these epicurean cannibals as the most delicious morsel of their unsocial banquet. It may be difficult for the English reader to believe this hitherto unrecorded story of the flesh-abhorring Hindoos; as well, perhaps, as the now fully authenticated facts of their prodigality of human life. Anecdotes to a considerable extent might easily be collected of the sanguinary propensity of these people; such as would startle those who have imbibed certain opinions from the relations of travellers, on the character and habits of the abstinent and flesh-abhorring Hindoos, and brahmins with souls as unspotted as the robes they wear."

In many Indian customs mentioned by the Greek historian, we find the same traits of character as among the modern Hindoos; others appear so extremely dissimilar that little credit is given them: such for instance are the Padæi, whom he describes as leading a pastoral life, and living on raw flesh; when any man was diseased, he was put to death by his nearest connections; if a woman was ill her female relations treated her in the same manner: the more aged among them were regularly killed and eaten; few indeed attained to old age, because in case of sickness they put every one to death.

Whether the existence of Hindoo anthropophagi is believed or not, there can be no doubt of the aged parents and diseased relations being at this day frequently carried by their nearest connection to the banks of the Ganges; where, after their mouths and nostrils have been stopped with the sacred mud, they are left to be carried away by the stream as food for alligators. It is well known that in some of the districts near Bengal, there are a tribe of people called *Sheep-eaters,* who seize the animal alive, and actually devour wool, skin, flesh, and entrails, until nothing remains but the skeleton. Lady Anstruther, who made a valuable collection of drawings during her residence in India, has a set of paintings in water-colours, done by a native, which contain the whole process of these extraordinary gluttons, from the first seizure of the unfortunate animal, until it is completely devoured.

Herodotus further says, that in India is a set of people, who, entirely different from the Padæi, put no animal to death, sow no grain, have no fixed habitation, and live solely upon vegetables. These were no doubt Yogees, Senassees, and wandering Gymnosophists, who live entirely in the same manner at the present day. The Massagetæ and Nasamenes of Africa, who were allowed promiscuous marriage, and during cohabitation with an individual, fixed a staff before the door, resemble in that respect the Nairs of Malabar.

I now take leave of the pagan Malabars, who differ in so many respects from the northern Hindoos: the facts mentioned from my own knowledge, especially concerning the degraded situation of the Pooleah and Pariah castes, having often excited a doubt in the minds of my English friends, when I have related such extraordinary anecdotes, I shall not apologize for confirming them by a few quotations from Dr. Francis Buchanan's interesting journey in the Malabar province, the beginning of the present century.

" The Pooleahs are called *churmun*, a term applied to slaves in general: the Pooleahs are divided into many different clans, who can eat together, and intermarry: they have no hereditary chiefs; all the business of the caste is settled in assemblies of their elders: they never excommunicate any person, but they impose fines: when they can procure it, they eat animal food, and drink spirituous liquors, but reject carrion: none of them can read. When a man becomes tired of his wife, and she gives her consent, he may sell her to any other person who will pay back the expense incurred at the marriage; which in presents to the girl's master, her parents, cloth for the bride and bridegroom, and charges of the wedding dinner, generally amounts to twenty-four fanams, or sixteen shillings sterling. The goddess worshipped by the Pooleahs is named *Paradévatá*, and is represented by a stone placed on a mound in the open air: they have a sort of priests, but never give any thing to the brahmins, nor do they pray to the great gods whom they worship. The Pariars are also divided into clans: the highest eat carrion, and even beef; so that they are looked upon as equally impure with Mussulmans or Christians; and they may lawfully drink spirituous liquors. Even among these wretched creatures the pride of caste has full influence; and if a Pooleah be touched by one of the Pariar tribe, he is defiled, and must wash his head, and pray."

About a fourth part of the inhabitants of Malabar are Moplahs, or Mahomedans, descended from the Moors and Arabians, who have settled there at different times, and married Malabar women: they are the principal merchants in the country, both for foreign and home trade: many are proprietors of trading vessels, navigated by Mahomedan commanders and seamen, in which they make an annual voyage to the Persian and Arabian gulfs; and after disposing of pepper, cassia, cardamoms, cotton-cloth, coir-ropes, and other productions of Malabar, they return with coffee, drugs, dates, and dried fruits. Those on the sea-coast use a corrupt language between the Arabic and Malabar: the Koran, and the few books they possess, are written in Arabic. The Moplahs engaged in commerce, and enjoying an intercourse with other people, are tolerably courteous and orderly; those in the interior, who are too proud to work or engage in agricultural pursuits, are generally an idle worthless race; parading about the country with a broadsword, or murdering time in one of the swings already mentioned. These are of a most turbulent revengeful spirit, prone to mischief, especially against the Nairs, whom they consider as infidels, proud and haughty as themselves. When intoxicated with bhang, or opium, they frequently run *a-muck*, and in a dreadful state of phrenzy, murder every person they meet, until they are overpowered and destroyed.

The Nairs are at constant variance with the Moplahs; and the king of Travencore, jealous of their ambitious revengeful temper, keeps them in great subjection, and levies frequent contributions on their property; to which they reluctantly submit, from knowing they would experience the same treatment from other governments. At one period the Moplahs created great commotions in Travencore, and towards the end of the seventeenth century massacred the chief of Anjengo, and all the English gentlemen belonging to the settlement, when on a public visit to the queen of Attinga: the sanguinary deed was committed near her palace; some were even murdered in her presence, whom she in vain attempted to rescue from their fury, although at that time sovereign of the country.

There was still a nominal queen of Attinga when I resided at Anjengo; who, like the rajah sovereign of the Mahrattas, was little more than a state prisoner, while the king of Travencore, the usurper of her dominions, imitating the peshwa of Poonah, styled himself duan, or minister to the queen of Attinga.

I shall say nothing more of the Moplahs, thus dispersed along the coast of Malabar from Tellicherry to Cape Comorin; but the Syriac churches, or Christians of St. Thomé, settled in Travencore, are objects of great interest and curiosity. I occasionally heard of such a people in the neighbouring country of Anjengo, but I had no idea of their number or respectability: as our accounts generally came through the medium of the Portugueze priests and Romish missionaries, it was not to be expected their intelligence would be impartial or favourable.

My own knowledge on this interesting subject being limited, I shall make a few extracts from Mr. Wrede's satisfactory account of the St. Thomé Christians; who were not unknown to Vasco de Gama, and the first navigators to India: to whom the unexpected discovery of Christians on the Malabar coast, was a matter of the greatest surprise and satisfaction; for they were not more enthusiastic in extending their military glory and conquests, than in propagating their religion among the infidels in the remotest quarters of the world. Their exultation, however, was temporary; for, upon nearer investigation, they found that these Christians followed the doctrine of NESTORIUS, and acknowledged, instead of the Pope, the patriarch of that sect residing in Syria, for their ecclesiastical supreme chief.

" Their number must have been very considerable in the beginning of the sixteenth century, when the Portugueze became first acquainted with them; since they possessed about one hundred and ten churches in the countries now subject to the Travencore and Cochin rajahs: and at this present time, after the manifold persecutions, oppressions, and successive revolutions that have almost depopulated the whole coast, they are computed to amount to no less than one hundred and fifty thousand souls.

" They are indiscriminately called St. Thomé Christians, Nestorians, Syrians, and sometimes the Malabar Christians of the mountains, by the Portugueze writers of that time, and by the subsequent missionaries from Rome. The most common name given to them by the Hindoos of the country, is that of *Nazaranee, Mapila*, and more frequently *Surians*, or *Surianee Mapila*.

" The Portugueze were fond of bestowing upon them the name of St. Thomé Christians, though this appellation does not appear to have been, or now to be, very common amongst themselves. It originates probably from the chief who settled the first colony of Syrians on the coast, and who was, according to their tradition, their first bishop, and founder of their religion in these countries; and whose name was MAR THOME. This is corroborated by the curious circumstance of their giving the name of MAR THOME to every ecclesiastical chief, or bishop of theirs, although his real name be JOSEPH or ABRAHAM; not improbably in compliment to their first bishop and founder, for whom they have still a religious veneration. His arrival and settlement on the coast, may perhaps at a future period be ascertained, with historical accuracy, to have taken place during the violent persecution of the sect of NESTORIUS under THEODOSIUS the Second, or some time after. But the bigotted Portugueze missionaries laid hold of this name to renew the story of the arrival of ST. THOMAS the Apostle in India; who they pretended had converted a great number of idolaters on the coast of Malabar, and afterwards on the other side of India, as far as *Malliapoor*, now *St. Thomé*, where he suffered martyrdom.

" All traditions and Malabar records agree, that the Syrian Christians, or Nazaranee Mapilas, were known, and had been settled on the Malabar coast long before either the Arabs or Jews. In the Malabar histories, the first mention of a Syrian colony of the Christians is made in the reign of COCOORANGON PERUMAL, who probably lived in the sixth century; a wealthy Syrian merchant, of the name of THOME CANNANES, is said to have landed at *Oranganore*, where he was well received, and induced to settle, by great privileges granted to him by the PERUMAL. He afterwards married two wives; one of the *Nair*, and one of some low caste; by whom he had a very numerous progeny, who after his death had great disputes about his inheritance.

" We find again mention made of two Syrian, or Chaldean bishops, at *Coilan*, or *Quilone*, about one hundred years after its foundation; where they were extremely well received by the rajah, and permitted to build a church, which was still extant when CABRAL first visited Quilone. The grants and privileges which they received from the rajah were engraved upon copper plates; which many centuries afterwards, were shewn to Archbishop de Menezes at *Tevalacáree*.

"If one adds to these historical dates the name of Syrians retained by the St. Thomé Christians, their distinct features, and complexion somewhat fairer than the rest of the Malabars, the style of their building, especially their churches; but above all, the general use of the Syrian, or rather Chaldæan language, which is still preserved in all their religious functions, even in those churches which have since embraced the Roman rite, and that to this day they take their Christian and family names from the Syrian or Chaldæan idiom, no doubt can remain but that the St. Thomé Christians are originally a colony of *Nestorians*, who fled from the dominion of the Greek emperors, after THEODOSIUS the Second began to persecute the followers of the sect."

"They made at first some proselytes among the brahmins and Nairs, and were on that account much respected by the native princes; so that even at present they consider themselves equal in rank to either of the above two castes. They are in fact in much greater estimation among the Hindoos than the Christians converted by the Portugueze, and mostly picked up from the lowest caste. Many of the St. Thomé Christians now preserve the manners and mode of life of the brahmins as to cleanliness, and abstaining from animal food.

"We learn from the Portugueze writers, that these Christians possessed upwards of one hundred villages, situated mostly in the mountainous part of the southern division of Malabar. Their habitations were distinguished from those of the Hindoos by being mostly solid buildings, and collected in villages; not scattered and dispersed as those of the brahmins and Nairs. They obeyed their Archbishop, both in ecclesiastical and civil matters, paying a very moderate tribute to the different rajahs in whose territory they lived, who very little interfered in their concerns. When any complaints in civil affairs were preferred to the Archbishop, he used to appoint arbitrators or judges, whose sentence was final; they never condemned any person to death, and most crimes were expiated with pecuniary fines. They paid no tithes to their clergy, but at weddings they offered the tenth of the marriage gifts to their churches. On these occasions they were very profuse and ostentatious, and celebrated their nuptials with great pomp; it was then principally that they made a shew of the privileges granted to them by one of the PERUMALS; as of the bride and bridegroom riding upon elephants, of having the hair ornamented with flowers of gold, of musical instruments, also of flags of different colours carried before them. They all wore swords and targets, and some of them had firelocks; they were great marksmen, and from their eighth year frequented the firing schools: husbandry and trade were their principal occupations, and, next to the brahmins, the St. Thomé Christians furnished the greatest quantity of pepper to the Portugueze.

" As to their religious tenets, they followed generally the doctrine of NESTORIUS. They admitted no images of saints in their churches, where the Holy Cross alone was to be seen. They had only three sacraments, baptism, eucharist, and the orders; and would not admit transubstantiation in the manner the Roman catholics do. They knew nothing of purgatory; and the saints they said were not admitted to the presence of GOD, but were kept in a third place till the day of judgment. Their priests were permitted to marry, at least once in their life. Their rite was the Chaldæan, or Syrian.

"The St. Thomé, or Syrian Christians, never claimed the particular protection of either the Portugueze or Dutch, which the new Christians generally do, but considered themselves as subjects of the different rajahs in whose districts they lived; and, as long as the old Hindoo system, and the former division of the country, under a variety of petty rajahs, was preserved, they appear to have enjoyed the same degree of freedom, ease, and consideration, as the Nairs. But when the rajahs of *Travencore* and *Cochin* had subjected to themselves all the petty *rajahs* and chiefs, whose respective territories were situated within the lines of Travencore, they also overturned the whole political system established by CHERUMA PERUMAL; and by setting aside the immunities and privileges of the higher castes, they established a most oppressive despotism in the room of the former mild limited oligarchy; and we ought not to be much surprised to behold the present comparatively wretched situation of these Syrian villages, since we see the brahmins and Nairs stript of their old prerogatives, and subject to almost the same oppressions and extortions."

Dr. Claudius Buchanan, who visited the Syrian churches in 1806, under the sanction of the Marquis Wellesley, confirms the preceding account, and has given an interesting and affecting detail of his reception by Mar Dionysius the bishop and the pastor of the Christian churches in Malabar: he describes the venerable metropolitan, at the age of seventy-eight, in his episcopal mitre and crozier, as a man of highly respectable character, eminent for piety, and devoted attention to his pastoral functions: in a conversation with the English divine the Bishop said, "You have come to visit a declining church, and I am now an old man: but the hopes of its seeing better days cheer my old age, though I may not live to see them." On Dr. Buchanan's submitting to the venerable prelate his wishes in regard to the translation and printing of the holy scriptures, he replied, "I have already fully considered the subject; I have determined to superintend the work myself, and to call the most learned of the clergy to my aid: it is a work which will illuminate these dark regions, and God will give it his blessing."

Dr. Buchanan collected an ancient Syrian bible, and several valuable manuscripts among these churches; and the king of Travencore acceded to his request for sending a catalogue of all the Hindoo manuscripts in the temples of Travencore to the English college at Calcutta; a measure to which the brahmins were very averse. Those manuscripts are supposed to contain most of the Hindoo literature of the south of India.

The Christians in Travencore, who exceeded two hundred thousand in number, were much in want of printed versions of the holy scriptures, having only a very few manuscript copies belonging to all the churches. This Syriac version was carried to India, according to the popular belief, at the beginning of the fourth century, before the year 325 of the Christian æra; at which time Johannes, bishop of India, signed his name at the council of Nice. Dr. Buchanan, in company with Colonel Macaulay, the British resident in Travencore, visited Udiamper, where Beliarte, king of the Christians, kept his court; for the Syrian Christians had formerly regal power in Malabar, and when Vasco de Gama arrived at Cochin in 1503, he saw the sceptre once swayed by their monarchs. At Udiamper is the Syrian church, at which Archbishop Menezes, from Goa, convened the synod of the Syrian clergy in 1599, when he burned the Syriac and Chaldaic books.

This well authenticated account of these churches affords many delightful sensations to a reflecting mind, and eminently displays the protecting power of the heavenly Shepherd. Numerous as the Syrian Christians now are, they were formerly a more extensive and flourishing body: and we have every reason to hope there will again be a glorious revival among a people so well prepared; a people who preserved a pure and spiritual worship when Europe was immersed in a gloom, emphatically styled the *dark age*. The uncontrouled power of Papal Rome had not then reached the Syrian churches in Travencore: they preserved their independence, and remained for ages unmolested, until the maritime discovery of India by de Gama: after which, priests and inquisitors from Goa disturbed their peace, burnt their unadulterated versions of the sacred scriptures, and compelled many of their churches to acknowledge the pope's supremacy.

The extensive tract of country, now denominated the Malabar Province, having since the fall of Tippoo Sultan, formed part of the British empire in India, and been placed under the management of the Company's servants, a more accurate and comprehensive detail of the subjects slightly touched upon during my voyage on the Malabar coast, and residence in Travencore, will most probably be communicated to the public. The pride and insolence of the Nambouri brahmins and Nairs will be checked under the English government, and by that means many new channels of information, which could not have been accessible forty years ago, will be attainable. A faithful narrative of the civil and natural history of Malabar will be a valuable acquisition to the northern Asiatic Researches: it is a country which affords an ample field for such investigation, especially in botanical pursuits: in that respect the copious descriptions and accurate plates of the Hortus Malabaricus, are truly valuable; but it is a very voluminous, expensive, and scarce work; and, being written in Latin, cannot be generally read. Dr. Roxburgh's beautiful collection of Coromandel plants contains many of those common in Malabar; but others, indigenous to the mountains and vallies of Travencore, are not introduced into that elegant and classical work.

I now close my own account of this singular country, and its more singular inhabitants, with a few very curious remarks by Lewis Vertomannus, a gentleman of Rome, who visited it in 1503, and published his travels in Arabia, Persia, and India, "containing many notable and strange things," upwards of three hundred years ago. His descriptions in Malabar are so curious, lively, and interesting, that I give them in the old English, into which they were soon after translated from the Latin.

"The chiefest idolaters, and of the greatest dignity in Malabar, are the Bramini. They of the second order are named Nairi; whose office it is when they go abroad to bear swords, targets, bows, and lances: the third order consisteth of mechanics or handy-craft men; with those that gather pepper, fruits, and spices. The basest sort of all are in such subjection to the Bramini and Nairi, that on pain of death they may approach no nearer unto them than fifty paces: and therefore they lie lurking in certain shadows, and dark places, and marshes, lest they should suddenly chance to meet with them. Wherefore when they come abroad, that they may be heard afar off, they cry with a loud voice, that they may be heard of the same Bramini and Nairi; lest being suddenly betrayed, they should be put to death.

"The higher sort of these idolaters, to shew great courtesie and friendship one to the other, use sometimes to change wives; but the children remain with the first husband: they have also divers other customs; for among some of them, one woman is married to seven husbands: when she hath brought forth a child, she may father it to which of them she listeth; who may in no case refuse it.

"When they pray to their idols in the morning before the sun-rise, they resort to the pools or rivers to wash them. Their weapons are certain crooked swords, bowes, and lances: lying along on the ground, they eat their meat out of a tray of copper; for spoons, they use certain leaves of trees: the ruder sort eat so filthily, that putting their foul hands into the pot, they take out rice by handfuls, and so thrust it into their mouths. Among the better sort the women have none other charge or care than to dress and beautify themselves; for their husbands like to have them curiously washed, and perfumed with sundry sweet savours. When these women go abroad, it is marvellous to behold how they are behanged with jewels and precious stones, on their ears, arms, and legs.

"When the king, or any of the priests or gentlemen die, their bodies are burnt in a great fire, made of a pile of wood; then all the while they sacrifice unto the devil. Whiles the bodies are burning, they cast in the fire all manner of sweet savours, as aloes, myrrh, frankincense, storax, sandal, coral, and innumerable other sweet gums, spices, and trees: these make the fire much greater, increasing the flame by reason of their gummosity: the wife also of the burned king or priest standeth by the fire alone, without the company of any other woman, lamenting and beating her breast. Within fifteen days after, the wife biddeth to a banquet all her husband's kinsfolks; and when they come at a day appointed, they go all to the place where her husband was burnt, and at the same hour of the night: then cometh forth the wife, garnished with all her jewels, and best apparel: in the same place is made a pit, no deeper than may serve to receive the woman; this pit is set about with reeds covered with silk, that the pit may not be seen. In the mean time a fire is made in the pit with sundry sorts of sweet woods; and the wife, after that her guests have well banqueted, eateth very much of a certain thing called betel, which troubleth her mind, as though she was half mad, or drunken. After the ceremonies are finished, she taketh her leave of all her kinsfolks, and then with sudden outrage, and a loud cry, lifting up her hands, she hurleth herself into the burning pit; which done, her kinsfolks, standing near unto the fire, cover her with little faggots of sweet wood; hurling also thereon much pitch, that the body may the sooner be consumed: and except the wife should do this after the death of her husband, she should ever after be esteemed an evil woman, be hated of all men, and in fine, in danger to be slain both of her own kinsfolks and her husband's, and therefore she goeth to it the more willingly. The king himself is present at these pompes; which are not commonly used for all men; but only for kings, priests, and noblemen."

As no traces now remain of the ancient city of Calicut, it is impossible to speak of its magnificence when Vertomannus wrote: but, considering the wealth and power of the Mahomedans, and the splendour of their cities in the north of India at that period; many of which, as well as Bezenagur, the metropolis of the great Hindoo empire of Narsinga, the Roman traveller had just visited; it is singular he should call Calicut the "chiefest, and metropolitan of all the cities of India; whose king in royal majesty exceeded all the kings of the east; and was therefore in the Malabar language called *Samory*, or *Zamorine*, that is to say, God on the earth.

That Calicut was the principal city in Malabar, and perhaps the greatest emporium in the east, there is little doubt; although now reduced to a stragging village of fishermen: but as Vertomannus describes the capital of Narsinga to be a city eight miles in circuit, and of proportionable wealth and grandeur, a monarch maintaining four hundred war elephants, and when he rode out or went a hunting, attended by six thousand horsemen, it appears extraordinary he should speak of Calicut in such high terms: not so much of the city as the palace, which, he says, "containeth no less than a mile in circuit; the wall is not high; the building is fair, with beams well joining the frame, clumsily wrought, and carved with the figures and shapes of devils on every side. What pearls and precious stones the king weareth upon him, cannot be expressed for the greatness of the thing; for doubtless it exceedeth all estimation: although at the time of my being there, he was not given to joyfulness, but lived in grief of mind, as well for the wars which the Portugals made against him, as for a grievous sickness; nevertheless his ears, arms, hands, legs, and feet, were so beautifully and richly garnished with all sorts of jewels and precious stones, that it cannot be spoken. His treasure is esteemed so unmeasurable, that it cannot be contained in two wonderful great rooms; it consisteth of precious stones, plates of gold, and also so much coined gold, as may suffice to lade a hundred mules; as their Bramini report, to whom it is best known: this treasure was gathered and reserved by twelve kings before him, and contains besides a coffer of three spans in length, and two in breadth, full of only precious stones, of price inestimable."

"In the hall of the palace are seen ten or twelve candlesticks, very fair, and of cunning workmanship; much like unto goodly fountains, and of the height of a man. In each of them are divers vessels, and in every vessel three candles light, of two spans long; and great plenty of oil.

"The king of Calicut and his people are given to idolatry, and serving of the devil: he hath a chapel in his palace where he worships him; the entrance is by a door of wood, garnished with carved work, containing divers monstrous forms and shapes of devils. In the midst of the chapel is a seat of majesty made of copper, with also a devil of copper sitting on it: this devil hath on his head a crown, after the manner of the Bishop of Rome; but this hath overplus four horns, his mouth gaping, with four notable teeth, a deformed nose, louring and grim eyes, a threatening look, crooked hands like a flesh hook, and feet not much unlike the feet of a cock: a monster horrible and fearful to behold. They sacrifice a cock to him once a week; they kill the cock with a silver knife, and the knife also being rayed with blood, they put often in the fire, that no part of the blood be lost. When the king hath left eating, the priests carry away all that is left to certain crows, which they keep for the purpose: these crows are therefore esteemed holy; and it is not lawful for any man to hurt them. When the king marries, the queen is first appropriated to the chief brahmin, to whom the king giveth fifty pieces of gold: which they say is one cause, that after the death of the king, if he have any male children living, they succeed not to the kingdom; for of ancient law and custom the sceptre pertaineth to the king's sister's sons. When the king goeth a hunting the Bramini keep the queen at home, and remain near about her; for there is nothing more acceptable to the king than that the priests should so keep company with the queen."

Many of these singular customs of the high caste of the Tamuri Raja, or Zamorin, mentioned by Vertomannus, are confirmed by Dr. Francis Buchanan, who travelled in this country three hundred years afterwards: sic transit gloria mundi! for so altered is the whole system within that space, that the present Zamorin, instead of possessing the power, wealth, and dignity of his ancestors, is reduced to a cypher, and subsists on a pension from the English East India Company. Notwithstanding his degradation and poverty, Dr. Buchanan says, that all the males of his family are called Tamburans, and all the ladies Tamburetti, appellations of high distinction: as the tamuri pretend to be of a higher rank than the brahmins, and to be inferior only to the invisible gods; a pretension that was acknowledged by his subjects, but which is held as abominable by the brahmins. All the children of the Tamburetti, or females of the family, are still of the highest dignity: these ladies are generally impregnated by Namburi brahmins; for any intercourse between them and their husbands would be reckoned scandalous: they live in the houses of their brothers, and the eldest man of the family is the Tamuri rajah, called by Europeans the zamorin.

CHAPTER XIV.

AN ACCOUNT OF THE ANCIENT TEMPLES, AND OTHER EXCAVATIONS ON THE ISLANDS OF SALSETTE AND ELEPHANTA.

1774.

What does not fade? The tower that long had stood
The crush of thunder, and the warring winds
Shook by the slow but sure destroyer Time,
Now hangs in doubtful ruins o'er its base;
And flinty pyramids, and walls of brass,
Descend: the Babylonian spires are sunk;
Achaia, Rome, and Egypt moulder down.
Time shakes the stable tyranny of thrones,
And tottering empires crush by their own weight;
This huge rotundity we tread grows old,
And all those worlds that roll around the sun.
The sun himself shall die, and ancient night
Again involve the desolate abyss,
Till the great FATHER through the lifeless gloom
Extend his arm to light another world,
And bid new planets roll by other laws. ARMSTRONG.

CONTENTS.

by the exiled Pandoos—similar grottos in Egypt—written mountains in Arabia—remarkable passage in the book of Job—engravings on rocks and stones—cemetery in the desert of Sinai.

Conquest of Salsette, Curanjah, Elephanta, and some smaller islands, by the English in 1774—siege of Tannah—description of those new acquisitions.

CHAPTER XIV.

During my residence at Bombay I frequently visited the excavations of Canara and Elephanta: the former are hewn in the central mountains on the island of Salsette, contiguous to Bombay; the latter in a similar situation on the isle of Elephanta, seven miles from thence, and nearer to the continent. Soon after my return to England, an engraving was published from my drawing of the large temple at the Elephanta; and the views of those stupendous works on both islands, since delineated by Mr. Daniell with the accuracy and effect which characterize all his productions, give a correct idea of their general appearance.

The nations of Asia, as well as of Europe, continued long ignorant of the origin and purport of these extraordinary caverns: later researches have thrown a light on their obscurity: the author of the "Indian Antiquities" has taken great pains to illustrate them; his minute investigations have the glow of oriental poetry, and are enriched by interesting anecdotes. If his comparisons between the tenets of the Hindoo religion and the rites of the Eleusinian mysteries, together with his other hypotheses, do not entirely satisfy, they at least afford pleasure to the inquiring mind.

My first visit to Salsette was in the beginning of 1774; that island then belonging to the Mahrattas, we obtained a passport from the Pundit for our journey; and crossing a narrow arm of the sea which divides Bombay from Salsette, proceeded in palanquins towards the caves. Our party consisted of six English gentlemen, a small escort, and numerous attendants; which were as necessary on this excursion as in the former journey in the Concan, from being obliged to carry beds, provisions, and every thing wanted, on the heads of the villagers.

The first part of the road was through salt marshes and rice-fields, with few trees, or interesting objects: at sun-set we ascended a pleasant hill, and took up our quarters in a Portugueze church, near an extensive lake, bordered by mango-trees: the priest did every thing for our accommodation, partook of our supper, and at midnight left us to repose in his spacious dormitory.

At day-break next morning we renewed our journey to another church, five miles from the principal excavation: the country improved in beauty and fertility; its produce chiefly consisting of rice-fields, mango groves, and palmyra trees. After breakfast we proceeded towards mountains of difficult ascent, through narrow rocky paths rendered almost impervious by thickets and jungle grass; through which our palanquin bearers could not penetrate, and we finished the journey on foot.

At noon we reached the great temple, excavated at some distance from the summit of a steep mountain, in a commanding situation. This stupendous work is upwards of ninety feet long, thirty-eight wide, and of a proportionable height, hewn out of the solid rock; and forming an oblong square, with a fluted concave roof: the area is divided into three aisles by regular colonnades;

similar to the ancient basilic, a pile of building twice as long as it was wide: one of the extremities terminating in a hemicycle; two rows of columns formed a spacious area in the centre, leaving a narrow walk between the columns and the wall; in these basilici the Roman emperors of the east frequently administered justice. The largest excavation at Salsette seems to be on the same plan, although doubtless intended for a place of worship: towards the termination of the temple, fronting the entrance, is a circular pile of solid rock, nineteen feet high, and forty-eight in circumference, most probably a representation of the *lingam*, the symbol of Seva. There are no images in this temple, nor any kind of sculpture except on the capitals of the pillars, which are generally finished in a masterly style, and are little impaired by time; some have been left in an unfinished state; on the summit of others is something like a bell, between elephants, horses, lions, and animals of different kinds.

The lofty pillars and concave roof of the principal temple at Salsette present a much grander appearance than the largest excavation at the Elephanta, although that is much richer in statues and bassi-relievi than any of those on Salsette: I annex a drawing of the pillars on each island, as they have a characteristic difference. The portico at Salsette, of the same height and breadth as the temple, is richly decorated; on each side a large niche contains a colossal statue well executed; facing the entrance are small single figures, and groups in various attitudes; the whole in good preservation. The outer front of the portico, and the area before it, corresponding in grandeur with the interior, are now injured by time, and the mouldering sculpture intermingled with clematis and a variety of rock-plants. We copied several lines from the long inscriptions on the square pillars at the entrance; the characters were obsolete, and had not been deciphered when I left India.

The following are the exact dimensions of the large temple, or principal excavation at Salsette.

Length of the interior, ninety-one feet, six inches.

Breadth, thirty-eight feet.

Depth of the portico, twelve feet.

Portico-wall, or support of rock, five feet.

Front-wall, or support of rock, three feet.

Area, twenty-eight feet.

Outer-wall, or support of rock, two feet eight inches.

The length of the whole temple, portico and area, leading to it, is one hundred and forty-two feet two inches.

After remaining some hours in the large temple, we proceeded further up the mountain by a flight of steps hewn in the rock, and continued to the summit. By various intricate paths they lead to smaller excavations; most of which consist of two rooms, a portico and benches, cut in the rock: to each is annexed a cistern of water of about three cubic feet, also hewn in the rock, for the preservation of rain water; which we found very cool and grateful after a sultry walk.

Some of these excavations are larger and better finished than others; a few in their general effect resemble the principal temple, though inferior in size and decoration. The whole appearance of this excavated mountain indicates it to have had a city hewn in its rocky sides capable of containing many thousand inhabitants: the largest temple was doubtless their principal place of worship;

the smaller, on the same plan, inferior dewals; the rest were appropriated as dwellings for the inhabitants, differing in size and accommodation according to their respective ranks in society; or, as is still more probable, these habitations were the abode of religious brahmins and their pupils when India was the nurse of art and science, and the nations of Europe were involved in ignorance and barbarism.

Southey has introduced these excavations, with good effect, into the "Curse of Kehama;" which, however extravagant, contains many true pictures of oriental scenery.

> "In solitude the ancient temples stood,
> Once resonant with instruments and song,
> And solemn dance of festive multitude;
> Now as the weary ages pass along,
> Hearing no voice save of the ocean flood,
> Which roars for ever on the restless shores;
> Or, visiting their solitary caves,
> The lonely sound of winds, that moan around,
> Accordant to the melancholy waves.
> High over-head, sublime,
> The mighty gate-way's storied roof was spread,
> Dwarfing the puny piles of younger time.
> With the deeds of days of yore
> The ample roof was sculptur'd o'er,
> And many a god-like form there met the eye,
> And many an emblem dark of mystery.
> Such was the city, whose superb abodes
> Seem'd scoop'd by giants for the immortal gods,
> Now all is silence dread,
> Silence profound and dead,
> The everlasting stillness of the deep!"

The summit of this wonderful mountain commands an extensive view; the island of Salsette appears like a map around the spectator, presenting a fine champaign of rice fields, cocoa-groves, villages, and cattle; woody hills and fertile vales: the surrounding mountains form a fore-ground of grey rocks, covered with trees, or hollowed into gloomy caverns, the haunt of tigers, serpents, bats, and bees, in immense swarms; the horizon is bounded on the south by the island of Bombay with the harbour and shipping, east by the continent, north by Bassein and the adjacent mountains, and west by the ocean. In various parts of Salsette are romantic views, embellished by the ruins of Portugueze churches, convents, and villas; once large and splendid, but suffered to decay since the Mahrattas conquered the island.

The enjoyment of the picturesque and fertile scenery of Salsette is interrupted by the tigers which infest the mountains and descend to the plains: they not only prey upon the sheep and oxen near the villages, but sometimes carry off the human species. During our short stay, a poor woman gathering fuel on the skirts of a wood, laid her infant on the grass, when a tiger sprung from the cover and carried it to his den, in sight of the wretched mother!

Another of these ferocious animals prowling in a garden near Tannah, the capital of the island, suddenly put his head and fore-feet through the small window of a summer house where a friend of mine was sitting. Alarmed at his danger, he kept his eye stedfastly fixed on the enemy, rightly judging that the aperture was too small for the admission of his body; the gentleman then ran speedily to the house, and returning immediately with two or three armed servants, shot the monster through the heart, he having never moved from the spot.

The island of Elephanta, about two leagues from Bombay, does not exceed three miles in circumference; consisting of two rocky mountains, covered with trees and brush-wood, and a small valley of rice-fields, cultivated by a few Hindoo farmers, whose cottages and cattle enliven the scene. Near the landing place is the figure of an elephant the size of life, shaped out of a rock, which probably gave its name to the island; that by which the natives distinguish it being very different.

Ascending the mountain by a narrow path, winding among rocks, trees, and underwood, we arrive at the excavation, which has long excited the attention of the curious, and afforded ample scope for the discussion of antiquarians. The principal temple, and adjoining apartments, are two hundred and twenty feet long, and one hundred and fifty broad; in these dimensions exceeding the largest work at Salsette: but being very inferior in height, notwithstanding the numerous and richer decorations at the Elephanta, the spectator is constantly reminded of being in a cave; at Salsette, the lofty concave roof and noble columns have a majestic appearance. Yet the observer feels more surprize and admiration at the Elephanta than at Salsette: he beholds four rows of massive columns cut out of the solid rock, uniform in their order, and placed at regular distances, so as to form three magnificent avenues from the principal entrance to the grand idol which terminates the middle vista; the general effect being heightened by the blueness of the light, or rather gloom, peculiar to the situation. The central image is composed of three colossal heads, reaching nearly from the floor to the roof, a height of fifteen feet: it represents the triad deity in the Hindoo mythology, *Brahma*, *Vishnoo*, and *Seeva*, in the characters of the creator, preserver, and destroyer: the middle face displays regular features and a mild and serene character; the towering head-dress is much ornamented, as are those on each side, which appear in profile, lofty and richly adorned with jewels: the countenance of Vishnoo has the same mild aspect as Brahma: the visage of Seeva is very different; severity and revenge, characteristic of his destroying attribute, are strongly depicted; one of the hands embraces a large cobra de capello; while the others contain fruit, flowers, and blessings for mankind; the lotos and pomegranate are easily distinguished. The lotos, so often introduced into the Hindoo mythology, forms a principal object in the sculpture and paintings in their temples, is the ornament of their sacred lakes, and the most conspicuous beauty in their flowery sacrifices. Whether the *Bali-putras*, or *Palibothra* kings, mentioned in Alexander's invasion of India, were the same with the more ancient dynasty of *Bali-putra*, or *Patali-putra*, is, perhaps, not yet determined; but the *Bhagavata* mentions one of the titles of *Maha-Bali*, the founder of that dynasty, to have been *Maha-padma*, *Pati-Nanda*, the "*Great Lord of the Lotos.*"

The lotos is often seen in the Egyptian and Grecian sculpture; and that a triad deity was an object of worship in the mythology of those ancient nations is an hypothesis well supported in Maurice's Indian Antiquities.

On either side of the Elephanta triad is a gigantic figure leaning on a dwarf, an object frequently introduced in these excavations. The giants guard the triple deity, and separate it from a large recess filled with a variety of figures, male and female, in different attitudes; they are in tolerable proportion, but express no particular character of countenance: one conspicuous female, like the Amazons, is single breasted; the rest, whether intended for goddesses or mortals, are generally adorned, like the modern Hindoo women, with bracelets, and rings for the ancles; the men have bracelets only. The intervening space between these large figures is occupied by small aërial beings, hovering about them, in infinite variety. I know not whether I am correct in saying the larger images in these groups are in alto-relievo, and most of the smaller in basso-relievo, brought sufficiently forward from the rock to produce a good effect.

The sides of the temple are adorned with similar compositions, placed at regular distances, and terminating the avenues formed by the colonnades, so that only one group is seen at a time, except on a near approach; the regularity and proportion of the whole are remarkably striking. The figures are generally in graceful attitudes; but those of herculean stature indicate no muscular strength. I believe in the finest works of Greece and Rome there is some peculiar distinction in this respect between the statues of deities and mortals: in the Apollo Belvidere the graceful attitude, majestic demeanor, and finely proportioned limbs, unite delicate softness with manly strength; or, to use the language of a celebrated enthusiast, " his stature is more than human; the beauty of youth is diffused over the manly perfection of his frame, and gracefully displayed in the noble configuration of the limbs: there seems nothing mortal; the body is neither warmed by veins, nor agitated by nerves; a celestial spirit like a gentle stream circulates over the contour of the figure." Certainly my first impressions on beholding this master-piece of art, surpassed those excited by the Venus di Medici, in her velvet tribune, at Florence; and greater than either was the effect of the Laocoon. The agony expressed in the countenance, and strongly marked by every vein and muscle stretched and swelling over the body, especially in the feet, admirably display the power and exquisite skill of the artist.

Nothing of this kind is observable in the Elephanta; among many thousand figures, few of the countenances express any particular passion, or mark a decided character: they have generally a sleepy aspect, and bear a greater resemblance to the tame sculpture of Egypt than the animated works of the Grecian chisel.

The columns at the Elephanta are of a singular shape, and in all respects differ from the beautiful orders of ancient Greece: the shafts are massive in proportion to their height; the large capitals, swelling over the ornaments, give the appearance of pressure by the superincumbent mountain; a form appropriate to their function in this wonderful work.

From the right and left avenues of the principal temple are passages to smaller excavations on each side: that on the right is much decayed, and very little of the sculpture remains entire; a pool of water penetrates from it into a dark cavern far under the rock; whether natural or artificial is not determined. A small corresponding temple on the left side, contains two baths, one of them elegantly finished: the front is open, and the roof supported by pillars of a different order from those in the large temple; the sides are adorned with sculpture, and the roof and cornice painted in mosaic patterns; some of the colours are still bright. The opposite bath of the same proportions, is less ornamented; between them a room detached from the rock contains a colossal representation of the lingam. Several small caves branch out from the grand excavations.

I remained on one occasion four days at the isle of Elephanta, and paid more than one visit to the sculptured mountains of Canara, sketching the most striking features of these wonderful works. I once accompanied an eminent English artist on his first visit to the Elephanta; I had been lavish in its praise; too much so, as I had reason to conclude, on our arrival at the great temple. After the glare of a tropical sun, during the walk from the landing-place, it was sometime before the eye had accommodated itself to the gloom of these subterraneous chambers sufficiently to discriminate objects in that sombre light. We remained for several minutes without speaking, or looking particularly at each other: at length, when more familiarized to the cavern, my companion still remaining silent, I expressed some fear of having been too warm in my description, and that, like most other objects, the reality fell short of the anticipated pleasure: he soon relieved my anxiety by declaring, that, however highly he had raised his imagination, on entering this stupendous scene he was so absorbed in astonishment and delight as to forget where he was. He had seen the most striking objects of art in Italy and Greece, but never any thing which filled his mind with such extraordinary sensations. So enraptured was he with the spot, that after staying until a late hour he reluctantly accompanied me to the hospitable mansion of an

English officer at Butcher's island; whither we repaired every evening, and returned on the following morning to revisit the Elephanta, as the nocturnal damps render it dangerous to sleep in the caverns, and the cottages of the natives cannot accommodate Europeans.

I do not wish to insinuate from this gentleman's surprize and delight in the caverns of the Elephanta, that he placed the Hindoo sculpture in competition with the Grecian temples and statues; it was the general effect which struck him. However these gigantic statues, and others of similar form, in the caves of Elora and Salsette, may astonish a common observer, the man of taste looks in vain for proportion of form and expression of countenance.

The Elephanta caves especially cause admiration when we contemplate the immensity of the undertaking, the number of artificers employed, and the extraordinary genius of its first projector, in a country until lately accounted rude and barbarous, by the now-enlightened nations of Europe. It is a work which would be admired by the curious, had it been raised from a foundation, like other structures; but when we consider it is hewn inch by inch in the hard and solid rock, we cannot but be astonished at the conception and completion of the undertaking. In Egypt are many excavations similar to those in Hindostan, which, with great reason, are supposed to be derived from the same origin; nor is it extravagant to pronounce, with Maurice, that the caves of Elephanta bear a great resemblance to what was exhibited in vision to the prophet Ezekiel; when, looking in, he saw every form of creeping things, and abominable beasts, and all the idols of the house of Israel pourtrayed upon the wall round about: and the worshippers therein had their faces towards the east, and they worshipped the sun toward the east.

I am far from advocating the cause of Hinduism; but I confess, that a view of these excavations has often caused pious meditation and filled my mind with awe, though I was surrounded by idols. My opinion of modern Brahminism is apparent throughout these pages; but many circumstances authorize a conclusion, that there was a time when the more enlightened brachmans worshipped God in his unity; and perhaps in these very temples sung the praises of Jehovah, without the medium of subordinate divinities; which are said to have been introduced only for vulgar minds: however erroneous the principle, we must subscribe to the opinion of Sir William Jones, that "the inextricable difficulties attending the vulgar notion of material substances, concerning which

"We know this only, that we nothing know,"

induced many of the wisest among the ancients, and some of the most enlightened among the moderns, to believe that the whole creation was rather an energy than a work, by which the Infinite Being, who is present at all times and in all places, exhibits to the minds of his creatures a set of perceptions, like a wonderful picture or piece of music, always varied, yet always uniform; so that all bodies and their qualities exist, indeed, to every wise and useful purpose, but exist only as far as they are perceived; a theory no less pious than sublime, and as different from any principle of atheism, as the brightest sun-shine differs from the blackest midnight. This illusive operation of the deity the Hindoo philosophers call máya, or deception."

The above is extracted from the argument of the hymn to Narayena, one of the most sublime and beautiful compositions in any language, translated by our great orientalist: the first stanza represents the sublimest attributes of the Supreme Being, and the three forms in which they most clearly appear to us, power, wisdom, and goodness; or, in the language of Orpheus and his disciples, love. I shall only copy the first stanza of this divine poem, and the concluding lines; although every part of it would delight a refined and pious mind, and enlighten the most obscure recesses appropriated to such an object of worship.

The Spirit of God, called Narayena, or *moving on the water*, has a multitude of other epithets in the Sanscrit, the principal of which are introduced in different parts of the hymn.

HYMN TO NARAYENA.

Spirit of spirits, who, through every part
Of space expanded and of endless time,
Beyond the stretch of labouring thought sublime,
Badst uproar into beauteous order start,
Before heaven was, thou art:
Ere spheres beneath us roll'd or spheres above,
Ere earth in firmamental ether hung,
Thou satst alone, 'till through thy mystic love,
Things unexisting to existence sprung,
And grateful descant sung.
What first impell'd thee to exert thy might?
Goodness unlimited. What glorious light
Thy power directed? wisdom without bound.
What prov'd it first? Oh! guide my fancy right;

Oh! raise from cumb'rous ground
My soul in rapture drown'd,
That fearless it may soar on wings of fire;
For thou, who only know'st, thou only canst inspire!

* * * * * * * * *

My soul absorb'd ONE only being knows,
Of all perceptions ONE abundant source,
Whence every object every moment flows:
Suns hence derive their force,
Hence planets learn their course;
But suns and fading worlds I view no more:
GOD only I perceive, GOD only I adore!

Various are the conjectures of d'Anquitel, Niebuhr, and other travellers, respecting these caverns, but none satisfactory; the author of the Indian Antiquities, and several writers who have recently published their investigations are more explanatory. Before I proceed to that part of the subject, I shall transcribe Dr. Fryer's entertaining account of his visit to the excavated mountains at Salsette, a century before I saw them.

" Curiosity led me to visit the island of Canorein, or Salsette; nor went I alone, some of the best quality on the island of Bombain being led by the same desire, joined themselves with me: we carried a train of horses, palanquins, and servants, which were ferried over before us; and we coming soon after, were met by some members of the convent of Jesuits, and conducted to the fathers, who detained us till afternoon by a stately banquet, shewing us the civility of the church and college, diverting us both with instrumental and vocal music, and very good wine: and wherever we came afterwards, we received, by the kindness of the padre-superior, presents of the best fruits and wines, and whatever we wanted.

"Here, not adjoining to any town, in a sweet air, stood a magnificent rural church; in the way to which, and indeed all up and down this island, are pleasant aldeas, or country seats of the gentry, where they live like petty monarchs, all that is born on the ground being theirs; holding them in a perfect state of villainage, they being lords paramount. (It may perhaps be necessary for me to remark, that the island of Salsette belonged at that time to the crown of Portugal.)

"From hence, when we had baited, the same night we travelled easily to Magatana, using our fowling-pieces all the way; being here presented with rich game, as peacocks, doves, and pigeons, chitrels or spotted deer. When we came to the town, two several churches strove to receive us: we accepted of one; and as soon as we came in, the servitors fetched us warm water to wash our feet, which was very refreshing; it put us in mind of Lot's courtesy to the angels. This night we fared well: next morn before break of day we directed our steps to the anciently famed, but now ruined city of Canorein: the way to it is so delightsome, I thought I had been in England; fine arable, pasture, and coppices: thus we passed five miles to the foot of the hill on which the city stands; and had passed half a mile through a thick wood, peopled by apes, tigers, wild buffaloes, and jackals: here were some flocks of parroquets.

"When we alighted, the sun began to mount the horizon over the hills, and under our feet, as if he had newly bathed his fiery coursers: there appeared the mouth of a tank, or aqueduct, out of a rock, whose steaming breath was very hot, but water cold: from hence it is thought the whole city to be supplied with water; for as we ascend, we find such places, where convenient, filled with limpid water, not over-matched in India: if it be so, as I know not how to contradict it, that it should have its current upwards through the hard rocks artificially cut, the world cannot parallel so wonderful a water-course. From hence the passage is uneasy and inaccessible for more than two abreast, till we come to the city, all cut out of a rock; where is presented Vulcan's forge, supported by two mighty colosses, bellied in the middle with two globes. Next a temple with a beautiful frontispiece, not unlike the portico of St. Paul's west gate: within the porch on each side stand two monstrous giants, where two lesser and one great gate give a noble entrance: it can receive no light but at the doors and windows of the porch, whereby it looks more solemnly: the roof is arched, seeming to be born up by huge pillars of the same rock; some round, some square, thirty-four in number, and the cornice work of elephants, horses, lions. At the upper end it rounds like a bow; near where stands a great offertory somewhat oval, the body of it without pillars; they only making a narrow piazza about, leaving the nave open: it may be an hundred feet in length, in height sixty feet or more.

"Beyond this, by the same *mole-like* industry, was worked out a court of judicature, (as those going to show it will needs give it names) or place of audience, fifty feet square, all bestuck with imagery, well engraven according to old sculpture. On the side over against the door, sat one superintendant, to whom the brahmin who went with us paid great reverence, not speaking of him without a token of worship; whom he called Jogee, or the holy man: under this the way being made into handsome marble steps, are the king's stables, not different from the fashion of our noblemen's stables; only at the head of every stall seems to be a dormitory, or place for devotion, with images; which gave occasion to doubt if ever for that end; or rather made for an heathen seminary of devotees, and these their cells or chapels, and the open place their common hall, or school: more aloft stood the king's palace, large, stately, and magnificent; surrounded with lesser of the nobility.

"To see all would require a month's time; but that we might see as much as we could in our allotted time, we got upon the highest part of the mountain, where we feasted our eyes with innumerable entrances of these coney-burrows, but could not see one quarter part. Whose labour this should be, or for what purpose, is out of memory: but this place by the gentiles is much adored: some contend for Alexander; and, as a proof, think they have said enough, when it is received by tradition, that a great gap was cut by him out of a solid rock to make this an island: but this is contradictory to the story delivered of Alexander, that he sailed up the Indus, and encountered king Porus; of whom some little remains may be collected, they speaking of that king by the name of Por, in Cambaia.

"Returning to Magatana, we spent some days in riding about the country, which we found every where provided with churches. The chief city of this island is Tanaw, in which are seven churches and colleges, the chiefest one of the Paulistines: the houses tiled, but low: here are made good stuffs of silk and cotton. The Portugals suffer none but christians here; it has no rivers, only inlets from the sea; but good springs from the rocks; the ground excellently fertile, either of itself, or by the care of the inhabitants; that it yields good cabbages, coleworts, and better radishes than ever I yet saw: besides garden fruit, here are incomparable water-melons, and onions as sweet and as well tasted as an apple; and for the natural growth of the soil, it is known not only to supply the adjoining islands, but Goa also: it is more than twenty miles in length, and seventy in circumference."

Dr. Fryer's account of the excavated mountains at Salsette, and the temples at the Elephanta, though very entertaining, throw no light on their origin: I did not pursue his route of Alexander, as it is foreign to the subject; and it appears almost ridiculous to mention the opinion of those travellers who conjecture the excavations to have been made in the reign of Solomon, by artists who sailed in his fleet from Ezion-geber to Ophir, for the commodities of India; and as a proof of this assertion, point out a sculptured group at the Elephanta, where they pretend to trace the story of the celebrated judgment of that monarch in the case of the two harlots: this is too groundless for discussion. Many attribute them to Alexander, as remarked by Dr. Fryer; but after crossing the Indus, and entering the Punjab, that country watered by five rivers, the Macedonian hero made little progress into the southern provinces of Hindostan; for, on the banks of the river Chelum, or Betah, the ancient Hydaspes, he was opposed by Porus, the Indian sovereign, as appears from Arrian's history, taken from the journals of Aristobulus, Nearchus, and the other generals who accompanied Alexander: the hardships his veteran Greeks had undergone in their marches during the rainy season, made them refuse to advance further; although he doubtless meant to have extended his conquests to the banks of the Ganges. The river Hyphasis, now called the Beyah, was the boundary of his march from Persia; from thence he commenced his return to that kingdom, and there he erected several monuments in memory of his achievements. Nearchus fitted out a fleet of near two thousand vessels, of various size and construction, on the Hydaspes, a branch of the Indus, with which he entered that noble river, and following its stream to the ocean, proceeded by the Persian gulph to the Euphrates; while Alexander himself returned, with the remainder of his army, through Persia. The other parts of Hindostan had then remained unpenetrated by the conqueror; this would abundantly disprove all connexion between these works and Alexander's expedition, did not the total absence of any thing Grecian, in the style of architecture, or the character of the mythological figures, preclude any such idea.

Sir Charles Malet's judicious remarks on the excavations at Ellora, which are similar, and most probably contemporary with those at Salsette and the Elephanta, throw considerable light on these wonderful productions; although in his letter to Lord Teignmouth he does not allow his inquiries to have been entirely satisfactory. "Doubtless they are the works of people whose religion and mythology were purely Hindoo, and most of the excavations carry strong marks of dedication to MAHDEW, as the presiding deity. The fanciful analogies of some travellers, (particularly that attributed to the eight-handed figure of VEER BUDDER, holding up rajah DUTZ in one hand, and a drawn sword in the other, with the famous judgment of Solomon) now vanish; and we no longer seek for colonies of *Jews*, *Egyptians*, *Ethiopians*, or *Pheni-cians*, to supercede the more rational mode of accounting for such works, in the enthusiastic labour and ingenuity of the natives of the country; by which means the wonder is at least simplified."

"The difference of the inscriptions in some of the caves, from the present known characters of Hindostan, may be objected to their being the produce of Hindoo artists; but it is well known that the formation of letters undergoes great changes in the course of ages, and that such is the case with respect to the excavations on the western side of India, may be fairly inferred, from the difficulty with which the ingenious Mr. Charles Wilkins traced and recovered, as I have been informed, some inscriptions in the neighbourhood of Ghya. But I am inclined to think that we are not sufficiently acquainted with the characters of the south of India, such as the *Tumbole*, *Arvee*, *Kenaraa*, and *Telinghee*, to pronounce on their affinity to those in the excavations, which will be fully submitted to the scrutiny of the learned in an intended publication by Mr. Wales; whose fine taste, masterly pencil, and laudable industry, are mentioned in my former letter; he has already made great progress in such a collection of these wonderful antiquities, many of them hitherto unheard of by Europeans, and first discovered by his inquiries, as, with the addition of those at Ellora, will at once engage and satisfy the expectations of the learned and the curious.

"Though I have mentioned my persuasion that the generality of the excavations I have seen, not only at Ellora, but elsewhere, are dedicated to MAHDEW; yet I do not mean thereby to abandon an idea, that the most northerly caves of Ellora, occupied by the sitting and standing figures, are the works of the *Sewras* or *Juttees*, who by the brahmins are esteemed schismatics; and whose sect, called *Shawuk*, is very numerous in Guzerat. The tenets, observances, and habits of the Sewras are peculiar and, in many points, very different from other Hindoos. Their adoration of the deity is conveyed through the mediation of ADNAUT and PARISNAUT, the visible objects of their worship, personified as a naked man, sitting or standing. This sect is supposed to be of a comparatively modern origin; if so, and if the foregoing hypothesis of the dedication of the temples to their idol, be admitted, the limit of their possible antiquity follows, but without ascertaining, or affecting that of the others."

"Whether we consider the design, or contemplate the execution, of these extraordinary works, we are lost in wonder at the idea of forming a vast mountain into almost eternal mansions. The mythological symbols and figures throughout the whole, leave no room to doubt their owing their existence to religious zeal: the most powerful and most universal agitator of the human mind."

Sir Charles Malet's account of the temple at Ellora was preceded in the Asiatic researches by a description of the excavations at the island of Elephanta, by Mr. Goldingham, whose investigations corroborate Sir Charles's so far as to prove that neither Egyptians, Jews, nor Greeks, had any share in the undertaking.

Mr. Goldingham's descriptions of the several compartments of figures and of the detached baths and temples, are very accurate, and discriminated with judgment; he justly supposes the triple bust to be a personification of the three grand Hindoo attributes of that Being for whom the ancient Hindoos entertained the most profound veneration, and of whom they had the most sublime conceptions. The middle head represents Brahma, or the creative attribute; that on the left Vishnu, or the preserving; and the head on the right, Siva, or the destructive or changing attribute. The figure with one breast appears to be a representation of the consort of Siva exhibiting the active power of her lord, not only as Bawani, or courage, but as Isani, or the goddess of nature, considered as male and female, and presiding over generation, and also as Durga. Here we find the bull of Iswara (one of Siva's names), and the figure bearing his trisule or trident. The beautiful figure on the elephant is Cama, or the Hindoo god of love; the figure with four heads supported by birds, is a representation of Brahma, and that with four arms mounted on the shoulders of another, is Vishnu. The two principal figures in the niche to the left, represent, perhaps, Siva and his goddess as Parvati, with Brahma and Vishnu in the back ground.

The terrific figure with eight arms has been supposed by some to represent Solomon threatening to divide the harlot's child; others suppose it to be the tyrant Cansa attempting the life of the infant god Crishna when fostered by the herdsman Ananda. But in this, the third attribute, or the destroyer in action, is too well represented to be mistaken: the distant scene, where the smaller figures appear in distress and pain, is perhaps the infernal regions. The figures, male and female, sitting, with a bull couching at the feet of the former, are Siva and his goddess; and thus they are represented in the temples of the present day. The figure with the human body and elephant's head, cannot be mistaken for any other than Ganésa, the Hindoo god of wisdom, and the first-born of Siva; and the lingam is a sufficient testimony of Siva's having presided in this ancient Hindoo temple.

Mr. Goldingham does not attempt to deduce the æra of the fabrication of this wonderful structure; but a considerable light is thrown on the subject by Mr. Wilford, whose erudition has been conspicuously displayed in the transactions of the Asiatic Society. He has discovered some of the inscriptions in the caves at Salsette to be the pure Sanscrit dialect, and the characters, though uncouth and barbarous, of the same language; others again are engraved in an ancient vernacular dialect, and in characters derived from the original, or primeval Sanscrit, since they are established on the same elements, although very different in form from those at present in use. The subject of these inscriptions would perhaps have been of little importance, had they not led to a very valuable discovery of ancient alphabets; which may hereafter facilitate the deciphering of other inscriptions of greater consequence.

In the literature of India there is no legend more celebrated than the wars of the Kooroos and Pandoos, the sons of Detrarashtra and Pandoo, for the dominion of Hindostan—a subject which has given birth to the Mahabarat, a poem that, among the Hindoos, has the credit of divine inspiration, and which Mr. Hastings has compared with the Iliad of Homer.

Detrarashtra and Pandoo were the sons of Veectreetraveerga, who was succeeded in the empire by Pandoo in consequence of his elder brother being incapacitated by blindness. Detrarashtra is said to have had a hundred sons, of whom Doorgadun was the eldest, and in fact the representative of that branch of the family distinguished under the name of Kooroos: the sons of Pandoo were five; Yoodishter, Bheem, Arjoon, Nekool, and Sahader.

Upon the death of Pandoo, Doorgadun, his nephew, succeeded to the throne; hence divisions were excited, and conspiracies were alternately formed, on the one hand, to usurp the government, and on the other, to extirpate the race of Pandoo. At length, to terminate the feuds, it was agreed between Doorgadun and Yoodishter to divide the kingdom; when Doorgadun conceived an artifice by which he might remove his rival, without occasioning those contentions to which the empire had before been a prey. To effect this purpose he challenged Yoodishter to a game of chance; which being accepted, Doorgadun, by means of false dice, won all his adversary's wealth and kingdom; and having thus succeeded, he agreed to give him one chance more of redeeming his loss, if, in case of failure, he would retire with his brothers for twelve years into such strict banishment, that they should not within that time be seen by any man. These terms were consented to, Doorgadun prevailed, and the Pandoos entered upon their exile into forests the most unfrequented. The term of their seclusion from society being expired, they addressed Doorgadun, by Vedum and Vyasa, to be restored; when, their overtures being rejected with contempt, they assembled a large army, and effected by force what they failed in by entreaty; for in a pitched battle fought between the two armies near the city of Tanassar, the Kooroos were vanquished, and Yoodishter succeeded to the throne.

It is to these exiles in the forests that the inscriptions are found to relate; they consist of short obscure sentences, supposed to have been engraven on rocks and stones by Vedum and Vyasa, the friends of the Pandoos, communicating to them, by their means, such intelligence as was necessary to their safety; consoling them in their misfortunes, and warning them against the arts of Doorgadun.

These transactions are supposed to have happened in the commencement of Kalee Youg, a period between four thousand eight hundred, and five thousand years ago: and some of the most respectable Hindoos of the present day, entertain a firm conviction that these inscriptions are the authentic works of Vedum and Vyasa. It may be interesting to the lovers of Hindoo literature to be informed that this Vyasa is the reputed author of the Puranas.

Such is the recent account of those inscriptions, and certainly there are many corroborating circumstances in the sculpture, especially in the caves at the Elephanta, to strengthen this opinion; and particularly so at Mont-pesser, or Mundip Ishwur, on Salsette: at a little distance from whence there still remain six obelisks, in tolerable preservation. On some of them is a representation, in basso-relievo, of sea and land battles; the vessels engaged in a furious combat are extremely well represented: on others are carved the emblems of peace, and similar subjects, which may perhaps relate to the æra just mentioned.

Before I conclude my account of these excavations, I must not omit the striking resemblance which has been observed between them and the sculptured grottos in Egypt; a circumstance which seems to imply that either the Egyptians copied from the Hindoos, or the Hindoos from them; the former is now generally allowed. Not far from the city of Assuan, the ancient Syen described by

Strabo, on the confines of Ethiopia, the rocks on the western banks of the Nile are hewn into grottoes, with places of worship, columns, pilasters, and hieroglyphics, as particularly mentioned by modern travellers. Strabo also describes the adjacent island of Elephantina, with its surrounding rocks in the Nile; from whence were hewn those enormous masses used in the magnificent structures of Egypt, and especially of that amazing cube, each side measuring sixty feet, in which the sanctuary of Butis was cut. The island of Elephantina in the time of Strabo contained a small town, with the temple of Cneph, and a celebrated Nilometer.

I have often been struck with the idea that there may be some affinity between the *written mountains* in Arabia, and the *excavated mountains* in Hindostan; I mean only as far as relates to such records or memorials in times of remote antiquity. The book of Job is allowed to be of a very ancient date; coeval, if not antecedent, to the writings of Moses. In his sublime and pathetic apostrophe the afflicted patriarch exclaims, "O that my words were now written! oh that they were printed in a book! that they were graven with an iron pen and lead in the rock for ever! for I know that my REDEEMER liveth, and that he shall stand at the latter day upon the earth: and though worms destroy this body, yet in my flesh shall I see GOD; whom I shall see for myself; and mine eyes shall behold, and not another!"

In this memorable speech to his misjudging and uncharitable friends, uttered by the venerable sufferer, in strong faith and fervent hope, he not only makes this animated appeal, but ardently wishes to have it recorded for the consolation of the latest posterity. Printing, so improperly introduced by the English translators, was then unknown; manuscripts were perishing, but the rock was permanent. On an adamantine rock, therefore, did the pious prince wish that his words might be engraved, the characters filled up with lead, and remain indelible for ever! All this must certainly allude to a custom then known: most probably the written mountains in Arabia, the very country in which they lived, were extant at the time, and familiar to his hearers.

Engraving on stones was generally practised in Egypt: their hieroglyphics were cut in the hardest granite; the obelisks were sculptured in intaglio, filled with cement of various colours; which is probably what our translators have meant by lead. These memorials brought into Europe by the Roman emperors, the remains of excavated hills and sculptured rocks still extant in Egypt, united with the accounts of the Greek historians, undoubtedly prove the antiquity of works similar to those in India. The written mountains of Arabia appear to be a strong confirmation that such memorials were not uncommon in those early ages The characters engraved on the portals of the excavated mountains in Hindostan, and the adjacent rocks, have very lately been deciphered: I copied several lines from the entrance of the caves of Canara, which were then pronounced obsolete, and past finding out: Mr. Wilford has proved the contrary. Possibly, in this enlightened age, the characters on the Arabian mountains may yet be explained.

In the bishop of Clogher's account of the written mountains in Arabia, he says, " the Prefetto of Egypt writes in his journal, that after disengaging ourselves from the mountains of Faran, we came to a large plain, surrounded by high hills; at the foot of which we reposed ourselves in our tents. These hills are called *Gebel el Mokatab*, that is, the *Written Mountains:* for as soon as we had parted from the mountains of Faran, we passed by several others for an hour together, engraved with ancient unknown characters, which were cut in the hard marble rock, so high as to be in many places at twelve or fourteen feet distance from the ground; and though we had in our company persons who were acquainted with the Arabic, Greek, Hebrew, Syriac, Coptic, Latin, Armenian, Turkish, Illyrian, and other languages, yet none of them had any knowledge of these characters; which have nevertheless been cut into the hard rock, with the greatest industry, in a place where there is neither water, nor any thing to be gotten to eat. It is probable, therefore, these unknown characters contain some very secret mysteries; and that they were engraved either by the Chaldeans, or some other persons, long before the Christian era."

Niebuhr mentions a large cemetery in the desert of Sinai, where a great many stones are set up in an erect position, on a high and steep mountain, covered with as beautiful hieroglyphics as those of the Egyptian mountains. The Arabs carried them to this burial place, which is more remarkable than the written mountains, seen and described by other travellers in this desert; for so many well-cut stones could never be the monuments of wandering Arabs, but must necessarily owe their origin to the inhabitants of some great city near this place, which is, however, now a desert.

Most of the preceding remarks formed the subject of a letter written in 1774, after my first visit to the excavations on Salsette. I shall not at present enter into the political disputes and civil wars then subsisting in the Mahratta state; they are detailed in a future chapter: towards the end of that year those commotions afforded the government of Bombay an opportunity of obtaining the islands of Salsette, Caranjah and Elephanta; the former was an acquisition of great importance to Bombay. In consequence of a treaty between the Select Committee of Bombay, and Ragonath Row, Peshwa of the Mahratta empire, by which those islands were ceded to the Company, a detachment of 120 European artillery, 200 artillery Lascars, 500 European infantry, and 1000 Sepoys, under the command of General Gordon, proceeded to Tannah, the principal fortress on Salsette; which, in consequence of orders from the Mahratta ministers at Poonah, the Killedar refused to surrender, they being then engaged in a civil war against Ragonath Row.

The English batteries opened on the 20th of December, and the breach was effected on the 24th, when the general resolved to storm. While our troops were filling the ditch during the night a heavy fire from the fort obliged them to retire with the loss of near an hundred Europeans, and several officers wounded: they stormed again on the 28th, and obtained possession with a trifling loss on our side, but a dreadful slaughter of the garrison, who made an obstinate resistance.

During the siege of Tannah, a detachment, under the command of Lieutenant Colonel Keating, marched against Versava, a small fortress on the west side of Salsette, which surrendered on the fourth day when the batteries opened, after our troops had been twice repulsed in attempting an escalade. Colonel Keating then proceeded with another detachment to the island of

Caranjah, situated on the east side of Bombay harbour; the fortress was soon evacuated, and the Elephanta and Hog-island, at that time belonging to the Mahrattas, were surrendered to the English without opposition.

Thus did the Company acquire these desirable possessions in the vicinity of Bombay; they have since been guaranteed by the Mahratta government, and form a part of the Bombay establishment.

I paid an early visit to these new conquests: it is a pleasant passage of a few hours from Bombay to Tannah, which so soon after the siege made a desolate appearance. The fort was a pentagon, with regular bastions, curtains, and towers, mounting more than a hundred cannon; most of which were damaged or dismounted during the siege: it was built by the Portugueze when masters of the island, and altered by the Mahrattas, who conquered Salsette and Bassein during the Peshwaship of Bajerow. When in possession of the Mahrattas, the houses and gardens at Tannah reached very near the fortifications; the English engineer immediately removed them, to form an esplanade of five hundred yards from the east to the north-west tower; the other sides were rendered inaccessible by the river and morasses. Half a mile from the fort is a Portugueze church, pleasantly situated on the side of a large tank, surrounded by mango and tamarind groves; the spires and domes of mosques and Hindoo temples rising amid their dark foliage, produce a good effect.

I sailed from Salsette to Caranjah, and landed about two miles from the principal town, situated between two lofty mountains, on the west side: it was nothing more than a large Mahratta village, with low straggling houses, near a tank covered with wild ducks and water-fowl, hitherto unmolested by Europeans. On its banks a small fort, a Portugueze church, and a Hindoo temple embellished the view. The principal fort stands on the summit of a lofty mountain, romantically diversified by woods and rock: the ascent is steep and difficult. This castle, small, badly constructed, and mounting only fourteen guns, was incapable of defence, but its situation rendered it almost inaccessible. It commands a western view of the town and harbour of Bombay, Salsette, and all the adjacent islands, and to the east the mountains of the continent, and nearer plains of Caranjah; abounding with rice-fields, cocoa-nut, palmyra, mango, and tamarind trees, filled with monkeys, parrots, owls, and singing-birds of various kinds.

Engraved by J. Greig

Interior View of the principal Excavated TEMPLE on the Island of ELEPHANTA.

Jam. Forbes, 1774

Published by White Cochrane & Co. Fleet Street, June 1st 1812.

Engraved by J. Shury.

Comparative View of two principal Pillars, in the Excavations at SALSETTE and ELEPHANTA.

Jam. Forbes. 1774.

Engraved by J. Stone

HILL FORT *on the Island of* CARANJAH.

Jam. Forbes. 1774.

Published by White, Cochrane & Co. Fleet Street, June 1st 1812.

CHAPTER XV.

HISTORY OF THE MAHRATTA EMPIRE FROM ITS FIRST FOUNDATION, TO THE MURDER OF NARRAIN ROW IN 1773; AND THE COMMENCEMENT OF THE CIVIL WAR BETWEEN RAGONAUTH ROW, AND THE CONFEDERATE CHIEFTAINS. 1775.

One part of mankind is naturally curious to learn the sentiments, manners, and condition of the rest; and every mind that has leisure or power to extend its views, must be desirous of knowing in what proportion Providence has distributed the blessings of nature, or the advantages of art, among the several nations of the earth. DR. JOHNSON.

CONTENTS.

The author obtains an appointment among the civil servants attached to the British detachment ordered from Bombay, to assist Ragonath-Row, peshwa of the Mahrattas, then driven from his capital, and at the head of an army in Guzerat—origin of the Mahratta empire—epitome of the Hindoos in general—derivation of the Mahratta name—Shajee the founder of the empire—his son, Sevajee, assumes the title of rajah—his wars with Aurungzebe, depredations in the Mogul empire, and death in 1680—*misfortunes and death of his son Sambajee by Aurungzebe—military character of the Mahrattas—great increase of their army—Raje-Ram—his widow assumes the government—dreadful scenes in the Mogul empire on the death of Aurungzebe—its rapid decline, subsequent plunder of Delhi by Nadir Shah, and wanton cruelties on the destruction of the Mogul power at the conclusion of the eighteenth century—Saojee, the son of Sambojee, escapes from the Moguls, and ascends the Mahratta throne—constitutes the great council—rapid rise of the brahmin family of Ballajee—Ballajee advanced to the dignity of peshwa—supersedes the power and splendour of the rajah, and becomes in fact sovereign of the Mahrattas—success of the Mahrattas, and increase of their dominions, under the administration of Ballajee Bajerow and Nanna Saib—situation of Poonah, the capital of the empire—progress of the Mahrattas in the art of war—battle of Paniput—death of Nanna Saib—accession of Mhadarow—disputes with his uncle Ragobah—foreign wars—success—and death of Mhaderow—conduct to his brother Narrain*

Row on his death-bed—last interview with his wife—his noble behaviour and provision for her widowhood—her resolution to devote herself on his funeral pyre; fortitude and dignity on that trying occasion—accession of Narrain Row; weak and irresolute character of that prince—machinations of his uncle Ragobah—massacre of Narrain Row—Ragobah claims the title of peshwa—and assumes the government—Ragobah's imprudent conduct respecting the murderers of Narrain Row—the mother and widow of Narrain Row appear in public view—character of the former—the latter declares herself pregnant—ceremony of investing Ragobah with the honours of peshwa procrastinated on that account—Narrain Row's widow delivered of a prince—Ragobah leaves Poonah, and marches against the Nizam—confederation of the ministers in favour of the infant peshwa, and commencement of the civil war—Ragobah applies to the Bombay government for a detachment of British troops, and enters into a treaty—embarkation of the English detachment to join his army in Guzerat.

CHAPTER XV.

Soon after the conquest of Salsette I obtained one of the appointments generally given to the civil servants, with the detachment of British forces sent from Bombay to the assistance of Ragonath-Row, at that time the reigning sovereign of the Mahrattas, though he had then been driven from his capital by the confederate ministers; and when the Bombay government resolved to reinstate him on the musnud at Poonah, he was encamped with his army in the province of Guzerat, waiting for the junction of the English troops.

That a war, which, in its consequences, has engaged the East India Company in various treaties and alliances with the Mahrattas, may be better understood, I shall give some account of that extraordinary nation; who, by their caste, are accounted among the lower tribes of the Hindoos; but by courage, policy, and perseverance, are become the most powerful and formidable people in Hindostan.

Having already described the Hindoos, in their national and individual character, it is only necessary, in this place, to recapitulate a few circumstances, in which the Mahrattas are generally included. Their religious tenets are mild and benevolent; and, although mixed with many errors, and bewildered in the mazes of polytheism, their definition of the Supreme Being is truly sublime; their rites and ceremonies, with a few exceptions, are pious, inoffensive, and suited to the climate. The high caste of brahmins are their priests and philosophers; the physicians of their bodies, and the guardians of their souls: I now allude to the recluse sects of this order, who minister in the temples, and preside in the colleges and religious ceremonies; or abstemiously retire from the world, to spend their days in pious exercises and superstitious penance.

The brahmins, banians, and superior castes of the Hindoos, are generally innocent and peaceable; they never taste any thing that either has or can have life, abstaining even from eggs, because they contain the vital principle; nor will they put to death the most noxious reptile. Many of these enthusiasts carry a small broom to sweep the ground before they sit down, lest they should crush some insect, and wear a cloth before their mouth from the fear of inhaling them with their breath. The diet of the higher tribes of Hindoos consists of grain, pulse, fruit, milk, and vegetables, except onions and garlic: made into curries, seasoned with spices and butter, to be eaten with rice, constitute their principal meal: the Rajepoots, Mahrattas, and many of the inferior castes, eat mutton, pork, goat, venison, and fish: but no one, on any consideration, will taste the flesh of the ox or cow, an animal held in the highest degree of veneration by every Hindoo.

After this brief recapitulation of the Hindoos in general, I shall confine myself to the Mahrattas, who are said to derive their name and origin from *Mah'rat*, signifying the great province, or country;

and designating a large, although an undefined portion of that part of Hindostan called Deccan, or Deckshan, meaning the south country, as situated south of the river Narbudda. From a state of rustic obscurity, and rigorous vassalage, the Mahrattas, within the last century, have become a mighty power; and, in that period, precipitated and completed the ruin of the Mogul empire, which had commenced in its own vices.

The founder of the Mahratta preeminence was Sahjee, or Shajee, of the Bhosla tribe, for among the Mahrattas are many distinct tribes; but the first who assumed the title of rajah, or king, was his son Sevajee: after an infinite variety of fortune, and being led captive by Aurungzebe, he escaped from the hands of that powerful emperor; and by the wonderful exertions of his own genius, seconded by his hardy countrymen, established the foundation of his power, amidst the inaccessible mountains and fortresses of the Deccan, and extended his predatory excursions to the rich provinces of Guzerat and Carnatic. In the fortieth year of his age he assumed the title and honours of rajah, and ascended the regal throne in the fort of Rairee, A. D. 1673. From that time Sevajee waged such an incessant war against the Moguls, that Aurungzebe, although next to Acber, the most warlike and vigorous of their emperors, was baffled and distracted by the innumerable and indefatigable invaders; who, like the barbarians on the Roman empire, poured down from their mountains, and devastated his fairest provinces.

Sevajee's career closed with his life in 1680, leaving two sons, Sambajee and Raja-Ram; the former succeeded his father on the throne, and therewith to hostilities with the Moguls. To his brother he gave the fort and principality of Pannella; and his successors retain it to this day. His own destiny was less fortunate; for having been made a prisoner by Aurungzebe, through the treachery of Cablis Caun, whom he esteemed as his most confidential friend, he was brought into the imperial presence, and on refusing to apostatize, the bigotted despot condemned him to a cruel death; so cruel, and so strikingly descriptive of Aurungzebe's character, that I shall transcribe the tragic scene from Orme's Historical Fragments.

" Sambajee appeared before Aurungzebe with undaunted brow; who reproached Cablis Caun, not with his treachery, but the encouragement which his prostituted ministry had given to vices which at length had led his sovereign to ruin, and ordered him to instant death. To Sambajee he proffered life, and rank in his service, if he would turn Mahomedan; who answered by an invective against the prophet, and the land of his own gods. On which he was dressed in the fantastic ornaments of a wandering Indian devotee, who beg in villages with a rattle and a cap with bells. In this garb he was tied, looking backwards, upon a camel, and led through the camp, calling upon all the Rajepoots he saw to kill him; but nonc dared. After the procession, his tongue was cut out, as the penalty of blaspheming Mahomet. In this forlorn condition, Aurungzebe, by a message, again offered to preserve his life, if he would be converted; when he wrote, " Not if you would give me your daughter in marriage:" on which his execution was ordered, and performed, by cutting out his heart; after which his limbs and body were separated, and altogether were thrown to dogs prepared to devour them."

For having thus emerged from obscurity, and the rustic habits of pastoral and agricultural society, to the dominion of vast and opulent regions, the Mahrattas are indebted to the two preceding heroes: from them the nation assumed a military character, priding themselves more on their proficiency in arms than in letters; leaving the revenue-department and management of the exchequer to the brahmins, who have since become so powerful in the empire. Although descended from a rural race, a spirit of enterprize, plunder, and usurpation, is now the prevailing characteristic of this restless nation, ever ready to engage in a desultory kind of warfare, which they conduct with great ease and profit to themselves, to the dreadful annoyance of their neighbours. This enterprising spirit keeps them in almost perpetual actions, either with foreign enemies, domestic rivals, or in military expeditions to collect their choute in different and distinct parts of Hindostan.

The Mahratta army made a rapid increase under the unfortunate Sambajee: the number of their cavalry and infantry, either at that period, or the present day, cannot be exactly ascertained: in the middle of the eighteenth century their united forces amounted to at least two hundred thousand horse, and fifty thousand foot, which they can at any time increase considerably without the least coercion: that indeed forms no part of their system: voluntary levies supply ample recruits to an army where no rigour of discipline or subordination obstructs the general taste for war and predatory excursions.

Rajée Ram succeeded to the government on the death of his brother Sambajee, and the captivity of his nephew Suojee, who had been made a prisoner with his father. He maintained his situation through a variety of fortune, against the power of Aurungzebe, until the year 1707, when death carried off the Mogul and Mahratta sovereign within a very short period of each other. On this event *Tarrabhye,* the widow of Rajeé Ram, assumed the reins of the Mahratta government, although she had a son by her husband, then living, called Sevajee Raja; and rajee Ram left another son, named Sambajee Raja, by *Rajusbhye,* to whom also he was married.

On the death of Aurúngzebe, dreadful was the contest for succession to the Mogul empire between his two sons, Sultan Aazim and Sultan Moazim, called also Azem Shah, and Mahommed Mauzim: the victor, treading in the footsteps of his cruel father, wore a crown of thorns, and deluged the musnud with fraternal blood: his three short-lived successors were dethroned and murdered by the SEYDS, Abdalla and Hossan, who at length in 1729 established Mahommed Shah on the vacant throne, which he occupied until the irruption of Nadir Shah in 1738, when Delhi was plundered of all its money and jewels, the accumulated wealth of ages. The savage cruelties of Mahmood, Timur, and the northern conquerors were renewed, and again an hundred thousand of the wretched inhabitants were tortured and massacred to discover their hoarded treasures: the plunder amounted to seventy millions sterling, including the peacock-throne, which cost Aurungzebe's father eleven millions. After these devastations, Mahommed Shah was reinstated by his conqueror on a throne, less splendid, and to the government of an empire then shook to its foundation. From that period, to the conclusion of a century which Aurungzebe commenced in the meridian of power, wealth, and dignity, seldom equalled, this immense fabric fell to ruin, until in 1788 Gholaum Kaudir, a Rohilla chief, for the last time plundered Delhi, with a cruelty surpassing even the atrocities of Timur and Nadir Shah. After robbing the palace of every valuable left by the latter fifty years before, Gholaum Kaudir concluded the tragedy by plucking out the eyes of the aged emperor, and consigning him to poverty and wretchedness. This monster of barbarity surpassed the tyrant whose portrait, drawn by himself, has been thus transmitted by Orme. A dervise had the boldness to present a writing to the Persian conqueror conceived in these words: "If "thou art a god, act as a god; if thou art a prophet, conduct us "in the way of salvation; if thou art a king, render the people "happy, and do not destroy them!" To this the barbarian replied, "I am no god, to act as a god; nor a prophet, to shew the "way of salvation; nor a king to render the people happy: but I "am he whom GOD sends to the nations which he has determined "to visit with his wrath!"

During the rivalship between Aurungzebe's sons, which eventually ruined the Mogul empire, sultan Aazim liberated Saojee, the captive son of the Mahratta sovereign Sambojee, murdered by his father, and sent him into the Deccan to recover his patrimony. On his arrival, Tarrabhye, pretending he was an impostor, disallowed his claims, and rejected his admission; in this emergency Saojee being joined by several powerful Mahratta chieftains, and especially by Pursojee Bhosla, from whom are descended the Nagpore rajahs, he overcame all opposition, and triumphantly ascended the throne in Sattara. Tarrabhye, with her son and adherents, retired into the strong hold of Pannella.

Saojee, who was from this period called the Sasu-rajah, proceeded with energy to reestablish the deranged system of the Mahratta government. The first and most important measure he adopted was the constituting the great council of the empire. In the course of these official arrangements, Ballajee Wissarath became a prominent character: he was a brahmin of the Concan, and had previously served Dunnajee Jaddoo, the Seyna-Puttee, or generalissimo; but attracting the rajah's notice, he was first employed as seyna-kurtee, or deputy of his old master; from which he was advanced to the dignity of *peshwa*, or acting general of the forces, and subsequently exalted to a place among the eight grand counsellors, with the title of *pundit purdhan*, or purdhan pud. This is the foundation of that vicarial power which, under the well known title of *peshwa*, or leader, has superseded the actual power and splendour of the Mahratta rajahs; who indeed continue to exist, with a certain degree of regal state, in the fortress of Sattara, but under such restraint as the reigning peshwa may think proper to impose, the title and forms of supremacy being still ascribed to the existing rajah, from whom the peshwa professes to derive his insignia of authority; which consists of a khellat, or investiture, a dagger and a seal, with an inscription describing the peshwa as paramount to the sovereign.

Under this dispensation (ably administered by Ballajee Wissanath and his two immediate successors, amidst the confusion that followed the death of Aurungzebe, and from which the Mogul empire was never more entirely extricated) the Mahrattas utterly subverted and levelled with the dust the vast and mighty fabric of Mogul power, and are themselves beginning to experience the ascendancy of the British dominion over those internal weaknesses and vices which have been produced by civil discord out of their national prosperity. May heaven long avert the same evils from the British!

On the death of Ballajee Wissanath in 1723, after a series of important services to the state, his eldest son Badjerow was appointed by Sao rajah to succeed him as peshwa; and his youngest son, Chimnajee Appa, was made duan, or principal minister. During the administration of Badjerow the important island and fortress of Bassein, with several other subordinate stations, were conquered by the Mahrattas from the Portugueze, about the same time that the Mogul armies were defeated, and Delhi taken by Nadir Shah. The consequent weakness of these disasters greatly assisted the Mahrattas in their expeditions towards the northern provinces; in which, under the auspices of Badjerow, the tribes of Sindia and Holkar became conspicuous, and Malhar Row Holkar, and Rancojee Sindia were entrusted by him with large commands.

The overwhelming power of the Mahrattas, whose tributary exactions were now, under various denominations, almost universally established, would probably have soon annihilated the neighbouring Mogul power in the Deccan, had not the resistance to it been directed by the great talents of the nabob Nizam al Doula, father of the present Nizam al Mulk; the death of Badjerow is attributed to his dejection after a defeat which he sustained from Nassir Jung, the nabob's son, in the neighbourhood of Aurungabad.

On Badjerow's death, in 1743, his eldest son, Ballajee Row,

more generally known by the appellation of the Nanna, or Nanna Saib, succeeded him as peshwa; his second son was called indiscriminately Ragonath Row, Ragobah, and Dadda Saib, names which I shall hereafter explain. Ballajee Row was invested by Saò rajah at Satarra, with the dignities of peshwa and purdun pud: he made his constant abode at Pòonah, an open town in the latitude of 18° 30′ north, and 73° 55′ east longitude, situated at the conflux of the rivers *Moota* and *Moolah*, which, for the convenience of assembling and subsisting the large armies of the Mahratta cavalry, had become the favourite residence of the peshwas, and has since grown into the capital of the Mahratta empire.

Under the administration of Ballajee Row, the Mahrattas established a tribute on the eastern provinces of Bengal: great confusion took place in the Deccan on the death of Nizam al Doula; the subsequent assassination of his eldest son, Ghazd al Deen, and his second son, Massir Jung, previous to the settlement of the Mogul vice-royalty of the Deccan in the person of the third son, Sullabat Jung, who afterwards made way for his brother, the present Nizam ul Mulk. Under this peshwa the Mahrattas became well acquainted with the operations of European regular troops, the French having been introduced by the competitors for the succession of Nizam al Doula, and the Mahrattas having entertained some corps under native and European partizans, to facilitate their operations against fortified places; in his time also the great members of the Mahratta aristocracy, the Bhosla family in Nagpore, under Ragojee, and the Gugkwar in Guzerat, under Damojee, having assumed too much independence, were reduced to subjection: and although he had lost the able assistance of his uncle,

Chimnajee Appa, the success of his arms and councils was great and uninterrupted. He enjoyed the unrivalled favour and confidence of his sovereign, Saò rajah; who, with little personal exertion or interposition in the government, devoted himself to the pleasures of the field and domestic conviviality; and having been happily conducted, by the fidelity and abilities of wise and active ministers, through a long and prosperous reign, he closed it by a natural and tranquil death, in his palace at Satarra, about the year 1749.

Saò Rajah leaving no issue, Rajah Ram, his grand-nephew, and grandson of the preceding prince of the same name, was placed by the peshwa Ballajee Row on the vacant throne, the latter assuming to himself the absolute government of the state, with the assistance of his brother Ragobah, and Sudobah, the son of his deceased uncle, Chimnajee Appa, to whom were occasionally associated his sons, Wiswas Row and Mhada Row; by whose exertions the Mahrattas made great progress against the Moguls in the north of Hindostan, and in the Deccan. The splendid administration of this peshwa was at length clouded by the most decisive and bloody defeat of the Mahratta army by the Afghans under Ahmed Shah Abdallee, in the neighbourhood of Panniput. The Mahrattas were commanded by Sudobah, Wiswas Row, Shumsheen Bhadur, a natural son of the peshwa, and many of the great feudatory chieftains. To those three principal leaders, who were lost in this tremendous battle, are to be added several others of the highest rank and fame in the empire; in fact two only are said to have escaped, Malhar Row, chief of the Holkar, and Damojee, of the Guykwar families. No estimate has ever been ventured of the general slaughter, nor of the whole plunder of this signal overthrow; it is certain that twenty-five thousand prisoners, fifty thousand horses, five hundred elephants, two hundred thousand baggage-oxen, several thousand camels, all the ordnance, and the whole camp, stored with the vast riches attendant on an assemblage of such great chieftains, fell into the hands of the victors.

It is worthy of notice, that the Mahrattas had a large body of regular infantry, and a numerous train of artillery, at the battle of Panniput, under the command of Ibrahim Khan, who had been educated by Monsieur Bussy; he was made prisoner, and put to death by Ahmed Shah's order.

Ballajee Row, accompanied by Jannojee Bhosla, was on his march from the Deccan to succour Sudobah and his sons, when he received intelligence of this disaster, which so deeply affected him, that giving orders for a retreat, he sickened and died in about a month, in 1760, leaving two surviving sons, Mhadarow and Narrainrow. The former, accompanied by his uncle Ragobah, waited on the Saò rajah at Sattara, who with every mark of favour conferred on Mhadārow the dignity of peshwa, purdhan pud, with the other honours and distinctions of his family.

The administration of Mhadarow was chequered by domestic and foreign vicissitudes; the former arising from jealousies which led to hostilities between him and his uncle Ragobah, who was finally subdued and imprisoned; and by the secession of Jannojee Bhosla and Gopal Row, who leagued with Nizam Ally Khan after deposing his brother Sallabut Jung, and assuming the government of the Mogul part of the Deccan. This unnatural coalition caused a temporary ascendency of the Nizam's arms, which was followed by the capture and pillage of Poonah; but the speedy return of the seceding chieftains reestablished the predominance of the Mahrattas, and enabled Mhadarow to direct it with effect against Hyder Ally, who had become formidable in the southern countries of upper Carnatic and Mysore, as also to threaten Mahomed Ally Khan in the lower Carnatic. The northern expeditions of this peshwa were chiefly conducted by Vissajee Krishun, in command of the peshwa's troops, and by the northern feudatories, Tookajee Holkar and Mhadajee Sindia, at the head of their respective quotas, which gave them a decided influence over the Mogul affairs in that quarter.

Mhadarow having administered the government, and supported it vigorously against domestic feuds and foreign foes, during a period of twelve years, died in 1772, much lamented by his country, without issue, at the age of twenty-six, and with him expired the prosperity of the Mahrattas.

Aware of his approaching dissolution, Mhadarow sent for his brother Narrain Row, and knowing the weakness of his understanding, and general incapacity for government, advised him, when invested with the dignity of peshwa by the Saò rajah, to follow a different plan from that which he had adopted, particularly respecting their uncle Ragobah: cautioning him rather to imitate the example of their father, by placing confidence in him, and making him of consequence in the administration. He further counselled him to cultivate the friendship of the old ministers, and attached adherents to their family, from whom alone he could derive assistance, should Ragobah's ambition create any future disturbance.

Mhadarow was endowed with uncommon talents, and possessed a mind unfettered by the restraints and superstitious tenets of the Hindoos: after parting with Narrain Row, he had a last interview with his wife, a woman of beauty and virtue; her personal charms and engaging manners had beguiled the cares of government, and cheered his retired hours in the haram: his actions now testified the sincerity of his affection. To preserve her dignity, and to free her from that degraded state to which the Hindoo widows of every rank are subjected, he settled on her a large jaghire, or annual income, with the supreme controul over a rich and populous country; to this he added a considerable sum of money, and a profusion of jewels. Deprived of such a husband, to her this munificence was of no importance; nothing afforded her consolation but the resolution she immediately adopted, to immolate herself on his funeral pile.

One of the causes usually assigned for this extraordinary sacrifice, could have had no influence on Mhadarow's widow, that of being reduced to a state of dependance and comparative insignificance in her husband's family: this young princess was left her own mistress, and enabled to vie in wealth and dignity with the first nobles in the realm; but, exalted above all sublunary honours, she resolved to add her name to those illustrious females who had accompanied their husbands to the upper world. After bequeathing her property, and dividing her jewels among her friends, she followed Mhadarow's corpse to the spot prepared for its cremation, and having performed the prescribed ceremonies, ascended the awful eminence with admirable dignity and fortitude, and with her own hand set fire to the sandal-pile, which the brahmins fed with clarified butter and aromatic oils.

When Narrain Row succeeded his brother as peshwa in November 1772, he was only twenty years of age; a weak indolent prince, destitute of all talent and resolution; placing no confidence in his ministers, and breaking the most solemn promises: the enfeebling pleasures of the haram had early seduced him from the path of glory: a stranger to every noble virtue, and a slave to sensuality, he lavished immense sums on dancing-girls, fire-works, and similar pursuits, seeming to be placed in a sphere of life he was unworthy to possess, and incapable of sustaining.

In consequence of Narrain Row's last interview with his brother, Ragobah obtained his liberty immediately after his decease: but, far from treating his uncle with the confidence desired, or endeavouring to gain the affection of the Mahratta chieftains, Narrain Row carried himself so haughtily in the durbar, that he entirely lost the esteem of the old friends of his family; and dismissing them from his council, he raised a set of low dissipated characters to the highest and most splendid situations. He behaved with more duplicity to Ragobah than the courtiers he disbanded: to deceive both him and the Saó rajah, he persuaded his uncle to accompany him to Satarra, on his first public visit, when he was to be invested with the insignia of peshwa, promising he should have the title and honours of naib, or vizier, conferred on him by the imprisoned sovereign, which was accordingly performed by the Saó rajah, with all the usual ceremonies. On their return to Poonah, Narrain Row, far from confirming Ragobah in his new appointment, deprived him of the little power he was before intrusted with; and although not immediately remanded to prison, he was surrounded by spies, and ordered not to move from the capital.

Narrain Row's duplicity and ill treatment at length occasioned Ragobah to concert measures with Hyder Ally's ambassador to effect his escape, which being known by the young peshwa, he confined him in his palace, suffering no friend to visit him, nor any of his own servants to attend him. Being all brahmins, Narrain Row could proceed no further, there being then no instance of one of that sacred order taking away the life of another.

Having thus once more imprisoned his uncle, Narrain Row gave himself up to every evil propensity; sensual pleasures, useless pomp, and an ostentatious display of wealth, constituted his chief delight: in a few months he thus squandered the immense treasures amassed by his predecessors for the emergencies of the state. This weakness of character, and insolent behaviour to his ministers, beame every day more disgusting, and the hearts of the people were entirely alienated. At length, conscious of defects which he was too weak and irresolute to amend, and dreading a revolution in favour of Ragobah, he confined him with yet more rigorous severity.

Whether from weariness of life, or to intimidate his nephew, Ragobah now entered into a solemn vow to starve himself, when, his death being attributed to Narrain Row's cruelty, the nation would stigmatize him as the murderer: thus resolved, he put his vow into execution, and, for the space of eighteen days, took no other sustenance than two ounces of deer's milk each day, until being nearly exhausted, Narrain Row relented, and promised, if he would procure brahminical absolution from his vow, he should have the government of a district with five castles, and a jaghire of twelve lacs of rupees per annum, provided some of the great chieftains would become surety for his future conduct; to which they readily assented: but, unmindful of his solemn protestations, the prince, actuated by suspicion and jealousy, again treated his uncle with unrelenting rigour.

Such was the state of affairs in the month of August 1773, when, to the astonishment of all the powers in India, Narrain Row was assassinated in his palace. The accounts of this catastrophe are variously related: the peshwa family and a large part of the nation accused Ragobah of the murder; some of the Mahratta chiefs, and numerous partizans, asserted his innocence. When we consider his ambitious character, and his peculiar situation at the time, it is difficult to exculpate him. When the murder was committed, Ragobah was confined in a small room near Narrain Row's private apartment: Sobal Sing, who commanded the peshwa's body-guard, had also the immediate charge of Ragobah's person, which afforded them frequent opportunities for private conversation. He is supposed, by large promises, to have been prevailed upon, with another officer, named Esoof Khan, to perpetrate the horrid deed.

Seizing the opportunity when Narrain Row had retired from the public durbar, Sobal Sing entered officially, as if to receive orders, but instead of the respect due to his prince, Narrain Row was surprized by his abusive language and insolent behaviour: when beginning to expostulate, on a signal from Sobal Sing, Esoof

Khan, and several armed men, entered the room. The unhappy prince dreading his approaching fate, fled through a private door to his uncle's prison, where, throwing himself at his feet, he claimed his forgiveness and protection. Ragobah, whether ignorant, or pretending ignorance of the plot, opened his arms and embraced his nephew: the assassins, in a well-feigned rage, ordered Ragobah to withdraw, or share his fate; he instantly obeyed, and Narrain Row was stabbed to the heart, after a short reign of eight months.

These commotions in the palace alarmed the city; but, as the gates were shut, they remained for some time ignorant of the murder, and only surmised that some mischief was transacting, the majority naturally concluding that Ragobah's sufferings were terminated. The ministers now assembled, sent two letters to the durbar, one addressed to the peshwa, the other to Ragobah, in which they mentioned the general alarm, and the suspicion of some dark transaction; assuring the injured prince he should meet with every redress in their power, and requesting the gates might be opened. On reading the letter, Ragobah immediately ordered the ministers to be admitted, and standing near the body, solemnly declared his innocence, imprecating divine vengeance on the perpetrators of the horrid deed. Few believed his protestations, and all retired with horror from his presence, the Hindoo annals having never before recorded the murder of a brahmin; and the dagger directed by a near relation of the same sacred caste, dreadfully increased its atrocity.

On the accession of a sovereign to the throne, it has often been the cruel policy of Asiatic despots to destroy every male relation capable of creating an insurrection, especially in the Mogul, Turkish, and Persian courts. The history of the house of Timur is filled with tales of woe: there seemed no alternative between the musnud and a grave; it was only to be ascended through a deluge of blood: no predilection for private pursuits, nor choice of religious retirement, could screen the royal princes from suspicion. The fate of Aurungzebe's brothers, and their descendants, is almost too tragical for recital: but the murder of Narrain Row had been committed on a Hindoo prince of the sacred caste of brahmins, every where most highly venerated.

It appears extraordinary, as Ragobah was so generally considered to be the author of his nephew's assassination, that he should have been quietly permitted to succeed him: it is difficult to determine whether it was occasioned by the general disaffection to the deceased peshwa, or that the leading men then thought the revolution necessary: it is certain, Ragobah assumed the government in course, and for some months ruled the empire with all the power of his predecessors, and remained undisturbed at Poonah. Still there were many obstacles to surmount: had he perserved the bravery, activity, and generosity, which had formerly distinguished him, he might have triumphed over all; but his conduct was unaccountably the reverse: he became timid, indolent, and suspicious; his understanding seemed clouded by superstition, and his mind weakened, either by the severities he had lately suffered, or the distractions of a wounded conscience.

The first act of his government was to reward Sobal Sing and

Esoof Khan, who were universally detested, thereby attaching to himself the foul stigma of this murder. The general discontent and sullen silence that pervaded the capital, soon spread through the empire: there seemed only wanting an enterprising spirit to stand forth and effect a revolution. This calm had not been of long duration, when two formidable enemies appeared in the highest female characters of the empire; the mother and the widow of Narrain Row, the decased peshwa.

The name of the former was Gopicabhye, the widow of Ballajee Row, and mother of Mhadarow and Narrain Row; a woman, who, during her husband's life, had great influence in the Mahratta court: at that time her character was not very correct, and afterwards she became extremely dissolute. Instead of immolating herself on the funeral pyre of her husband, she preferred a longer abode among the sons of men, to indulge in the most licentious conduct: false, malicious, and tyrannical, her state intrigues were marked by cruelty and oppression, and, instead of a decent retirement, and chaste deportment, her widowhood was devoted to shameless levity. This woman was emphatically styled the scourge of her country: to an undue influence over her husband and her sons, the three succeeding peshwas, were imputed all the troubles which had for so many years disturbed the court of Poonah, especially in the distrust and imprisonment of Ragobah. Being now deprived of her only surviving son by means of the man she so much detested, she gave loose to the whole fury of her revenge.

Actuated by sentiments equally inimical to the new peshwa,

Gungabhye, the youthful widow of Narrain Row, came forth to public view: being declared pregnant, she was exempt by the *Suttee*-law, had she been so inclined, of becoming, like the wife of Mahdarow, a devoted victim to the manes of her murdered husband. The promulgation of this interesting circumstance fixed the attention of the whole nation in the most anxious state of expectancy, and attracted around the young widow all those, who, from attachment to her husband, or enmity to her murderer, were eager to excite, or ready to execute her revenge. Under these circumstances, and sanctioned by the two widowed princesses, a conspiracy was formed; in due time the posthumous prince appeared, and religious ceremonies, thanksgivings, and rejoicings generally prevailed throughout the empire.

During that period Ragobah went twice to Satarrah, to be invested with the khelaut, as peshwa; but the rajah, at the instigation of the ministers, procrastinated the ceremony; at first alleging, that decency required him to wait until the expiration of the mourning for his nephew. It was afterwards deferred until the birth of the expected child.

On this second disappointment Ragobah marched with a large army against the nizam, at the time a secret rebellion was pervading his own capital. Previous to his departure, he removed most of the old ministers from their stations, and replaced them by others of more obscure character. These discarded officers, who were men of the first families and influence in the state, justly incensed at such conduct, no longer concealed their design; but immediately on Ragobah's departure, twelve of the principal chieftains formed themselves into a legislative body, levied a considerable army, and commenced hostilities against him.

Thus this infatuated peshwa left the Mahratta capital, no more to return. Among many extraordinary instances of weakness and folly, on marching against the nizam, he carried with him only fifteen lacs of rupees from the public treasury at Poonah, leaving a much larger sum of ready money to be seized by the confederates, which gave them a decided advantage. Mhadajee Sindia and Tookajee Holcar, two of the great chieftains of the empire, collected the principal jaghiredars, and instantly summoned the *husserat*, or household troops, who compose a select body of twenty thousand cavalry, and hold their lands by military tenure, stipulating their appearance, completely armed, and well mounted, when called forth on public service: these are esteemed the most valiant of the Deccan horse; they have always distinguished themselves in the path of glory, and are far superior to the occasional hirelings in the Mahratta armies. A full treasury enabled the confederate chieftains to add to this valuable corps a large body of common Mahratta horse, and as many Patan, Scindian, and Arabian infantry as they deemed necessary.

Thus commenced the civil wars in the Mahratta empire. Ragobah, on hearing of the proceedings at Poonah, too late relinquished foreign conquest to suppress rebellion at home. Both armies took the field; but nothing decisive being effected, Ragobah sent an ambassador to Bombay, to request the assistance of the English government in furnishing him with troops and a field train of artillery, to be paid by him, and for which he assigned a considerable territory on the continent, and the valuable acquisition of Salsette, with some smaller islands contiguous to Bombay. A treaty to this effect was concluded between Ragobah and the Bombay government, in behalf of the English East India Company; and a considerable detachment of European infantry and sepoys, and a large train of artillery, were embarked from thence in March 1775, and sailed to Surat, in hopes of effecting a junction with Ragobah's forces in Guzerat; which, according to the latest intelligence, were then encamped on the banks of the river Myhi, not far from Cambay: the army of the confederate chieftains was reported to be on the opposite side of the river.

END OF VOL. I.

T. Bensley, Printer,
Bolt Court, Fleet Street, London.